THE RISE AND FALL OF
PHILANTHROPY
IN EAST AFRICA

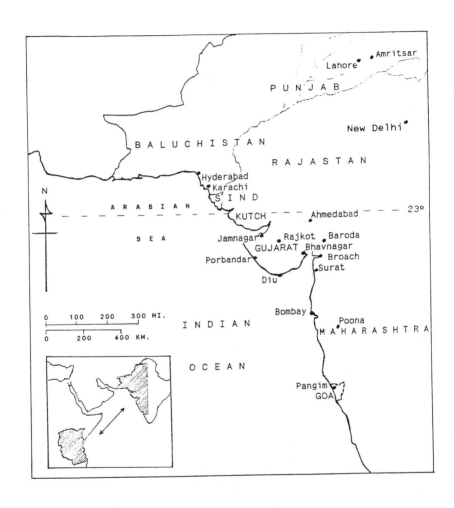

MAP 1
NORTH-WEST INDIA, 1890–47 Areas of Asian Emigration to East Africa

THE RISE AND FALL OF PHILANTHROPY IN EAST AFRICA

The Asian Contribution

Robert G. Gregory

Transaction Publishers
New Brunswick (U.S.A.) and London (U.K.)

1-15-7

Library of Congress Catalog Number: 91-19903
ISBN: 1-56000-007-4
Printed in the United States of America

Library of Congress Cataloging-in-Publication Data

Gregory, Robert G.
    The rise and fall of philanthropy in East Africa: the Asian contribution/Robert G. Gregory.
    p.   cm.
    Includes bibliographical references and index.
    ISBN 1-56000-007-4
    1. East Indians—Africa, East—Charities—History—20th century. 2. Charities—Africa, East—History—20th century. 3. East Indians—Africa, East—History—20th century. I. Title
HV3199.E232A3534   1991
361.7'09676—dc20   91-19903
                                                                CIP

For
R. P. Chandaria
and
K. P. Chandaria

Contents

Preface

After completing *India and East Africa: a History of Race Relations within the British Empire, 1890–1939*, which was mainly a political study of the policies of Britain and India toward the settlement of South Asians in East Africa, I decided to undertake a further study specifically on the Asians. There was no comprehensive history of these important people. Eventually two additional volumes were completed: one on the Asians' political history with a concentration on the period since 1939; and the other an overall survey of the Asians' economic and social history during the nine important decades from 1890 to 1980. The study of the Asians led to the discovery that philanthropy had become a prominent feature of their society and also an important determinant of East African economic and social history. Yet philanthropy, it appeared, had received virtually no attention from scholars focusing on East Africa, and, surprisingly, the subject has received very little attention throughout the non-Western world. Obviously, the Asians' philanthropic history deserved description.

Since this study is a by-product of the others, the same sources are pertinent. When the study was begun, Syracuse University had undertaken with the Kenya National Archives a seven-year cooperative project for the microfilming of historical records. Most of the records of the British colonial administration, from the files in the Kenya district offices to the correspondence in the British Colonial Office, and many newspapers and private records were being collected and filmed. In directing the microfilming, which eventually produced nearly three thousand reels, I was able to include nearly all the extant Asian records: those of the community's political and economic organizations as well as newspapers and private papers.

The research in the British and Asian sources, nearly all of which contain some information on the Asians, consumed a number of years. Fortunately, during one year in East Africa I had the help of three senior graduate students—Charles Bennett, Martha Honey, and Dana Seidenberg—who were writing Ph.D. dissertations on the Asians. They assisted not only in the examination of written sources in Kenya and Tanzania, including Zanzibar, but also in the interviewing of Asians from these areas and Uganda. Subsequently I was able to undertake further interviewing and the examination of written sources in India and Britain. In all approximately two hundred Asians, most of whom were communal leaders, were interviewed. The records of these interviews, together with the written sources, constitute an invaluable collection of information on the Asians and East Africa.

A number of organizations and individuals facilitated the research and writing. The National Science Foundation and the National Endowment for the Humanities joined Syracuse University in supporting the microfilming and the compilation of indexes. Bachulal Gathani, Amritlal Raishi, Nitin Madhvani, R. P. Chandaria, I. T. Inamdar, Hansa Pandya, Pritam Pandya, Dana Seidenberg, William Stinchcombe, Vernon Snow, and my wife Pat, who assisted in almost all the research and interviewing, read all or much of the manuscript. To all these, including the three assistants, and to the many others who cheerfully provided information, I wish to express my gratitude.

Introduction

Social Welfare is not, of course, a new activity in India. It is as old as India itself.
— Jawaharlal Nehru

These words by Jawaharlal Nehru refer to what is generally termed "philanthropy." Meaning literally in its Greek origin "love of mankind," *philanthropy* may be defined as essentially a self-sacrifice on behalf of needy individuals outside the donor's extended family. It is expressed mainly by the sharing of wealth but also by the devotion of time and energy for the benefit of others. One's basic impulse is to care primarily for one's spouse and children and secondarily for close relatives on both sides of the nuclear family. Caring for those who are not closely related is more difficult. The first step beyond the extended family is to serve the needs of those who share the same culture, those who are neighbors, fellow villagers, and, somewhat more remote, those who are of the same caste, the same religious sect, or the same nationality. This requires a higher degree of self-sacrifice, and it is here that *philanthropy, altruism, beneficence, benevolence, munificence, voluntarism,* or *charity*—terms that society has applied to this form of the sharing of wealth, time, and energy—begin.

It is possible for philanthropy to advance to a further stage by embracing the needs of humanity without distinction of culture, race, or creed. It then is a true humanitarianism. This is by far the

1

most difficult stage of self-sacrifice, for it is often beyond the realm of interpersonal association and in conflict with highly esteemed group loyalties including patriotism and nationalism.

Voluntary service or *social work,* which is often equated with philanthropy, is a somewhat narrower term in that it emphasizes individual action apart from the sharing of wealth. It has been aptly defined as "a labour of love given by individuals or groups by free choice and under no external compulsion, to help individuals, groups or communities in social, economic or spiritual need." Lord Beveridge called it "a private enterprise for social progress." [1] Voluntary service is sometimes referred to as the "third sector" or "public sector" to distinguish it from the open market economy and from state welfare.[2]

The reasons for philanthropy cannot be defined with certainty, but they seem to be inherent in the nature of humans and society. Philanthropy is a response to conditions in the environment that induce suffering and obviate the fulfillment of basic human needs and the realization of common goals. It can be inspired, augmented, and directed by religion, which itself is shaped by factors in the environment. It can also be stimulated and reinforced by rational thought such as that associated with the Enlightenment. Essentially, perhaps, philanthropy is a product of the human power of imagination, the ability to project one's self into another's position and to develop an empathy that motivates one to charitable endeavor. It seems to have been practiced by all peoples.

The physical environment of South Asia was an underlying determinant of philanthropy. The northern river valleys, blessed with rich deposits of alluvial soil, fostered an abundance of plant and animal life and a high density of population. South of those valleys, however, most of the subcontinent was a semidesert reliant on the annual southwest monsoons for support of agriculture, and many people eked out a precarious existence in scattered villages. The fickle winds often brought disaster in the form of floods in the river valleys or drought in the Deccan plains. The tropical location and dense population also fostered a plethora of disease from typhoid, cholera, and dysentery to leprosy, malaria, and bubonic plague. Lacking in nearly all instances a government that could alleviate the environmental problems, the people were constrained to provide for their own welfare. Villages, religious groups, and castes undertook to care for the disadvantaged among their peoples. Communal responsibility for the social welfare became a prominent feature of society, and charity a duty prescribed by religion.

All the South Asian religions supported philanthropy. "Charity," in the words of A. R. Wadia, director of the Tata Institute of Social Sciences in Bombay, "is a virtue which has flourished on the soil of religion. . . . True religion means service of man." [3] Wadia has stressed the concept that *dharma* in Brahmin society entailed duties of mutual service within caste. "Everyone had to help whether in building the village road or village tank, the village temple or the village school." [4] The endowment of temples and shrines and the support of religious institutions generally were the primary obligations. Benevolence for religious purposes included gifts for the construction of *dharmsalas* (rest-houses) to assist pilgrims.

Buddhism is said to have added a missionary zeal and an expansion of benevolence beyond the caste and village. Teaching the eightfold path and stressing the universality of man, "Buddha became the very embodiment of mercy." [5] The *Jatakas,* which form a part of the Buddhist canonical literature, contain many stories of individual and collective charity.[6] Although Buddhism declined as a separate religion within South Asia, it contributed to the evolution of Hinduism as a fusion of Brahminist and Buddhist ideals. The Buddhist humanitarian concept is reflected in the Sanskrit dictum *Vasudhaiva kutumbakum* (The whole world is one family).[7]

Though constituting a different stream of South Asian religion, Islam also emphasized the importance of philanthropy. It apparently provided divine sanction for practices that had long prevailed among the Arabs. Mohammed foretold an eternity in Paradise for those who shared their wealth and "a woeful punishment" in Hell for those who hoarded it. In an early pronouncement recorded in the Koran he did not specify the quantity of alms that should be given, stating only, "Give what you can spare," but later he designated the amount as "one fifth of your spoils." [8]

> The righteous man is he who . . . gives his wealth to his kinsfolk, to the orphans, to the needy, to the wayfarers and to the beggars, and for the redemption of captives; who attends to his prayers and pays the alms-tax.
>
> Give generously for the cause of Allah. . . . Be charitable; Allah loves the charitable.
>
> To be charitable in public is good, but to give alms to the poor in private is better.

Charity was a prominent feature of Muslim India and was practiced by both subjects and rulers. People contributed to the construction of mosques with attached schools and colleges, built *serai* (roadside inns) for travelers, and even endowed hospitals for cats, dogs, and goats. The Tughluq sultans, who are noted for their concern with public welfare, dispersed free medicines, food, and drinks, subsidized marriages, and provided resources for the upliftment of slaves. The *Zakat,* an obligatory alms, could be paid in currency, cattle, grain, fruit, or merchandise.[9]

An idealism in support of philanthropy is evident in other religious sects. Mahavira, the twenty-fourth *Tirthankara,* or prophet, of the Jains, stressed not only nonviolence and self-restraint, but also the limitation of possessions.[10] Nanak, the Sikhs' guru, predicted, "The wealth of those who have not given alms shall slip away."[11] The Parsis have been "catholic in their charity," it is said, because their fundamental religious principle — *manasni, gavasni, kunasni* (pure thoughts, pure words, and pure deeds) — "teaches them to be pure in thoughts, words, and deeds not towards their co-religionists alone but also towards persons of other religions."[12]

Although religious traditions may have provided the primary motivation, donations on a large scale occurred regularly outside religious channels. Emergencies resulting from famines and other natural disasters always evoked a charitable response from political and commercial leaders. A duty to care for the ill or incapacitated resulted in the merchants' regularly reserving part of their earnings for the destitute. The wealthy also assumed a duty to provide for the social improvement of the community. It was a common practice for them to subsidize *gurukuls* (community schools) and colleges, support the copying of manuscripts, and in other ways contribute to education. People shared their food with students, planted shade trees for travelers, and dug tanks and wells for fellow villagers.[13]

Beginning in the late eighteenth century and extending into the twentieth, European influence in the form of evangelical Christianity and of the Enlightenment stimulated social welfare in India. After 1813, when revision of the East India Company's charter permitted their admission to British India, Protestant missionaries were surprisingly unsuccessful in winning Christian converts but helped to inspire a new movement of social reform. They introduced Western education, and "as the new knowledge spread, more and more thinking Indians were introduced to a new sense of values." [14] The missionaries also gave practical demonstrations of the gospel of Christ by establishing schools, hospitals, leprosariums, and foundling homes, caring for the disadvantaged in house-to-house visits, and crusading against *sati,* untouchability, caste discrimination, female infanticide, child marriage, and the ban on remarriage of widows.[15]

The result was a heightened awareness of the plight of the disadvantaged in society and a general movement aimed at social improvement. During the nineteenth century new, vital religious organizations, such as the Brahmo Samaj, Prarthana Samaj, Arya Samaj, Arya Mahila Samaj, Ramakrishna Mission, and Theosophical Society, emphasized the need for social reform.[16] Leaders associated with the religious fervor and the new rationalism, notably Ram Mohan Roy, Ishwar Chandra Vidyasagar, Behramji M. Malabari, Sasipada Bannerji, Dayanand Saraswati, Pandita Ramabai, Jyotiba Phule, Swami Vivekananda, Dr. R. G. Bhandarkar, Mahadev Govind Ranade, and Sir Syed Ahmed Khan, worked in various ways for the improvement of society. Periodicals, such as the *Indian Social Reformer* edited by Natarajan and the *Mohammadan Social Reformer* founded by Sir Syed, stressed the need for a collective approach to social change. The Indian National Congress, organized in 1885, and the Indian National Social Conference, which followed in 1887, became forums for discussion of Indian social conditions and the means for reform.[17]

The movement continued into the twentieth century. In numerous writings emphasizing reason as opposed to religious sentiment,

Gopal Ganesh Agarkar inspired a new approach to social reform. Within this context the Servants of India Society, founded by Gopal Krishna Gokhale in 1905, focused attention on India's economic and social problems and provided a vital leadership. Other organizations, such as the Bombay Presidency Infant Welfare Society and the Society for the Protection of Children in Western India, stressed the need for preventive measures. Beginning in 1925, the National Council of Women, inspired by Annie Besant and Margaret Cousins, campaigned against the disadvantaged position of Indian women. In 1936 the Sir Dorabji Tata Graduate School of Social Work was established to train specialists in combating a wide range of social evils. The Social Service Leagues and the YMCAs, operating in numerous urban centers, were among the many new private organizations designed to alleviate human suffering; these voluntary organizations are said to have numbered in the thousands.[18]

The most influential leader among the social reformers of the twentieth century was Mohandas K. Gandhi. "His political struggle," as one author has recognized, "brought a new force to bear on social reform." [19] "In his vision," as another has stated, "the social, the religious, the political and the economic did not appear as different aspects. He attempted to integrate these various approaches to voluntary work weaving them into a single pattern." [20] In his lectures and many writings Gandhi repeatedly stressed the duty of individual sacrifice and the need for collective action. "*Satyagraha* required every Indian," as the Gandhi scholar Bhikhu Parekh has explained, "to suffer and make sacrifices for his country . . . to follow a way of life involving identification with and an active service of his fellow men." [21] In his personal life, with his historic fast on behalf of the Harijans a foremost example, Gandhi became a model for emulation. The Harijan Sevak Sangh, All India Village Industries Association, Nai Talim Sangh, and Leper Society are but a few of the many voluntary organizations that he initiated or inspired.

In the philosophies and work of the nineteenth- and twentieth-century social reformers, culminating in those of Gandhi, a new direction to philanthropy is evident. There was a gradual but pronounced movement away from individual effort to collective action and organization. The social worker was assuming the role of the private philanthropist, and "social work" was becoming the catchphrase to denote the new form of voluntary action.

Implicit in the Indian nationalist movement, as in such movements in the colonial dependencies everywhere, was the ideal of devising a postcolonial nation-state that would unite the diverse peoples of South Asia and attend to all the needs of society. There were visions of creating an earthly utopia through a democratic, socialist state founded on the principle "to each according to his work" or, in an even more equitable sense, "to each according to his need." The state would assume not only the management of the economy, but also the responsibility for social welfare. Special government agencies, administered by a new class of salaried and professionally trained social workers, would care for the sick, the elderly, the destitute, and all others in need. Inherent in this design was the assumption that the extremes of wealth that previously had created both the need and the support for private philanthropy would no longer prevail. As the following words, expressed in 1959, indicate, Nehru clearly envisaged this result:

> We talk about a Welfare State and direct our energies towards its realization. That welfare must be the common property of everyone in India and not the monopoly of a privileged group, as it is today.[22]

It was not only India and other dependencies within the European imperial fold that aspired to this end. The Soviet Union, China, Albania, and Cuba were among the so-called communist countries that endeavored to eliminate the private sector of the economy and create a social welfare system managed entirely by the state. Even countries like Britain, France, Sweden, and the United States that sought a compromise between government ownership and free enterprise gravitated toward increased government control and various forms of the welfare state.

Five decades after becoming independent, the new nations of India and Pakistan, in common with the other new countries of the non-Western world, have yet to achieve their ideal. Illness, poverty, malnutrition, housing, education, and relief for drought, flooding, and earthquake victims were among the many continuing social problems that the governments alone could not solve. The gross national products and the acceptable levels of taxation were not sufficiently high to support the necessary welfare programs. Thus in these countries, as in the more industrialized welfare states, the need for philanthropy to cooperate with the governments in alleviating the social problems has continued. Fortunately, in India and Pakistan there have been sufficient private capital accumulated in previous years and sufficient dedication to voluntary service without remuneration to provide a significant philanthropic support. Because of their financial constraints, the governments have welcomed rather than discouraged this support. India's successive five-year plans, for instance, have "reiterated the importance of voluntary action as an instrument of public cooperation in welfare and development programs." [23]

The continuing role of philanthropy in South Asia is well illustrated by a Bombay Parsi family, the Tatas. Jamsetji Nusserwanji Tata (1839–1904), the commercial and industrial entrepreneur who founded the family fortune in the presocialist years, formulated a philosophy of "constructive philanthropy." "What advances a nation or a community," he maintained, "is not so much to prop up its weakest and most helpless members but to lift up the best and the most gifted, so as to make them of the greatest service to the country." [24] Jamsetji's principal aim was to foster India's industrialization. In 1892 he set up the J. N. Tata Endowment Scheme for Higher Education, which through the succeeding ninety years was to acquire an endowment of Rs. 9.3 million and grant more than Rs. 10 million for study abroad by India's future scientists, administrators, doctors, lawyers, and engineers. His plan to provide an equivalent higher education in India was implemented in 1911, after his death, when the Indian Institute of Science was inaugurated at Bangalore. It was this institute that was to develop India's nuclear capability.[25]

Jamsetji's "constructive philanthropy" was continued and significantly augmented after 1904 by his sons Dorab and Ratan and his cousin R. D. Tata. Jamsetji left three textile mills and Bombay's renowned Taj Mahal Hotel. To these were added iron and steel production—the largest in the British Empire—hydroelectric generation, oil, soap, and cement production, insurance, and the airline that was to become Air India. The sizeable increase in income from these endeavors made possible the establishment of eight more philanthropic foundations, the most important of which were the Sir Ratan Tata Trust (1918) and the Sir Dorab Tata Trust (1932). By 1983 through these two trusts alone the Tata family had donated Rs. 1.1 billion to Indian society. The family donations as a whole totaled more than Rs. 2 billion. Among the institutions established in India were the national center for the performing arts and the first institute of the social sciences, first cancer hospital, and first institute of fundamental research in mathematics and physics. One among every five employees in the Indian Civil Service was a J. N. Tata Scholar.[26]

The persistence of private philanthropy as illustrated in the contrasting ideals of Gandhi and the Tatas—the one deeply spiritual, founded in Indian religious traditions, and the other practical and pragmatic, a result of India's industrialization—provided two models of benevolence for the South Asian immigrants in East Africa. Because of the peculiar nature of the East African environment, as will be seen, most of the philanthropic leaders among the immigrants combined the two ideals. They were on the whole, like Gandhi, deeply religious and interested in preserving the spiritual traditions of their heritage, but they were also, like the Tatas, entrepreneurs interested in the industrialization and modernization of their society.

Contrary to the trend in other parts of the world, the pronounced transformation in ideology and methodology in the provision of assistance to the needy that was embodied in the welfare state and professional social work was to have very little impact on the East African Asians. Again, because of the peculiar character of the British colonial environment, the Asians were unable to develop or partake in a state system of welfare responsive to their needs and interests. Since the British administration concentrated on serving the needs of the European and African peoples, the Asians were constrained to devise their own means for social improvement. Thus during this twentieth century, when the peoples of India and most other countries were turning to state-conducted systems of social welfare, the Asians had to rely on the traditional system of private philanthropy. Fortunately, through most of the colonial period, they lived under conditions that offered unusual economic opportunity and imposed no serious restraints on the accumulation of private capital.

The conception of social work as an integral part of the welfare state seriously diminished scholarly concern with the history of philanthropy. Indian scholars had not devoted attention to the subject before the twentieth century, when a new cadre of university-trained social scientists began to contemplate the nature of the country's postcolonial nation-state and its social service organization. Beginning about two decades before Britain's withdrawal and continuing afterward, scholars compiled numerous books and articles appearing in social-science classification under the heading "social work." A few of the books contain an introductory chapter or two on the history of philanthropy before the twentieth century, but the emphasis, which forms the content of the remaining chapters, is on the present or future and on social work as a function of government.[27] Apart from the occasional biography of an industrial or commercial leader renowned for his munificence — such as Sir Dorab Tata — there seem to be no other books related to philanthropy.[28] What is true of scholarship in South Asia appears true of scholarship in other areas of the non-Western world.

Even in the Western world philanthropy is a relatively new study and poses serious problems for the scholar. As Stanley N. Katz, president of the American Council of Learned Societies, has explained:

> There is no general academic publication on philanthropy. Many books have been published, but their titles do not always clearly indicate that they concern philanthropy, and library cataloging generally does not identify them as such. Those who are not experts in a particular field will have great difficulty in locating literature on philanthropy, and even experts have a hard time.[29]

In Western scholarship the focus so far has been on the philanthropy of the Western world. Some scholars have traced the roots of modern European philanthropy to ancient Greece and Rome, and there are a number of studies of the history of benevolence within the separate European countries.[30] The British, who have taken great pride in the development of private and public social work within their own culture, seem to have assumed that philanthropy in the various territories of their vast empire was, if not exclusively a British phenomenon, at least a product of British initiative and example.[31] Scholars in the United States who have examined philanthropy in the non-Western world have concentrated either on the contributions of the large American foundations, such as Ford, Carnegie, and Rockefeller, those of USAID and other federal agencies, or those of the World Bank, World Health Organization, UNESCO, and other UN agencies.[32] Throughout the Western world there appears to have been an underlying assumption that philanthropy by the non-Western peoples is either not worthy of consideration or deserving of only low priority.

The Asians of East Africa offer a challenge to that assumption.

Notes

1. Quoted, N. P. Jain, "Historical Perspective of Voluntary Service," chap. 1 in *Voluntary Service in India* (New Delhi: Central Inst. of Research and Training in Public Co-operation, 1967), 1.
2. E.g., James Douglas, *Why Charity? The Case for a Third Sector* (Beverly Hills: Sage, 1983); and Walter W. Powell, ed., *Nonprofit Sector: A Research Handbook* (New Haven: Yale Univ. Press, 1987).
3. A. R. Wadia, ed., *Hist. and Philos. of Soc. Work in India,* 2d ed. (Bombay: Allied Pub., 1968), 6–7, 12.
4. Ibid., 7.
5. Ibid., 8.
6. R. C. Majumdar, "Soc. Work in Ancient and Medieval India," chap. 2, ibid., p. 8.
7. H. Pandya intv.
8. N. J. Dawood, trans., *The Koran* (Harmondsworth: Penguin, 1986), verses 2:117, 2:195, 2:269; see also 9:35. M. J. Gazdar, "Charities: Their Past, Present, and Future," chap. 9 in S. K. Khinduka, ed., *Soc. Work in India* (Allahabad: Kitab Mahal, 1965) 63.
9. Majumdar, "Soc. Work in Ancient," 22–23.
10. G. B. Shah, "Hist. of the Birth of the Oshwal Society," 3-page typescript presented during interview.
11. Quoted, Majumdar, "Soc. Work in Ancient," 22.
12. Letter signed "X.Y.Z," *E. Afn. Standard* (Nairobi), 8 May 1909, 16.
13. N. P. Jain, "Historical Perspective of Voluntary Service," chap. 1 in *Voluntary Service in India,* pp. 3–4.
14. Clifford Marquardt, "Social Work during the British Period," chap. 3, Wadia, *Hist. and Philos.,* 27.
15. Wadia, *Hist. and Philos.,* 9–10. M. S. Gore and I. E. Soares, "Historical Background of Soc. Work in India," chap. 1 in Planning Commission, *Soc. Welfare in India* (New Delhi: Govt. of India Publications Div., 1960), 2–3.
16. Marquardt, "Soc. Work during the British Period," 29.

17. Ibid., 30–31. Gore and Soares, "Historical Background," in Planning Commission, *Social Welfare in India,* 3.
18. Fifty-nine of them are described in Madhu Kohli, *Voluntary Action in India: Some Profiles* (New Delhi: National Institute of Public Cooperation and Child Development, c. 1982). For another listing, see *Sharan, Serving the Poor: Resource Directory* (New Delhi: Sharan Voluntary Agency, 1986).
19. Wadia, *Hist. and Philos.,* 5.
20. Jain, "Historical Perspective," 11–12.
21. Bhikhu Parekh, *Colonialism, Tradition, and Reform: An Analysis of Gandhi's Pol. Discourse* (London: Sage, 1989), 78. See also Ammu Menon Mazumdar, *Social Work in India: Mahatma Gandhi's Contributions* (Bombay: Asia Pub. House, 1964); and Herbert H. Aptekar, "Mahatma Gandhi's Contribution to Social Work," chap. 5 in Khinduka, *Soc. Work in India.*
22. Jawaharlal Nehru, "Foreword," in Planning Commission, *Social Welfare in India,* v.
23. Kohli, *Voluntary Action,* vi.
24. Quoted, J. R. D. Tata, "Foreword," in R. M. Lala, *Heartbeat of a Trust: Fifty Years of the Sir Dorabji Tata Trust* (New Delhi: Tata McGraw-Hill, 1984), xii. See also D. E. Wacha, *Life and Work of J. N. Tata* (Madras: Ganesh, 1914); and B. Sh. Saklatvala and K. Khosla, *Jamsetji Tata* (New Delhi: Govt. of India Publications Div., 1970).
25. Lala, *Heartbeat of a Trust,* 3–4, App. A.
26. Ibid., 3–6, App. A; Tata, "Foreword," ibid., xi–xiv.
27. Wadia's *Hist. of Soc. Work,* the anonymous *Voluntary Service in India,* and Planning Commission, *Social Welfare in India,* illustrate this emphasis.
28. Other examples of biographies of eminent philanthropists are Grish Ghosh, *Ramdoolal Dey, the Bengalee Millionaire* (Calcutta: Riddhi-India, 1978); Divijendra Tripathi, *Dynamics of a Tradition: Kasturbhai Lalbhai and His Entrepreneurship* (Ahmedabad: Manohar, 1981); V. S. M. De Mel, ed., *The de Soysa Charitaya or Hist. Pertaining to the Lives and Times of Charles Henry de Soysa J.P. and Other Members of the de Soysa Family* (Colombo, Sri Lanka: de Soysa & Co., 1986); and Paul Marett, *Meghji Pethraj Shah: His Life and Achievements* (Bombay: Bharatiya Vidya Bhavan, 1988).
29. Stanley N. Katz (president, Am. Council of Learned Societies), "Foreword," in Daphne Niobe Layton, *Philan. and Voluntarism: An Annotated Biblio.,* (New York: Foundation Center, 1987), x.
30. E.g., A. R. Hands, *Charities and Soc. Aid in Greece and Rome* (Ithaca: Cornell Univ. Press, 1968); Orvoell R. Gallagher, "Voluntary Associations in France," *Soc. Forces* 36 (1957): 153–60; and W. J. Mommsen, ed., *Emergence of the Welfare State in Britain and Germany, 1850–1950* (London: Croom Helm, 1981).
31. Wilbur K. Jordan, "English Background of Modern Philan.," *Am. Hist. Rev.* 66 (1961): 401–8. William Seward Hall, *The Empire of Philanthropy with a Portrature of Brit. Excellence as a National Example: A Dramatic Poem with Notes* (London: Hatachard & Son, 1822). Franklin Parker, *George Peabody, Founder of Modern Philanthropy* (Ann Arbor: Xerox Univ. Microfilms, 1974). John P. Halstead, *The Second Brit. Empire: Trade, Philanthropy, and Good Govt., 1820–90* (Westport, Conn.: Greenwood, 1983).
32. Robert F. Gorman, ed., *Pvt. Voluntary Organizations as Agents of Devt.*

(Boulder: Westview, 1984). Francis X. Sutton, *Role of Foundations in Devt.* (College Station: Texas A & M Univ. Press, 1982). E. Jefferson Murphey, *Creative Philan.: Carnegie Corp. and Africa, 1953–73* (New York: Teachers College Press, Columbia Univ., 1976). For a negative assessment, see Robert F. Arnove, ed., *Philan. and Cultural Imperialism: The Foundations at Home and Abroad* (Boston: G. K. Hall, 1980). Also, Edward H. Berman, *Influence of the Carnegie, Ford, and Rockefeller Foundations on Am. For. Policy: The Ideology of Philan.* (Albany: SUNY Press, 1983).

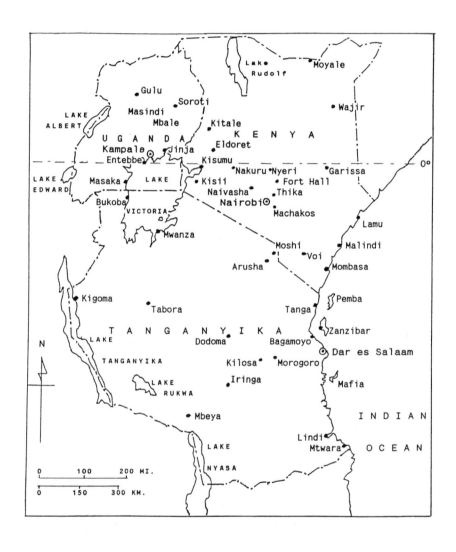

MAP 2
BRITISH EAST AFRICA, 1920–64 Main Political Centers

1

The Settlement in East Africa

Wealth imposes obligations.
—Sir Yusufali A. Karimjee Jeevanjee, ca. 1950

East Africa offered a unique opportunity for the elaboration and application of the philanthropic traditions and practices developed in India. By the Heligoland Treaty of 1890 the eight hundred miles of the African coast extending from the mainland opposite Lamu Island in the north to Cape Delgado in the south were divided into British and German spheres of influence. The two European powers then proceeded to annex the offshore islands and the mainland interior from the coast to the great lakes. This area of approximately 675,000 square miles—nearly half the size of India and Pakistan and seven times that of the United Kingdom—they divided into the British East Africa, Uganda, and Zanzibar protectorates, and the German East Africa Protectorate. After World War I Britain acquired German East Africa as a mandate, renaming it Tanganyika, and in recognition of the growing importance of European settlement, it also changed the name of its East Africa Protectorate to Kenya Colony. These four British dependencies, henceforth known collectively as British East Africa, became the area of concentration for the last great wave of migration from South Asia.

The Migration to East Africa

Nearly all the Asians came from northwest India, where monsoon winds had fostered an age-old trade with East Africa. The

15

indentured servants, who, beginning in 1895, were recruited to construct the Uganda Railway and other public works, were mainly from the Punjab and Sind. Most of the free immigrants came from the Gujarat, Kathiawar (Saurashtra), Kutch, and Mahrashtra; some also emigrated from Portuguese Goa. These peoples became mainly the shopkeepers and civil servants of East Africa. In the earlier years most of the migrants came from villages where they were engaged in agriculture. Later increasing numbers came from the towns and cities, mainly the port cities such as Bombay, Karachi, Broach, Surat, and Porbandar, but also from inland centers such as Ahmedabad, Baroda, Rajkot, and Poona. These Asians from cities and towns were mainly shopkeepers and professionals, but most of them had only recently left a farming occupation in the rural areas.

Life was difficult in northwest India. The Punjab, the land of five rivers where most of the indentured laborers were recruited, was fertile and well watered but overpopulated, and many small farmers had not sufficient land to sustain their families. Sind was a desert in which any livelihood was difficult to earn. The Gujarat, Kathiawar, Kutch, and Mahrashtra were fairly fertile but dependent on the summer monsoons for rainfall. In time of plentiful rain these lands could be green and luxurious. When the monsoons failed, they were dust bowls. Drought and famine, recurring every two or three years, kept the population density to half that of the Punjab.[1] Goa was a verdant, tropical paradise in all but employment opportunity. The Portuguese monopolized the higher positions in the civil service, and there were too many qualified Goans for the remainder.

Poverty was compounded by overpopulation. During the century before 1850 the population of India had remained fairly constant at approximately 130 million. During the latter half of the nineteenth century, coincidental with the opening of East Africa, a dramatic growth began. Because of modern medicine, sanitation, and transportation, the death rate from disease and famine declined markedly, and the population began to grow at an annual rate of more than 2 percent. As a result, India's population leaped from 133 million in 1847 to 236 million in 1901, to 251 million in 1921, to 317 million in 1941, and to 439 million in 1961. In the

Gujarat and Kathiawar the natural increase — averaging annually over 16 per 1,000 during 1941 – 50 — was the highest in all India. The figures would have been far higher if millions of Indians had not emigrated. Much of India's surplus population, usually at a young, productive age, poured into Burma, Ceylon, South Africa, Fiji, British Guiana, and the West Indies as well as East Africa.[2]

The impoverished peoples of western India endeavored in various ways to improve their situation. Many farmers supplemented their incomes by running small shops in their villages or transporting goods from one center to another. A large number of villagers sought new opportunities overseas or in India's towns and cities. Those who moved to the urban centers encountered not only stiff competition in employment, but severe problems of housing, sanitation, and disease. During the 1880s and 1890s, extending into the early decades of the twentieth century, Bombay, Karachi, and other port cities of western India suffered from a terrible epidemic of bubonic plague.[3] Those who moved directly to East Africa from the villages were soon joined by many from the urban centers. Increasingly the farmers, shopkeepers, artisans, and laborers were accompanied by a professional class. Doctors, lawyers, accountants, teachers, and engineers, after education and qualification in India or Britain, were drawn to East Africa.

The Asian migration can be divided into four chronological periods. The first, beginning at a remote time, perhaps several centuries B.C., extended to almost the end of the nineteenth century. Like the Arabs, the Asians for millennia plied the Indian Ocean in small sailing ships. Through the Persian Gulf they traded with ancient Babylon, and through the Red Sea with Egypt, Greece, Rome, Axum, and Kush. Near the end of the first century A.D., when the *Periplus* was written, they apparently were trading with Rhapta in the area of East Africa. The Asians left commercial agents in the places of barter, and from these initial trading posts sizeable settlements emerged. In 1497, when Vasco da Gama explored the area, there were many Asians on Zanzibar and Pemba, and along the coast in towns such as Kilwa Kivinje, Bagamoyo, Mombasa, and Malindi. During the eighteenth century, after the Portuguese decline and the end of Dutch rivalry, both Asians and Arabs expanded their trade and settlement. After 1840, when

TABLE 1.1

Asian Population of East Africa, 1887

Zanzibar Town	3,086	Mandani (Pemba)	133
Mombasa	533	Tanga	127
Bagamoyo	493	Pangani	123
Jumba	373	Dar es Salaam	107
Kilwa	252	Malindi	82
Lamu	230	Other places (24)	622
Kwale	184	Total	6,345

Seyyid Said moved from Oman to Zanzibar, many Asians resident in Oman followed, and during the latter half of the nineteenth century, Zanzibar flourished as the focal point of an extensive trade between the African mainland and the outside world.

By 1890, when East Africa had been partitioned among European powers and the old period of Arab ascendency was at an end, the Asians were the dominant economic community on Zanzibar and along the East African coast. An economic and social pattern had already been established in which the Asians constituted the vital middle class. Through the centuries they had proved that under conditions of relatively free competition, such as those provided by the Zanzibar sultanate, they could compete successfully with Arabs, Europeans, and Africans and attain a controlling interest, often a monopoly, in finance and commerce. The decline of the slave trade and slavery, which had been a source of profit to them as well as Arabs, had not seriously affected their commercial interests. Sensing opportunity on the mainland, they began to migrate from Zanzibar and Pemba in increasing numbers. In 1887, when a detailed census was taken, approximately half the Asians were already on the coast.[4]

A second wave of Asian migration, much larger than the first, occurred between 1890 and 1914. Within this period the British, employing Indian troops, established a firm control over the new East Africa and Uganda protectorates.[5] The Germans, also by means of military force, founded German East Africa. Both built railways to the great lakes, encouraged European settlement, and

TABLE 1.2

Asian Population of East Africa, 1921–62

	1921	1931	1939	1962
Kenya	25,253	43,623	46,897	176,613
Tanganyika	10,209	25,144	25,000	92,000
Uganda	5,200	14,150	17,300	77,400
Zanzibar	13,772	15,247	15,500	20,000
Totals	54,434	98,164	104,697	366,013

imported indentured labor from India. Between 1895 and 1914 the British imported 37,747 Asians, mainly from the Punjab, on three-year contracts to provide the labor essential for construction of the Uganda Railway and other public works. The Germans, utilizing more African labor, imported fewer than 200 Asians. Of the total indentured laborers, about 18 percent, some 7,000, elected to remain in East Africa on expiration of their contracts.[6] While some continued to work on the railway or took other employment in government service, most became artisans or merchants in the many towns that sprang up behind the advancing railhead. These towns had been swelled by a far more numerous free-immigrant population from western India.

Between 1890 and 1921 the expanding sphere of government protection, the provision of rail transportation, and the opportunity to supply the wants of European settlers and begin a trade with the Africans attracted between 10,000 and 20,000 Asian free immigrants. Judging from immigration statistics, the Asians throughout East Africa numbered about 34,000 in 1914. By the time of the census of 1921, shown in Table 1.2, the Asian population of East Africa had risen spectacularly to more than 54,000. The East Africa Protectorate attracted by far the greatest number, but Zanzibar, which was at the height of its prosperity, had a fourfold increase.[7]

A third wave of migration was coterminous with the interwar period. The great influx to the British East Africa and Uganda protectorates that was interrupted by World War I resumed with the armistice in 1918 and was extended to Tanganyika with the establishment of the British administration in 1920. Unlike before

1914, the Asian population after the war grew almost entirely because of free immigration and natural increase. Although 2,024 indentured Asians entered after 1914, a total of 2,905 returned to India on expiration of their contracts. As shown in Table 1.2, the Asians of East Africa numbered 98,000 in 1931 and nearly 105,000 in 1939.[8]

These figures indicate that nearly all the growth occurred during the first decade after the war. Between 1921 and 1931 the total Asian population nearly doubled; during the second decade, immigration almost ceased and the population apparently grew only by natural increase. That the economic depression of the thirties had so profound an effect on Asian immigration illustrates the continuing importance of economic opportunity as a motivation. Probably the relative lack of economic reward also explains the minimal increase on Zanzibar. New immigrants from South Asia went directly to the mainland, where, at least during the twenties, the opportunities for employment in government service, crafts and construction, and commerce and banking, especially in the wholesale-retail trade serving European and African needs, appeared exceptional.

The end of the Second World War in 1945 and the conferral of independence on the East African territories during 1961–63 mark the final period of extensive Asian migration. A comparison of the statistics for 1939 and 1962 reveals that the Asian population increased after the war by approximately 260,000. Again Kenya, offering the greatest economic opportunity, was the most attractive territory. After 1939 the number of Asians in Kenya grew by approximately 130,000 in comparison with 67,000 for Tanganyika, 60,000 for Uganda, and less than 5,000 for Zanzibar.[9]

Unlike in preceding periods, about half the increase in the Asian population was due to natural causes. In Kenya during the decade ending in 1960, for example, the natural increase and that from immigration were generally the same, at 2.5 percent per annum. A continuing high birth rate of at least 30 per 1,000 and a declining death rate were partly responsible, but independence in India and prospects for independence in East Africa made immigration less attractive. Although the number coming to East Africa grew almost every year, and the Asians continued to outnumber Europeans more than three to one, the proportion between Asian arrivals and residents steadily diminished.[10]

The Concentration on Business

After arrival in East Africa the immigrants often went through several weeks or months of uncertainty and privation while determining their initial location and employment. Although some had a smattering of English, very few knew any German, Arabic, or Swahili. Even among Asians they were strangers outside their own communities. In most cases, with a life of poverty behind them, they had borrowed the money for the voyage or spent nearly all their savings, and rarely did one arrive with more than a few rupees in his pocket. The Goans and the Patels, fairly versed in English, could hope for some government position. The peasant farmers, such as the Shahs or Punjabis, lacked an adequate knowledge of English and had no skill in crafts or firsthand experience in business. With neither opportunity nor inducement to continue as farmers, they could seek only some menial employment with someone from their own community who was already established. Even food posed a formidable problem. It was not only that most of the Hindus and Jains were vegetarians accustomed to the grains, legumes, garden vegetables, spices, curds, and ghee of their homeland. Nearly all the non-Muslims, because of religious prohibitions, could not eat food prepared by anyone outside their own communities or even their own castes.

Solutions to these problems were difficult. Many early immigrants were very young and had few, if any, contacts in Africa. In 1890 after a journey alone by dhow, Mohamedali Pirbhai, age sixteen, stayed in a community rest house in Dar es Salaam until he found work with a German provision store. As a clerk he earned Rs. 12 per month and had to provide his own food and lodging. In 1898 Gulamhusein Rajpar Ladak, only twelve years old, arrived in Bagamoyo alone after a similar voyage. After a few days during which a stranger helped him, he began a four-hundred-mile walk to Tukuyu, where eventually he found work escorting caravans at Rs. 7 per month. In 1912 Mepabhai Vershi Shah, after a voyage alone on a German steamer, joined the three to four hundred Asians in

Nairobi. He was thirteen, and his first employment was in a stone quarry at Rs. 50 per month.[11] For those who joined established relatives or were recruited while still in India, the transition was easier. During the twenties and later most immigrants were in this category. For those, however, who had to learn a business or trade, become fluent in new languages, and make the many social adjustments, the initial years were trying.

Industry, ingenuity, thrift, and education eventually combined with favorable factors in the environment to bring prosperity to many Asians. Though lacking important mineral resources, the country was rich in timber, stone, big game, and, in many areas, fertile, well-watered land. Africans, introduced to a monied economy, a great variety of commodities from abroad, and radically new concepts and values, were beginning a cultural revolution, and they offered a vast market for consumption of foreign goods and services. They also could be viewed as an unfathomable reservoir for labor. The Europeans, establishing the government, managing the railway, and settling the highlands, constituted another consumer market. Moreover, both they and the Africans could be expected to produce cash crops for export. Then there were the Asians themselves, who needed the spices, piece-goods, tools, and cooking utensils that they had known in India. They would be additional consumers. The combination of opportunities, therefore, was immense, and the Asians had the unique potential for providing a vital service to all three communities as middlemen — intermediaries not only among the three communities in East Africa, but also between the three and the world outside.

Business in the form of retail and wholesale shopkeeping, distribution and transport, money-lending and insurance, the building trades, and property rental posed the foremost opportunity. This is principally why the Shahs, Patels, and Ismailis so easily broke with the tradition of generations by transferring their interests from farming to business when they arrived in East Africa. It explains why so many indentured laborers forfeited their return passages to stay in the country, and why Asian clerks seldom remained in government service sufficiently long to retire with pensions. In fact it was common for the relatively few who did retire in government

TABLE 1.3

Occupations of Economically Active Asians, 1957–62

	Kenya 1962		Tanganyika 1957		Uganda 1959	
Commerce, banking	16,325	44.5%	9,247	50.0%	9,426	56.7%
Public services	11,474	31.3	1,953	10.5	1,542	9.3
Manufacturing	5,001	13.6	1,999	10.8	1,879	11.3
Construction	1,584	4.3	809	4.4	690	4.1
Private transport, communication	1,085	3.0	1,852	10.0	250	1.5
Agriculture, forestry, fishing	667	1.8	898	4.9	1,737	10.4
Electricity, water	124	.3	113	.6	95	.6
Mining, quarrying	73	.2	149	.8	76	.5
Other	320	.9	1,485	8.0	932	5.6
Totals	36,653	100.0%	18,505	100.0%	16,627	100.0%

service to invest their savings in founding new businesses. Even the professional people were attracted; doctors and lawyers frequently carried on one or more businesses in addition to their practices. Such activity is found to some degree in every capitalist economy, but it was extreme in East Africa not because the Asians were uniquely business-minded, as is so often assumed, but because the opportunities there were so bountiful.

The emphasis on business in the mainland territories is evident in Table 1.3, drawn from the last censuses before independence. Although comparable statistics are not available for Zanzibar, a similar emphasis prevailed there.[12]

A 1966–67 survey of 281 Asian businessmen in Nairobi showed an overwhelming preoccupation with retail and wholesale trade. As many as 36 percent of the businessmen were primarily in retailing and 31 percent in wholesaling. In contrast 13 percent were in manufacturing, 9 percent in service industries, 5 percent in building contracting, 4 percent in restaurant- or bar-keeping, 1 percent in transporting, and the remaining 1 percent in other types of business.[13] This distribution was probably fairly representative of all the Asian businessmen in East Africa.

Despite various forms of economic discrimination, the Asians' business activities were not seriously curtailed until the closing years of colonialism. Until then the Asians enjoyed a relatively free economy that permitted the accumulation of private capital essential for philanthropy. The railway rates and the customs duties established early in the colonial years were lower for the European settlers' imports and exports than for those of the Asians, and the taxation system was structured to impose a heavier burden on the Asians through onerous licensing fees on all kinds of business activity. More serious was the marketing legislation of the mid-thirties that restricted Asian commerce in African areas to designated rural trading centers. The Asians found alternatives, however, by organizing new commercial activities in the urban areas and initiating new forms of manufacturing. Not until the fifties, as explained in Chapter 10, did the managed economy, which was applied in all the territories after World War II, sharply curtail Asian enterprise.

On the eve of independence, as shown in Table 1.4, the Asians were situated mainly in the cities and larger towns. By then their activities in rural areas had been reduced, but far more than their brethren in India, these Asians, because of their focus on business, were an urban people. In Kenya 90 percent were concentrated in the sixteen largest urban centers. In Tanganyika 71 percent were in the twelve main centers, and in Uganda 62 percent were in sixteen. A large proportion of the Asians resided in the principal city in each territory. Nairobi held 49 percent of Kenya's Asians, Dar es Salaam 36 percent of those in Tanganyika, and Kampala 27 percent of those in Uganda. These statistics also reveal some major differences among the Asian settlements in the three territories. In Kenya almost all the Asians were in the urban centers, with a heavy concentration in Nairobi and Mombasa. In Tanganyika relatively fewer Asians lived in urban centers, and they were scattered more evenly among the towns. In Uganda, where the rural residence was the highest, these characteristics were more pronounced.[14]

TABLE 1.4

Asian Urban Population, 1957–62

Kenya (1962 Census)					
Nairobi	86,453	Kericho	1,462	Gilgil	593
Mombasa	43,713	Nyeri	1,147	Fort Hall	556
Kisumu	8,355	Nanyuki	982	Malindi	438
Nakuru	6,203	Machakos	719	Embu	404
Eldoret	3,758	Kisii	673	Lamu	233
Thika	2,336	Meru	662	Isiolo	218
Kitale	2,065	Kakamega	601	Elsewhere	15,042
				Total	176,613
Tanganyika (1957 Census)					
Dar S'm	27,441	Dodoma	2,269	Mtwara	593
Tanga	7,412	Lindi	1,804	Mikindani	370
Mwanga	3,956	Morogoro	1,525		
Arusha	3,496	Iringa	1,238	Elsewhere	22,388
Moshi	3,148	Mbeya	896		
				Total	76,536
Uganda (1959 Census)					
Kampala	19,268	Iganga	1,005	Gulu	571
Jinja	8,883	Mbarara	919	Fort Portal	519
Mbale	4,575	Entebbe	904	Arua	516
Masaka	2,139	Kamuli	817		
Soroti	1,833	Lira	671	Elsewhere	27,482
Tororo	1,220	Kabale	611		
				Total	71,933

The differences in urban-rural settlement among the three territories are explained largely by the fact that the major cities offered the most attractive economic and social opportunities. Kenya had the two most important cities, Nairobi and Mombasa. Nairobi was at the base of the highlands to serve the comparatively wealthy European settlers. It was also the capital, with a large number of government officials, and it was in a central position for trade with the Africans. Mombasa as a port and railway terminus was the import-export depot for both Kenya and Uganda. In Tanganyika Dar es Salaam had the unique combination of capital, railway, and port. In Uganda Kampala developed more rapidly than the capital, Entebbe, because it was in the heart of the rich Ganda kingdom and had the railway. Attractive initially only because of the opportunities for business, these cities later afforded the additional advantages of the most desirable educational, recreational, social, and cultural amenities as well as security.

Religious Communal Organization

Although changing rapidly from rural peasants to urban businessmen, the Asians clung to their communal religions throughout their long residence in East Africa. It was not the village, town, or city from which he emigrated nor his particular caste that determined an individual's social and economic association in East Africa, but rather his traditional religious community. Very early in their new residence the Asians discovered that their interests lay primarily with those of their own faith and that their needs were best served by organizations they could establish within their religious communities. Thus instead of diminishing their religious beliefs and practices within a colonial system in which European culture and westernization were emphasized, the Asians strengthened them. At the end of the colonial period, as shown in Table 1.5, the Asians were still most conveniently classified by religious affiliation:[15]

The Hindus and Jains, who are usually combined in East African statistics under the label Hindu, were predominant only in the later years. The Asians who first emigrated to Zanzibar and the mainland coast tended to share the Muslim faith of the Arab rulers. According to the census of 1887, the British Asians alone in this area included 4,866 Muslims and only 1,022 Hindu/Jains.[16] Not until the British assumed control did a change begin toward a proportion more representative of the population in India. In 1911, however, the Muslims of the East Africa Protectorate still outnum-

TABLE 1.5

Asian Religious Affiliation, 1958–62

	Hindu/Jain	Muslim	Sikh	Christian	Other
Numbers					
Kenya 1962	97,841	40,057	21,169	16,524	1,022
Tanganyika 1957	29,048	36,361	4,234	4,732	2,161
Uganda 1959	47,689	17,818	3,058	3,145	85
Zanzibar 1958	4,243	10,618	30	714	286
East Africa	178,821	104,854	28,491	25,115	3,554
Percentages					
Kenya 1962	55.4%	22.7%	12.0%	9.3%	0.6%
Tanganyika 1957	38.0	47.5	5.5	6.2	2.8
Uganda 1959	66.4	24.8	4.3	4.4	0.1
Zanzibar 1958	26.7	66.8	0.2	4.5	1.8
East Africa	52.5%	30.8%	8.4%	7.4%	1.0%

bered the Hindu/Jains by 5,939 to 3,205, and in Uganda by 1,102 to 674.[17] At the end of World War I the Hindu/Jains began to equal the Muslims in these two territories; afterward they increased far more rapidly. By 1948 they totaled 45,238 in Kenya as contrasted with 27,583 Muslims, and 20,441 in Uganda compared to 11,172 Muslims.[18] Tanganyika and Zanzibar retained a larger proportion of Muslims because they attracted comparatively few new immigrants from India. Tanganyika's Asian population, even during the period of British administration, grew largely through natural increase and immigration from Zanzibar.

The Hindus, not including the Jains, totaled on the eve of independence approximately 135,000—about 40 percent of all the Asians in East Africa—and were themselves fragmented.[19] The largest Hindu group, numbering well over 50,000 by 1970, was the Patels, who included not only the Asians of the surname Patel, but also some of the Desais and Amins. Mostly Gujarati-speaking, coming mainly from the area of Ahmedabad and Baroda as small farmers they were also known as Patidars, "land-owning peasants." [20] They were by tradition, however, members of the military Kshatriya caste, and many in India had become landlords, held political office, and received an above-average education. Nearly all who emigrated in the early years were poor. Because of their knowledge of English, they readily found employment in East Africa as clerks with the railway and other branches of government. Most, however, soon found business more rewarding than clerical service. The Patels were especially prominent in Uganda. A survey in the early fifties showed that 1,446 of the 5,819 Uganda Asians holding trading licenses—25 percent—were Patels, and that they were the most numerous—41 percent—among the Hindus. Because of their emphasis on education, the Patels became in the second and third generations the main professional people as lawyers, doctors, dentists, pharmacists, and teachers. Perhaps as a consequence, they were prominent philanthropists. [21]

Next to the Patels, the most numerous Hindu group was the Lohanas. By 1970 there were an estimated 40,000 Lohana adults in East Africa, with 14,000 in Uganda, slightly more in Kenya, and about 7,000 in Tanzania. Although they had been, with the Bhatias, the first Asians to settle on Zanzibar, they had emigrated from there to the mainland, and only a few remained on Zanzibar after the 1964 revolution. They came to East Africa mostly from Kutch and from several areas of Saurashtra. Like the Patels, the Lohanas in Africa quickly became associated with the banya merchant group. Not so well educated or urbane as the Patels when they left India—they had come from more rural areas—they moved directly into business on arrival in East Africa. Collectively they became perhaps the wealthiest of all the Asians. The two most affluent families, the Madhvanis and the Mehtas, were Lohanas, and both were outstanding as philanthropists. [22]

Though far less numerous than the Patels and Lohanas, other Hindu groups were influential in East Africa. Unfortunately, no coordinated survey was ever taken of them in the four British territories. There were at least a dozen others, the most prominent of whom were the Vanias and Brahmins. The Vanias, from whom the name "banya" is perhaps derived, were a large trading caste in northwest India. Like the Vanias, the Brahmins were a more significant group than their numbers indicate. In India they were priests by tradition, but largely soldiers, lawyers, teachers, and other professionals in practice. In East Africa, retaining this professional interest, comparatively few of the Brahmin immigrants concentrated on business.[23]

As a whole, the East African Hindus absorbed far more of Western culture than did their countrymen in India, but in many ways the appearances were deceiving. Though adopting English and a modified Hindustani, or in some instances Swahili, as a lingua franca, most still spoke within their homes and often in their community their traditional Gujarati, Kutchi, or Marathi. Most of the men by the end of the colonial period had long since abandoned the dhoti, sandals, cap or turban, and hairstyle still common in India in favor of a smart business suit, polished shoes, and hair trim of Western style, but some still clung to a single article — perhaps a Nehru jacket or a Gandhi cap — as a token of Indian identity, and the women nearly all still wore the sari, sandals, long hair, gold bangles and necklaces, and distinguishing red mark on their foreheads. Outwardly nearly all the Hindus appeared the same. They dressed alike, drove Peugeot and Mercedes cars, and lived, at least in the cities, in residential areas where all Asians were intermixed in separate homes and flats. Hindus of all types sat next to one another at the weekly Indian movie, mingled together in Lions and Rotary, and joined in various Asian chambers of commerce and political associations. Each remained, however, acutely aware of his or her origins in India and the pertinent religion, caste, and family traditions.

The Muslims, numbering approximately 110,000 in East Africa at the end of the colonial period, were overall only three-fifths as numerous as the Hindus but comprised nearly a third of the total Asian population. Like the Hindus, they came mainly from the Gujarat and Kutch rather than the more northern area that became Pakistan. They were attracted to Zanzibar and the African coast long before the European presence mainly because of the Arabs' hegemony, and many Muslim Asians accompanied Seyyid Said in the move from Oman. A census of the sultan's domain in 1887 revealed that they were by far the largest Asian community, 4,866 as compared to 1,340 Hindus.[24] Not until after World War I, as explained, did they become the minority. The great proportion of the Muslims who emigrated to East Africa were Shias rather than the orthodox Sunnis. They traced their spiritual descent to Ali, the Prophet's son-in-law, claimed that the caliphate was inherited rather than elected, and emphasized the importance of living spiritual leaders, the imams. In East Africa they shared a common religion with the Arabs and a large proportion of the Africans, and they associated with these other communities in Muslim Councils or Associations in most of the cities and towns. The Shia Asians, however, were sharply divided into three main sects: the Ismailis, Ithnasheris, and Bohras.[25]

The Ismailis became the most numerous and most prominent of the Shia Muslims in East Africa. From an origin in Persia the Ismailis had been led by their imam, the Aga Khan, into western India, where they converted many of the Lohanas in Kutch and spread into Bombay and a number of Gujarat towns. Accepted by neither the more numerous Sunni Muslims nor the Hindus, these Ismaili *Khojas* (honorable converts) were unable to rise in society, politics, or government and remained mostly petty traders. Early in the nineteenth century they began a migration to Zanzibar and the adjacent coastal towns and became the most numerous Asian community in East Africa. After 1926, when the Aga Khan directed his followers to settle the East African interior, they began an extensive movement into Uganda and western Tanganyika.[26]

Under the Aga Khan's leadership the Ismailis evolved a complex organization and a dedication to mutual service. The two Aga Khans important to the Asians' history in East Africa were Sultan Mohamed Shah (the third Aga Khan, who reigned from 1885 to 1957) and his successor, Shah Karim. Both were devoted to fostering their community's interests. In 1945 Sultan Mohamed Shah established the Diamond Jubilee Investment Trust to provide low-interest loans for business and housing, and in 1963 the Industrial Promotion Services for assistance in industry and agriculture. He also organized the Jubilee Insurance Company, a finance company, a building society, and schools, hospitals, clinics, orphanages, hostels, and hotels all for the benefit of the community. The gift of 10 percent of their income that he received annually from his followers was in large part returned in the form of these services. By the end of the colonial period the Ismailis rivaled the Lohanas in prosperity, and many had become outstanding lawyers, doctors, and teachers. Often viewed as the most liberal, progressive, and accomplished of the Asians, the Ismailis spoke English and wore Western dress. They had been the first to put their daughters to work and encourage them in professional attainment.[27]

The Ithnasheris (Ithna Ashariya) were the second major Muslim group. Like the Ismailis, with whom they had a common origin, the Ithnasheris represented a diverse background of merchants, farmers, and menial laborers, mostly poor and illiterate when they crossed the Indian Ocean. In the mid-nineteenth century, rejecting the Aga Khan and claiming that the imam was still in concealment, the Ithnasheris split from the Ismailis, and the resulting bitter conflict was a principal reason for their migration to East Africa. The Ithnasheris went initially to Zanzibar and then to the coastal towns in southern Tanganyika, where most of them remained through the colonial period. While the Ismailis spread into the interior, achieving a virtual monopoly of business in the Tanganyika highlands, the Ithnasheris became predominant along the southern coast. By 1960 they numbered about 12,000 in Tanganyika, 3,000 on Zanzibar and Pemba, 3,000 in Uganda, and 2,500 in Kenya, nearly 21,000 in all. In 1972 they were estimated at 30,000.[28]

In East Africa the Ithnasheris developed a culture considerably different from that of the Ismailis. They were not so tightly organized nor so intent on westernization, education, and communal assistance. A large proportion dropped Kutchi as the language in the home and adopted Swahili. They mingled more freely with Africans and sought earnestly to convert them. Like the Ismailis, however, the Ithnasheris were very successful in business. They specialized in the ivory trade, cotton ginning, coffee buying, sisal production, and other basic industries, and many became wealthy. Jaffer Samji was recognized, at least by his own community, as the "uncrowned King of Kilwa," Nasser Virjee as the "King of business in Tanganyika," and Abdulla Fazal as the "King of Coffee." [29]

The Daudi Bohras (Bohoras), the third Shia people in East Africa, traced their origin to a much more remote split with the

Ismailis but also regarded their imam as living in concealment. Pending his revelation, they entrusted supervision of the sect to a *Dai al mutlaq* who from a headquarters in Surat exercised many of the powers of an imam but, unlike the Aga Khan, held office by election and lacked a vital ownership of communal property. The Dai differed from the Aga Khan by opposing a rapid moderniza- tion, and the Bohras became renowned for their conservatism. They were cautioned by the Dai to avoid higher education and the professions. The focus was on the family directed by the father, and the women clung to saris and remained in the home.[30]

Like the Ismailis and Ithnasheris, the Bohras were attracted to East Africa by economic opportunity. From Kutch and some areas of the Gujarat they followed the usual pattern of migration to Zanzibar and the coastal towns. Remaining mainly on Zanzibar and the Kenya coast from Mombasa to Lamu, they grew to about 20,000 in East Africa at the time of independence. The Bohras remained almost exclusively businessmen and became a wealthy community. Two of the most outstanding trading families in East Africa were the Jeevanjees and Karimjees of the early colonial years, and at the time of independence a descendant of one of these Bohra families, A. Y. A. Karimjee, was the foremost leader of the Asian community in Tanganyika. At the lower levels of business on the coast, where petty traders and craftsmen competed daily with Africans and Arabs, there tended to be a free association between communities. Unlike other Shias, some Bohras took African or Arab wives.[31]

Together with the three Shia groups — the Ismailis, Ithnasheris, and Bohras — there were Muslims of Sunni and other beliefs, mostly from the Punjab. The most influential of the Punjabi Mus- lims were the Ahmadiyas, followers of Mirza Ghulam Ahmad, who in 1890 had declared himself the Mahdi. From Quadian, a village in the Punjab, Mirza and his successors, the "caliphs," had directed a missionary movement that quickly spread beyond India. Those who came to East Africa left a peasant background and became traders and artisans with a concentration in Nairobi. In 1924 the Ahmadiyas of East Africa began a campaign to convert Africans. They translated the Koran into Swahili, Luganda, Kikuyu, and other languages and built mosques, schools, and colleges. They moved into remote settlements and shared hardship with prospective converts. More than any other Asians, they lived in equality with Africans and readily accepted them into their organization and society. Not surprisingly, the only woman member of Parliament in Tanganyika, Sophia Mustafa, was an Ahmadiya.[32]

Among the Sunni Asians were several other communities with relatively small populations. The Memons (Memans), originally from Sind, had migrated into Kutch and the Gujarat to escape religious persecution, but they came to East Africa primarily as textile dealers seeking an expanded trade. They were among the first Asians on Zanzibar, and from there they moved to the Tanganyika coast to sell American cottons *(merecani)*. Exhibiting a common Sunni conservatism, they built their own schools and mosques, rarely married beyond the extended family, and were in effect a closed community. The Bhadias, reputedly the oldest immigrants of the coast, were seafarers who helped develop the coastal dhow trade. Khumbars, farmers from Kutch, established profitable little dairies around Mombasa and other coastal towns. Koknis carried on their traditional vocations as skilled mechanics, engineers, and captains or mates of coastal vessels. Baluchis, once the sultan's guards, turned to trade and, intermarrying with Arabs, gradually lost their separate identity. Another Sunni community, the Bhadalas, were exceptional in retaining their traditional status as laborers.[33]

Next to the Muslims the most numerous, and certainly the most conspicuous, Asians in East Africa were the Sikhs. Emerging in the fifteenth century as a separate religious community, the Sikhs were followers of Nanak, who defined their religious principles and urged them to resist with force any oppression from the Great Mogul. They were thus a martial people — every man was to carry a sword — and in the nineteenth century they forged an independent dominion in the Punjab. The "golden temple," which they erected in the middle of a lake in Amritsar, became their sanctuary, and the *Granth Sahib* (master book) their sacred text. Nearly all retained the name Singh (lion). Large of frame, robust, strong, proud, and aggressive, yet beset with poverty in the harsh conditions of their homeland, these independent farmers were logical recruits for work on the Uganda Railway. They were also suited to a career with the army or police.[34]

In East Africa the Sikhs who joined the railway acquired skills as artisans and after indenture, joined by other immigrants, took up construction at first as carpenters, masons, excavators, and iron-mongers, and later as electricians, plumbers, auto mechanics, building contractors, and merchants selling the tools and materials of their crafts. Their only noteworthy experiment with agriculture was in Kibos, near Kisumu, where the government, beginning in 1903, settled and nurtured a small colony of Sikh farmers to raise sugar cane. Though concentrated in Kenya, the Sikhs spread into Tanganyika and Uganda to fill the void between the Hindu and Muslim merchants and the African unskilled laborers. Their disregard of caste and willingness to work side by side with Africans were strong leveling influences. Although the men clung to their traditional beards and turbans through most of the colonial period, and the women to their long braids, chemise, pantaloons, and *dupita* (long scarf), the Sikhs adapted more readily than most Asians to the new way of life. Among them was Indar Singh Gill, a leading industrialist and philanthropist.[35]

Like the Sikhs, the Christian Asians were more influential than their numbers indicate. Although a few Protestant Asians came from various areas of western India, the great majority of the Christian immigrants were Roman Catholics from Portuguese Goa. In Kenya, where they were concentrated, the Goans in 1962 comprised 97 percent of the Christian Asians. Of Hindu antecedent in the Konkani-speaking area of western India, they had embraced Roman Catholicism, adopted many aspects of Western culture, and learned to speak and write Portuguese and some English for employment in the Portuguese colonial system. Comparatively well educated but suffering from lack of opportunity as the Portuguese Empire declined, they were attracted to the British East Africa Protectorate for clerical service in the rapidly expanding government, especially the railway. Goans of varied training, however, even professionals, arrived in considerable number from Mozambique as well as Goa during the initial years of British rule.[36]

Though adhering to many traditions, the Goans were a progressive, outgoing people within the Asian community. Far more than Hindus and Muslims, they adopted a western life-style and inter-married with Europeans. Their social and political organizations were models of their British counterparts. As competition developed with other Asians, the Goans did not remain prominent as merchants, but they became outstanding in government service and in education, law, medicine, and politics. Dr. Rozendo Ayres Ribeiro, the Nairobi doctor, John Maximian Nazareth, Q.C., legislative councillor and president of the East Africa Indian National Congress, Pio Gama Pinto, trade unionist, journalist, and champion of African nationalism, and Fitzval R. S. de Souza, lawyer, journalist, and founder of the Kenya Freedom party, deserve prominence in East African history.

Another vital Asian community was comprised of the Visa Oshwal immigrants, commonly known as the Shahs. The Shahs were a small segment of the world's Jains, a people dedicated to nonviolence whose antecedents in India are at least as old as the Buddhists'. Their religion was critical of landed wealth but condoned monetary accumulation, and it thus appealed to the commercial classes. The Shahs who came to East Africa differed from most Jains in that they were relatively poor, illiterate farmers. Clustered in fifty-two small villages around Jamnagar, where the sufferings from drought and famine, compounded by overpopulation, were most severe, they tilled small plots of land. To send a son to East Africa required a considerable sacrifice from the typical Shah family, which had to save, borrow, and pool resources to pay the cost of the voyage. The first two to leave, Hirji Kara Shah and Popat Vershi Shah, reached Mombasa in 1899 and encouraged others to follow. The word spread from village to village, and a mass movement to the East Africa Protectorate began. "Within thirty to forty years," as one remarked, "we emptied our part of Jamnagar." [37] Their focus of settlement was Nairobi, which by 1972 had 7,430 Shahs out of a total in East Africa of about 15,000, nearly all of whom were in Kenya.[38]

The Shahs' progress in the new environment was remarkable. Conforming to the usual Asian pattern of shopkeeping and regarded in the early years as banyas, they became to Kenya, it is often said, what the Patels were to Uganda. They dealt mainly in textiles, but also in hardware, crockery, and a variety of other goods—in nearly everything except provisions, which normally included meat, fish, and liquor, the particular items that conflicted with their Jain ideals of nonviolence and temperance. The Shahs also avoided the tourist industry with its emphasis on hunting safaris. Like most Asians, they worked hard, saved, and invested. While retaining close communal ties and preserving their religion, the Shahs emphasized modernization, organized for mutual service, and stressed education and professional attainment for women as well as men. After independence they perhaps surpassed the Ismailis as the best-educated Asian community. Some among them, notably Lakhamshi R. Shah, Meghji Pethraj Shah, and the Chandarias, expanded into manufacturing after successful commercial careers and, like the Mehtas and Madhvanis, contributed significantly to East Africa's industrial development.[39]

Though far less numerous than the Shahs and the other principal communities, the Parsis became important to the economic and social life of East Africa. Driven from Persia, where in the sixth century they had embraced the teachings of the prophet Zoroaster, the Parsis had settled in Bombay and other centers of western India, where they became highly successful as traders and bankers. In the East African environment they were involved in many activities including clerical and artisan work, engineering, and contracting. At the end of the colonial period the Parsis numbered about five hundred in Kenya and somewhat less in Tanganyika and Uganda. They were regarded, however, as an enlightened and progressive community that accorded women the same education, status, and freedom as men. More than any other Asians they were accepted socially by Europeans.[40]

Motivation for Philanthropy

The Asians' philanthropy is explained by a combination of factors. From South Asia the Asians inherited the religious mores of sharing one's wealth with the needy and the traditions of local voluntary contribution in serving the physical, economic, and social needs of the villages. They also brought with them the idealism of India's nationalist movement and a profound personal awareness of the nature of poverty. According to his biographer, Meghji Pethraj Shah, one of the foremost philanthropists, "never forgot what it had been like to be poor himself." [41] In the new environment of East Africa the Asians encountered conditions that reinforced their religious communalism and necessitated a high degree of voluntary contribution in providing the educational, medical, and other needs of the overall community. Fortunately, the Asians' ability to adjust and take advantage of the economic opportunities resulted in a monetary accumulation that enabled a high degree of philanthropy.

During their early years in East Africa the Asian immigrants had to rely almost entirely on their own resources not only for economic welfare, but also for all the social amenities. Immigrants from each village clung together, and these groups in time coalesced into ethnic units characterized chiefly by a common religion and language. Through self-help mostly in the form of voluntary monetary contribution, they provided on a rudimentary level most of their own educational, medical, social, and recreational facilities and services.

After World War I, as the colonial governments gradually assumed a responsibility for the provision of these services, the Asians in common with the Africans suffered from discrimination. Inequality was implicit in European colonialism. Through most of the colonial period the Asians were prohibited from owning land in the Kenya highlands and from establishing businesses outside designated locations in the urban centers. They were relegated to a middle position in the civil service with a salary scale and other provisions inferior to those of the Europeans, and they were denied trial by jury. Although their population through most of the colonial years was nearly three times as numerous as that of the Europeans, the Asians' representation in the central government and on municipal bodies was always far less. Residential areas, like the business zones, were segregated, and so were the schools, libraries, railway cars, and buses. Throughout colonial society a color bar extended from hotels, restaurants, and sport and recreational facilities to public lavatories. Despite Queen Victoria's proclamation of 1858 promising equal treatment to all British subjects under the imperial Crown, the Asians in the British territories were assigned by law and regulation as well as practice to a decidedly inferior position. In German East Africa the Asians were classified as "natives" on the assumption that they could not observe German civil law.[42]

In the application of state welfare the governments strongly favored the European and African communities. Despite Asian efforts to unite politically and campaign for equality, discrimination continued, and to narrow the gap between the European and the Asian levels of education, hospitalization, and other services, the Asians felt constrained to maintain a high level of voluntary self-help.

Other determinants of the Asians' philanthropy may have been their particular type of business formation and their association with the European community. With rare exception the Asians formed private rather than public companies. It may be that "corporate giving" in the impersonal public company is hindered by the shareholders' interest in earnings and dividends, whereas in private companies the individuals or partners and their families are the owners and managers and thus more likely to feel a personal responsibility to share their companies' earnings. Presumably, the Asians were also influenced toward charitable donation by the local European society, which, like that in Britain, participated in many philanthropic endeavors.

Essential changes in the evolution of the Asian community may have been additional determinants. During the interwar period the need for common effort led eventually to a new sense of unity and identity as South Asians. With this development the Asians began to contribute to services and facilities that would be enjoyed not by individual ethnic groups, but by the Asian community as a whole. After the war, despite estrangement between Muslims and other Asians paralleling the move toward partition in India, a philanthropy in the interests of all the communities continued.

That the Asians were to extend this beneficence to Europeans, Arabs, and Africans in a colonial environment characterized by segregation attests to the strength of their religions and traditions of social welfare.

Notes

1. Saurashtra and Kathiawar are names for the peninsula. The Gujarat, a name often loosely applied to include the peninsula, properly includes as a geographical term only the northeast part of the peninsula and extends inland. It is the flat land north of the Narbada River. Politically, Gujarat is now a state including Kutch, the peninsula, some of the coast to the south, and considerable inland territory. S. Chandrasekhar, *India's Pop.: Facts, Problems, and Policy* (Meerut: Meenakshi Prakashan, 1967), 16. Even in the more favorable circumstances some of these areas could not grow wheat and rice. F. Kapadia intv.
2. These figures are adjusted to India's present area from 1901. S. Chandrasekhar, *Infant Mortality, Pop. Growth, and Family Planning in India* (Chapel Hill: Univ. of North Carolina Press, 1972), 248. Chandrasekhar, *India's Pop.,* 16.
3. The epidemic is vividly described in the annual *Rept. on the Annual Admin. of the Bombay Presidency* (Bombay, Gov't Printer).
4. "Census of Brit. Indian subjects in dominions of Sultan of Zan.," in Maj. J. R. L. Macdonald to For. Office, 19 Dec. 1887, F.O. 84/1854. The census did not include Goans and Baluchis and was considered very conservative in its survey.
5. Robert G. Gregory, *India and E.A.: A Hist. of Race Relations within the Brit. Empire, 1890–1939* (Oxford: Clarendon, 1971), 118–20.
6. Ibid., 50–61.
7. Census figures through 1939 are from Robert R. Kuczynski, *Demographic Survey of the Brit. Colonial Empire* (3 vols., London, 1948), 2:144–45, 239, 326, 653–54. Those for 1962 are from the annual reports of each territory. See also statistics in Gregory, *India and E.A.,* 61, 372–74, 387, 394, 403, 455, 475, 484. Figures for 1939 are estimates, since the next detailed census after 1931 was in 1948. The 20,000 for Zanzibar was estimated in Michael F. Lofchie, *Zan.: Background to Revolution* (Princeton, N.J.: Princeton Univ. Press, 1965), 80. The 1958 Zanzibar census listed a total of 15,892 Asians.
8. Kuczynski, *Demographic Survey,* 2:653–54.
9. Agehananda Bharati, *Asians in E.A.: Jaihind and Uhuru* (Chicago: Nelson-Hall, 1972), 19–20.
10. Kenya, *Sessional Paper No. 4 of 1959/60* (Nairobi: Govt. Ptr., 1960), 5. *Kenya Pop. Census, 1962,* vol. 4, *Non-Afn. Pop.* (Nairobi: Govt. Ptr., 1966), 31, 54, 60, 68.
11. G. R. Ladak intv. Y. Pirbhai (son) intv. G. D. Shah (son) intv. D. P. Shah (nephew) intv.
12. *Kenya Pop. Census, 1962* 4:28. *Tang. Rept. for the Year 1960: part 2, Stats.* (London: HMSO, 1961), Colonial No. 349, p. 9. *Ug. Census, 1959: Non-Afn. Pop.* (Nairobi/Entebbe: E.A. Stat. Dept., 1960), 52.

13. Peter Marris and Anthony Somerset, *Afn. Businessmen: A Study of Entrepreneurship and Devt. in Kenya* (London: Routledge & Kegan Paul, 1971), 244.
14. *Kenya Pop. Census, 1962: Tables: Advance Rept. of vols. 1 and 2* (Nairobi: Govt. Ptr., 1964), 37–44. *Tang. Rept. for the Year 1960, part 2,* 5. *Ug. Census, 1959: Non-Afn. Pop.,* 10. Charles Bennett, "Persistence amid Adversity: The Growth and Spatial Distrib. of the Asian Pop. of Kenya, 1903–63," Ph.D. diss., Syracuse Univ., 1976.
15. *Kenya Pop. Census, 1962,* 4:28. *Tang. Rept. for the Year 1960, part 2,* 9. *Uganda Census, 1959: Non-Afn. Pop.,* 52. *Rept. on the Census of the Pop. of Zan. Prot. . . . 1958* (Zan.: Govt. Ptr., 1960), 109. Jains were apparently classified as Hindu in Kenya and Uganda, but perhaps not in Tanganyika. Zanzibar, which provided the most complete analysis, enumerated Hindus as 4,095, Jains 148, Parsis 241, and Buddhists 19. In Table 1.6 "Other" includes Parsis, Buddhists, "none," and "not stated."
16. "Census of Brit. Indian subjects . . . Zan."
17. Gregory, *India and E.A.,* 80, n. 5; 113, n. 4.
18. J. S. Mangat, *Hist. of the Asians in E.A., c. 1886 to 1945* (Oxford: Clarendon, 1969), 142.
19. Jains in East Africa were estimated as approximately 45,000 at independence by Amritlal Raishi (intv.). This figure is subtracted from that for Hindu/Jain in Table 1.5.
20. Bharati, *Asians in E.A.,* 48–49. Donald Rothchild, *Racial Bargaining in Independent Kenya* (New York: Oxford Univ. Press, 1973), 43.
21. Bharati, *Asians in E.A.,* 34, 44–47. In a strict sense, Patidars came from Charotar in the Gujarat, Kadva Patels from Saurashtra, and Kutchi Patels from Kutch. H. Pandya intv.
22. H. S. Morris, *Indians in Ug.* (Chicago: Univ. of Chicago Press, 1968), Table 6, 184–85. There is no date for this table, but it probably was compiled 1952–55 when Morris was in Uganda.
23. Z. Patel intv.
24. "Census of British Indian subjects . . . Zan."
25. Surendra Mehta and G. M. Wilson, "Asian Communities of Mombasa," chap. 6 in typescript, *Mombasa Soc. Survey, part 1,* ed. Gordon Wilson, Syracuse Univ. microfilm 2081, reel 12, 180–81.
26. Kurji, Feroz. Graduate student. 28 Feb. 1974, Dar es Salaam (Honey). At the Univ. of Nairobi in 1970–71 Kurji, an Ismaili, researched the geographical distribution of Ismailis in Kenya. K. R. Paroo, "Ismailia Settlement in E.A.," 6-page typescript presented to Gregory during interview. The most detailed study of the Ismailis in East Africa is Shirin Remtulla Walji, "Ismailis on Mainland Tanzania, 1850–1948," Ph.D. diss., Univ. of Wisconsin, 1969.
27. B. R. S. (Jimmy) Verjee, "Ismailism and the Challenge of the Seventies," address to Vancouver Jamat, 11 Dec. 1972, 19-page typescript, presented to Seidenberg during interview. For a penetrating study of the aga khan, see H. Stephen Morris, "Divine Kingship of the Aga Khan," *Southwestern J. of Anthropology* 14, no. 4 (1958): 454–72.
28. H. M. Jetha intv. Seyyid Saeed Ashtar Rizvi intv. A. Fazal intv. Morris, *Indians in Ug.,* 68–75 passim. Emigration to escape religious persecution and physical harm was stressed by Yusuf Sheriff (intv.).

29. Bharati, *Asians in E.A.,* 319. Rizvi intv. A. Sachoo intv.
30. Ali Mohamedjaffer Sheriff. intv. B. A. S. Versi intv. L. W. Hollingsworth, *Asians of E.A.* (London: Macmillan, 1960), 144–48. Mehta and Wilson, "Asian Communities of Mombasa," 163. Morris, *Indians in Ug.,* 87, 184–85.
31. Major F. B. Pearce, *Zan.: The Island Metropolis of Eastern Africa* (New York: Dutton, 1920), 255–56. I. M. Jivan intv. Akbarali Adamjee Mamujee, a Bohra raised in Mombasa, married an Arab from the Yemen (intv.). R. G. Datoo knew several instances of Bohra-African intermarriage in Mombasa (intv.).
32. Hazrat Mirza Bashir-ud-Din Mahmud Ahmad, *Admadiya Movt.* (Rabwah, W. Pakistan: Ahmadiya Muslim Foreign Missions, 1967). Franz Babinger, "Islam," *Religions of the World: Their Nature and Their Hist.,* ed. Carl Clemen, trans. from German by A. K. Dallas (Freeport, N.Y.: Books for Libraries Press, 1931), 470. Sophia Mustafa wrote one of the few Asian autobiographies, *Tang. Way: a Personal Story of Tang.'s Growth to Independence* (London: Oxford Univ. Press, 1962).
33. Mehta and Wilson, "Asian Communities of Mombasa," 17, 166–67. Zahid H. Adamjee, "Hist. and Life of the Memon People," research paper, Hist. Dept., Syracuse Univ., May 1974, based largely on Hashim Zakariya, *Memon kom ni itehas* (Karachi: Arafat, 1971).
34. Mehta and Wilson, "Asian Communities of Mombasa," 187–88. Otto Straus, "Indian Religion," *Religions of the World* (cited in n. 32), 131–32. There was also a small settlement of Jats, a subcaste who, as relatives of Indar Singh Gill, were placed by him on farms near Eldoret to grow wheat. Bharati, *Asians in E.A.,* 101–2.
35. Rothchild, *Racial Bargaining,* 46, 131.
36. Dr. A. Ribeiro intv. One informant proudly pointed out that all Figueiredo Goans were of Brahmin caste. H. S. Figueiredo intv.
37. A. Raishi intv. G. B. Shah, "Hist. of the Birth of the Oshwal Society" (see n. 10 to introduction). Mehta and Wilson, "Asian Communities of Mombasa," 178–79.
38. A. Raishi intv.
39. L. R. Shah intv. K. P. Shah intv.
40. Mehta and Wilson, "Asian Communities of Mombasa," 187–88.
41. Marett, *Meghji Pethraj Shah,* 95.
42. *Rept. on the German Colonies in Afa. and the S. Pacific* (London, 1894), F.O. Misc. Series No. 346, C. 7582-7, p. 40.

2

Asian Charitable Organizations and the Leading Benefactors

I think of people's needs, and see them as my own.
—Meghji Pethraj Shah, 1960

Although the organizations of the separate religious communities attended to many of the economic, social, and physical needs of the members, there were many other Asian organizations concerned with philanthropy. Most were designed primarily for other purposes and assumed charitable functions to meet needs that were not addressed by the colonial society. The Asian political and economic organizations were of this type. Some organizations, such as the Social Service Leagues and the wealthy Asians' private trusts, which served the Asian community at large and, in most instances, provided assistance also to Africans, Arabs, and Europeans without distinction of race or creed, were created specifically for charitable purposes. Nearly all the organizations were led in their philanthropic endeavors by individuals who provided models for emulation.

Political, Economic, and Social Organizations

The Asian political organizations, which served as collective organizations primarily for the expression of political opinion, were established in the main centers of settlement. The first such organization in East Africa was the Mombasa Indian Association organized in 1900 on the initiative of L. M. Savle. Described as "a fiery

43

Maratha who hunted elephants and ran a small business as Manufacturers' Representative at Mombasa," Savle had the enthusiastic support of three of the wealthiest and most influential Asians in East Africa — Allidina Visram and the brothers Alibhoy and Tayabali Mulla Jeevanjee.[1] Under the successive leadership of a number of prominent Mombasa Asians, the association was to continue as an important institution of coordination and protest through the colonial period. In 1906 at the instigation of Visram, who became the first president, a similar organization was founded in Nairobi, and during the ensuing decades it was to become even more influential than the one in Mombasa. After World War I, as Asian settlement expanded, political associations were established in Kisumu, Naivasha, Eldoret, Fort Hall, and nearly all the urban centers of Kenya.[2]

Asian political associations in the other territories appeared somewhat later and were never so numerous. In 1909 the Zanzibar community formed a Committee of Indians, which was to be renamed in 1914 the Indian National Association and to provide in succeeding decades most of the community's political representation. In German East Africa the first Indian Association was instituted at Tanga in 1914, and only in 1918 after the British had taken over was one organized in Dar es Salaam. Others followed in the other main centers of Tanganyika. In Uganda Indian Associations were established in Jinja in 1918, in Kampala and Mbale in 1919, and in most of the other towns during the twenties.[3]

To coordinate the goals and activities of the emerging local associations, the Mombasa Asians again took the lead by forming two interterritorial organizations. As early as 1907 they established a British East Africa Indian Association, but it soon became representative of only local interests and remained relatively unimportant. In March 1914 they met with representatives from all the territories to establish an East Africa Indian National Congress. Modeled on the congress in India, the new organization had a written constitution describing the goals, officers, and administrative procedures. In succeeding years as provided by the constitution, it held on the average of every two years an "open session" attended by delegates from the local political associations. At these sessions officers were elected, issues debated, and resolutions passed that set the basic policy. The daily function of the congress was entrusted to an executive committee and a standing committee on policy. The chief administrator was an honorary secretary aided by one or more assistant secretaries and a treasurer. There was also a president, whose chief function was delivery of the key address at the open session. After World War I the congress moved its head-quarters to Nairobi, which had succeeded Mombasa as the focal point of Asian activity.[4]

Despite its aim to become representative of Asians throughout East Africa, the congress from the outset concentrated on affairs in Kenya and in time became less and less representative of Asians in the other territories. In 1952, when the Asians in Tanganyika formed their own territory-wide organization, the Asian Associa-tion, the congress was renamed the Kenya Indian Congress. In Uganda the Asians organized their own Central Council of Indian Associations as early as 1920. In Tanganyika the Dar es Salaam Asian Association and in Zanzibar the Indian National Associa-tion were to serve similar coordinating functions for their territor-ies.[5]

After the partition of India the congress lost most of its Muslim members. Differences between Muslims and Hindus became ap-parent in East Africa as early as 1933 when the Kenya Muslims began to agitate for separate elections and separate representation in the Kenya legislature. In 1943 a Central Muslim Association was formed in Nairobi, and in 1953 it was superseded by a Kenya Muslim League. Differences between Hindus and Muslims never became pronounced in the other territories, but in Kenya, as will be evident in the discussion of the fund drive for the Coryndon Mu-seum, they had a profound effect on Asian philanthropy. They also led to the designation "Asians" rather than "Indians" as a collec-tive term for the Indians and Pakistanis of East Africa.[6]

Asian commercial organizations, like the political, were not formed expressly for philanthropic purposes but often undertook important benevolent activities. In Mombasa and Nairobi, where Europeans initiated the chambers of commerce and excluded all non-Europeans, the Asians set up merchants' chambers. In other major centers, such as Dar es Salaam, Jinja, Kampala, and Zanzi-bar, as well as in smaller places like Bukoba, the Asians established the chambers of commerce and, in most instances, opened them to the other racial communities. In 1932, to coordinate the Asian commercial organizations on the model of the congress, the Mombasa politician and businessman J. B. Pandya initiated the formation of the Federation of Indian Chambers of Commerce and Industry in Eastern Africa. Though originally situated in Mombasa, it followed the congress in moving its offices to Nairobi, and it remained an important organization beyond the colonial era. Its range of interest was narrower than that of the congress, but it cooperated in the major charitable endeavors.[7]

Next in importance to these political and commercial organizations, which initiated and managed many of the Asians' charitable activities, were the Social Service Leagues, which were primarily philanthropic in purpose. Established in the major urban centers expressly to promote social welfare, the leagues, like the congress and federation, united Asians of all creeds in benevolent activity and had a major impact on society. Because of their importance and the breadth of their activities, they are accorded separate description in Chapter 4.

Additional organizations, more social and religious than political and economic, were predominantly Asian in origin and membership. The Lions Clubs, most of which were formed in the late fifties and early sixties, eventually numbered fifty-eight in East Africa and Ethiopia. Composed mostly of Asians, but including many Europeans and Africans, they were involved in many charitable functions. For instance, the Lions of Kampala, formed in 1959 primarily by Sultan Jaffer, raised money for the Foundation for the Blind, the Sanyu Babies' Home, the Deaf and Dumb Society, the Red Cross, the Salvation Army, and the Muriel Obote Charities. In Mombasa the Lions added a leprosy ward to a hospital, built a children's park in a depressed African area, created swimming pools for African schoolchildren, and provided equipment for the handicapped. At least two Asians, Jaffer of Kampala and Rajam Patel of Mombasa, served as district governors in charge of the four territories, and Jagdish Sondhi of Mombasa became the Lions' international director for Africa.[8]

Rotary International differed from Lions in that it began earlier in East Africa—the first was in Nairobi in 1930—had fewer clubs, and in most centers, including Nairobi, was mostly European in membership. In Mombasa, however, Rotary before independence was almost exclusively Asian and, like Lions, was involved in many charitable activities beneficial to Africans. The leading Mombasa Rotarian was Anant J. Pandya, J. B. Pandya's son, who served two terms as Mombasa president and in 1965 – 66 was district governor of six African countries.[9]

In 1947 Pandya organized in Mombasa a Saturday Club, which was very similar to Rotary and Lions in its social and charitable functions. Meeting, as its name denotes, every Saturday, the club was composed at first of only ten members, all Asian men less than forty years old, but by the time of its silver jubilee in 1972 it had grown to more than sixty members including Africans and women without any age limitation. During the intervening years its guest speakers had included governors, ambassadors, judges, government ministers, physicians, professors, artists, "merchant princes," and "thinkers" of many kinds. At its height it had branches in Nairobi, Kampala, and Dar es Salaam. As Dr. Shankar D. Karve, its first speaker, noted, the club was designed essentially "to train the young Indian to socially take his place in our multi-racial Society." [10] The purposes described in the club's constitution denote a strong philanthropic emphasis. The club was to promote fellowship and the "study of intellectual and charitable activities," to instill a dedication "to due fulfillment of all civic duties," and to inspire the finding of "joy and happiness through service to humanity." [11] In time the club became an important fund-raising institution. In 1972 Councillor John Mambo praised the club for its eagerness "to work in the interest of the Public at large and in particular in organizing aids to charities and funds." [12]

An organization with a function somewhat similar to those of the Saturday Club, Rotary, and Lions was the Giants Club. Having emerged in India, where there were nearly three hundred branches, the Giants were first organized in East Africa in 1981. There were soon five separate clubs in Kenya; though initiated by Asians, they were nonracial in membership. Their main charitable activity was the institution of three camps for family planning.[13]

A few other Asian organizations deserve special mention for their philanthropic work. The Mombasa Indian Women's Association, which Mrs. V. V. Sondhi headed as president for thirty-four years (1939–73), conducted flag days and in other ways raised money for charitable causes. The Kampala Indian Women's Association performed many similar services, including the distribution of food, milk, and clothing to African mothers and children. In Tanganyika the various Indian Women's Associations were represented in a Tanganyika Council of Women, which had its headquarters in Dar es Salaam and carried on a range of activities. In Nairobi the Anjuman Himayat Islam spent several thousand pounds annually for African education and the building of schools and mosques, and the Batal Mal Committee built homes for the poor. In 1972, when the exodus from Uganda began, the 130 Hindu organizations in Kenya combined to form a Hindu Council of Kenya for administering to the needs of the refugees. Led successively by Virendra S. Sikand, S. Kantilal Raval, Tarlok Singh Nandhra, and Ramesh Manilal Desai, the council engaged in many other charitable activities.[14]

Asian youth organizations were also important. The Jain Youth League at Thika acquired a distinction in fund-raising through a series of very successful lotteries. In like manner the Lohana Welfare Youth Organization of Dar es Salaam supported many needy Asian and African families by raising money through the gambling game Tombala. Collecting in more orthodox ways, the Nairobi Young Muslim Association built an orphanage for Africans at Garissa.[15]

Not all such organizations were successful. During the early forties in Nairobi a group of young Asians led by Chanan Singh and Kantilal Punamchand Shah formed a nonsectarian, nonracial organization, the Nairobi Indian Youth League, chiefly to associate African and Asian youth in charitable endeavor. After failing to attract Africans, they dropped "Indian" from the title, but in 1948 the league died for lack of support from Asians as well as Africans.[16]

Families, Individuals, and Trusts

Although perhaps the greater portion of the Asians' charitable endeavor was expressed through the many organizations, a significant contribution came from Asians in family and individual capacities. A full account of the total donations of the pertinent families and individuals is difficult to obtain, since very few kept systematic records of their disbursements. Moreover, many seem to have shared the philosophy expressed by Indar Singh Gill that one should not donate to charities and then advertise it, because "then it isn't a donation." [17]

Among the prominent Asian trading families of East Africa, the Karimjee Jivanjees were apparently the first to be noted for their philanthropy. The founding member, Jivanjee Budhabhoy, a Bohra from Kutch-Mandvi, arrived at Zanzibar in the 1820s and started a small firm to export cloves and copra and import German and American cloth. In the 1860s his second son, Karimjee Jivanjee, began a new business engaged in a similar trade primarily between Zanzibar and Bombay. By the time of his death in 1898 Karimjee had developed a far-flung trade involving Zanzibar and Pemba, the more southern East African coastal towns, the seaports of western India, and Europe. Karimjee Jivanjee & Co. had become the foremost Asian firm in East Africa.[18]

During the twentieth century under the able leadership of Karimjee's three grandsons — Hassanali Alibhai Karimjee Jivanjee, Mohammedali A. Karimjee Jivanjee, and Yusufali A. Karimjee Jivanjee — and a nephew, Tayabali H. A. Karimjee, the expansion resumed. While continuing an import-export trade in many commodities and acquiring new shipping agencies, the Karimjees began to supply petroleum to East Africa, and they became the exclusive agents of Caltex for Tanganyika. They also invested in sisal and tea estates and formed an automobile dealership. In 1940 Karimjee Jivanjee & Co. Ltd., which had branches in Mombasa, Tanga, Lindi, and Mikindani, moved its headquarters from Zanzibar to Dar es Salaam.[19] There a younger member of the family, Yusufali's son Abdulkarim Y. A. Karimjee, assumed the management of the agricultural and auto sales and began an illustrious political career. He was five times mayor of Dar es Salaam, a prominent member of the colonial legislature, and the first speaker of the Parliament after independence. Meanwhile, for their many public services and their impressive philanthropic contributions, Yusufali and Tayabali had been awarded knighthoods.[20]

By 1963 Seth Tayabali Hassanali A. Karimjee, chairman of the

Karimjee Group of Companies, Zanzibar, had endowed the following institutions:[21]

Hassanali Karimjee General Hospital, Zanzibar	£ 67,500
Town Hall, Dar es Salaam	40,000
Muslim Girls' School, Zanzibar	26,000
Bohra School, Mombasa	25,000
Bohra Maternity Home, Dar es Salaam	22,500
Bohra Maternity Home, Mombasa	20,000
Bohra Jamnatkhana and Marriage Hall, Tanga	15,000
Bohra Nursery School, Dar es Salaam	12,500
Sports Stadium, Zanzibar	10,000
Nursery School, Tanga	10,000
Sports Gymkhana, Tanga	7,500
Total	£256,000

Tayabali's cousin A. Y. A. Karimjee, who directed the family business in Dar es Salaam, was the main donor of the Tanzania National Library. He also contributed substantially to the Faculty of Arts of the University of Dar es Salaam and to buildings for the Girl Guides, the Boy Scouts, and the SPCA. A. Y. A. professed to follow the example of his father, Sir Yusufali A. Karimjee, who left one-third of his money to charity. Sir Yusufali, applying his motto, "Wealth imposes obligations," bestowed a total of more than £150,000 on hospitals, dispensaries, schools, mosques, social halls, and sports pavilions. Donating mainly through three family trusts, the Karimjee companies began on Zanzibar in the 1920s to give 5 percent of their profits to charity in the good years and at least 3 percent in the bad.[22]

Two other families noted for philanthropy in the early colonial years were those of Allidina Visram and the brothers Alibhoy and Tayabali Mulla Jeevanjee. Unfortunately, there is very little specific information left about Allidina Visram, but his reputation for munificence remains. While the Karimjee Jivanjee family concentrated on Zanzibar and ultimately Tanganyika, Visram, an Ismaili from a small village in Kutch, became the foremost trader in the East Africa and Uganda protectorates. Arriving by dhow in 1863 at age twelve, Visram found employment with Sewa Haji Paroo, an Ismaili trader in Bagamoyo, the sultan's coastal town opposite

Zanzibar. At that time Bagamoyo was the base for most of the caravan trade to the great lakes. When Paroo died without children, Visram took over the business and joined another Ismaili pioneer, Nasser Virjee, in opening a chain of general stores from Bagamoyo to Ujiji.[23] In the nineties, as Germany acquired his trading area, Visram moved to the British sphere, where construction of the railway from Mombasa to Kisumu posed an extraordinary opportunity. As the railhead proceeded, Visram kept one stop ahead, building and outfitting his shops, and when the line reached Kisumu he moved into Uganda to found similar businesses along the caravan routes. Within a few years his Allidina Visram & Co. had over 170 branches.[24]

Like the Karimjee Jivanjees, Visram devoted his profits to many other forms of enterprise. He established a road transport business to serve the railway, and, purchasing a number of dhows and a small steamer, he set up a water transport system on Lake Victoria. Meanwhile, concentrating on Uganda, he acquired seven plantations and experimented with numerous crops. He also became involved in the processing of agricultural produce and was one of the first to gin cotton. While developing these many interests, Visram worked in close association with leaders of the British and African communities and won their respect. He was widely known as the friend of kings, kabakas, and chiefs, of ministers, generals, and admirals, and as the "uncrowned King of Uganda." Unfortunately, Visram's vast commercial, agricultural, and industrial empire was weakened by the war and the ensuing depression. Within the decade following his death in 1916, lacking his resourceful leadership, it all disappeared.[25]

Allidina and his son Abdul Rasul rank among the foremost Asians in their reputations for philanthropy. The biographer Shanti Pandit has well expressed the sentiment about Allidina: "His generosity to deserving charities and help to poor and needy and assistance to religious institutions [was] so universal that he was respected from the highest to the lowest — from the Governor to the lowest European as well as by the Asian and the African communities alike."[26] Streets in Kampala, Nairobi, and Mombasa were named after him, and his statue was erected in Mombasa. By the year of his death, Visram's charitable donations had amounted to Rs. 9 million. His son Abdul Rasul's endeavors to carry on the tradition culminated, as will be shown in Chapter 5, in the endowment of the Allidina Visram High School.

As the Karimjee Jivanjees developed Zanzibar and Tanganyika and Visram established a trading network with a headquarters in Uganda, another Muslim trader, Alibhoy Mulla Jeevanjee, a Bohra of no relation to the other family, assumed a unique role in the British East Africa Protectorate. During the 1880s, aided by his brother Tayabali, Jeevanjee developed a prosperous contracting, shipping, and trading concern, A. M. Jeevanjee & Co., in Bombay and his home city, Karachi. In 1890 he was employed by the Imperial British East Africa Company to import artisans and police from India. While recruiting these Asians, he began a business in Mombasa to serve the company further as stevedore and contractor. In 1895 he was hired by the East Africa Protectorate to recruit Asian workers, erect buildings, cut stone, prepare earthworks, and supply provisions for the projected Uganda Railway. By the time the railhead reached Nairobi, he was riding in a four-horse carriage and was the government's trusted ally. While performing an invaluable service for the new government, Jeevanjee rapidly acquired a fortune.[27]

Like many successful Asians, Jeevanjee combined business and politics. He was the first Asian appointed to the Legislative Council and the guiding spirit behind the early Asian political organization. His villa in Nairobi became the home of many of East Africa's British, American, and Indian visitors as well as the center of Asian political and social activity. Meanwhile Jeevanjee became a principal landowner, assumed an important role in building and construction, and founded the country's main newspaper. He also established two steamship lines for service from Bombay to Mauritius, Mombasa, and Aden.[28] During the first three decades of the new century, he was in many ways Kenya's leading Asian citizen. For his numerous public services Jeevanjee received an O.B.E., an exceptional honor in European-oriented Kenya. His economic empire, however, was another that endured little more than the one generation. His company was dissolved during the great depression.[31]

Although their records, like those of the Visrams, have not survived, some evidence of the Jeevanjees' philanthropy remains. The Nairobi Public Market and the adjacent Jeevanjee Garden with its statue of Queen Victoria are reminders of A. M. Jeevanjee's benevolence. So too is the old Nairobi Club, which in gratitude for a sizeable donation made Jeevanjee an honorary member. He was the only Asian ever admitted to this exclusive settler retreat. The Jeevanjees also endowed sports clubs, sangat mandals (associations for religious discussion), and religious bodies.[30]

Among the later philanthropic families, those of the Aga Khans, Mehtas, Madhvanis, and Chandarias are outstanding. Because of the Ismailis' policy of not revealing statistics on the third and fourth Aga Khans, who have reigned successively since 1885, no detailed account is possible. As will be apparent in the descriptions of Asian contributions to religious, educational, medical, and other charities, however, the Aga Khans gave generously in support of peoples outside the Ismaili community. The East African Muslim Welfare Society, established by the third Aga Khan, Sultan Mohamed Shah, in 1945, disbursed money not only for mosques, schools, and scholarships, many of which were designed for Africans, but for such projects as construction of the Vasini Island Water Reservoir. The Aga Khan normally matched all contributions made to the society by non-Ismailis and within the first four years donated Shs. 1,312,983.[31]

Nanji Kalidas Mehta, a Lohana Hindu, was the most successful of the Asians who built their fortunes from humble beginnings far in the African interior. Born in 1889 in a village near Porbandar, he came alone by dhow to German East Africa at age nine to seek his fortune. After three years of shopkeeping with his brother, who had preceded him, he moved to Uganda. In 1905 he opened a *duka* (shop) in Kamuli, forty miles north of Jinja, to purchase African produce and ivory, and in 1908 he set up a second duka in another location and began to buy the new African cotton. Within six years he had added a duka in Jinja and five more in the "north country."[32]

For Mehta as well as many other Asians, commerce provided a base for additional forms of enterprise. Sensing the opportunities for industrial and agricultural development, he left trading after World War I to concentrate on ginning cotton and planting sugar cane and quickly became Uganda's leading planter-industrialist. He developed a 6,000-acre sugar-cane estate at Lugazi, erected a factory, and in 1924 began to manufacture sugar. Ultimately he was to expand his acreage to 22,000 acres, reach a production capacity of 600,000 bags (60,000 tons), and employ 10,000 Africans.[33] Through the last three decades of colonial rule, Mehta was the most respected and influential Asian not only in Uganda, but probably in all East Africa. He appears to have been during those years East Africa's principal donor to libraries, hospitals, schools, temples, civic buildings, and recreational facilities in India as well as Africa.

In the postcolonial years, after Mehta returned to Porbandar, the family continued to exert a prominent influence on agricultural and industrial development. In India, as will be explained in Chapter 3, Mehta's eldest son, Dhirendrakumar, helped to establish and manage numerous industries. In East Africa the Mehta Group, led by another son, Mahendrakumar, continued to develop the Lugazi and Muhoroni sugar estates while undertaking new industrial ventures in Uganda and Tanzania.[34]

Under Nanji Kalidas and his sons, who contributed in their father's name, the Mehta family by 1973 had given a total of more than Rs. 24 million, of which a fourth went to charitable causes in East Africa. In addition to establishing schools, hospitals, and libraries in Lugazi, the Mehtas were the sole or principal donors in Kampala alone to the Town Park, the Town Hall, the Council of Chambers, the Arya Girls' School, and the Sports Club and Pavilion. With the Aga Khan, as will be described in Chapter 8, they were the main donors to the National Cultural Centre in Kampala, which included the National Theatre, a language hall, and film society. In Jinja the Mehtas endowed the public library. Among their many other donations in East Africa, the foremost, as will be explained, was the University of Nairobi. Like many other wealthy Asians, the Mehtas formed a trust to further their charitable donations. The trust, in the name of N. K. Mehta and his wife Santokben, began with an endowment of Rs. 700,000.[35]

In their commercial beginnings, industrial and agricultural development, and philanthropy, the Mehtas were closely paralleled by another Lohana family, the Madhvanis. Born in 1894 in a

Saurashtra village near Bileshwar, Muljibhai Prabhudas Madhvani at age twelve sailed to Uganda to join his elder brother in working for Vithaldas Haridas & Co. at a shop in Iganga. Eventually he rose to the position of the managing partner of the Jinja office and helped to establish at Kakira a sugar-cane plantation and factory very similar to that of the Mehtas. With the dissolution in 1946 of Vithaldas Haridas & Co., the company's subsidiaries were divided among its partners. While Muljibhai's elder brother Nanjibhai took over a sugar factory on the Kenya coast, Muljibhai retained the sugar complex at Kakira. By 1958, when he died at age sixty-four, he had not only expanded the Kakira sugar works, but also acquired two soap factories, three ginneries, a glass factory, a mill, a vegetable ghee factory, a jaggery plant, a sweets factory, and a tea plantation.[36]

Between 1958 and 1971 Jayant Madhvani, who succeeded his father at age twenty-six, developed the largest industrial, commercial, and agricultural complex in East Africa. He was to die in 1971, only forty-nine years old, but by then he controlled seventy-eight companies that employed a total of 22,500 Africans. His invested capital had increased from £1.9 million to £16.7 million and his annual turnover from £2 million to £26 million. He is said to have conducted 40 percent of Uganda's business and provided over one-tenth of its revenue. Apart from the sugar interests, his most important industry was the Steel Corporation of East Africa Ltd., the first steel-rolling mill in East Africa. Through other companies Jayant manufactured glassware, beer, textiles, matches, metal and paper boxes, soap, oil, tea, confectionery, and flour.[37]

A key reason for Jayant's remarkable success during a time of diminishing opportunity is that he merged his interests with those of Africans. He was one of the first Asians to apply for Uganda citizenship. He continued his father's program of providing educational, health, housing, and recreational facilities for his African employees, and whenever feasible he employed handicapped Africans. His sweets factory at Thika, for instance, included blind workers. Unlike most Asian company owners, he employed Africans in top management. For his agricultural employees he initiated an "outgrowers' scheme" providing loans, training, and encouragement for Africans to produce cane for the sugar factories.

For his factory workers he introduced the purchase of nonvoting but high-interest-bearing shares in his companies. His dedication to Uganda and its people was one of the main reasons for his nomination in 1970 as the first chairman of Uganda's vital parastatal, the Export and Import Corp. He was then also president of the Uganda Federation of Industries.[38]

The successive Mahdvani leaders — Muljibhai, Jayant, and after 1971 Jayant's son Nitin — rivaled the Mehtas in munificence. Their contributions in East Africa before 1972 were as follows:[39]

> £576,648 from the beginning through 1966
> 22,028 during 1967
> 34,429 during 1968
> 19,481 during 1969
> 21,339 during 1970
> 16,249 during 1971 to 11 December

During a typical year, 1968, the money was distributed among Makerere University, the President's Polio Appeal Fund, the Industrial Society (London), the Federation of Uganda Football Associations, the Girls' School in Jinja, the National Council of Sports, the Jinja Recreation Club, the Church of Uganda, the YMCA of Dar es Salaam, the Muljibhai Madhvani Hall at Kakira, and numerous scholarships. Through the years much of the money went to Jinja, where it provided the Town Hall and Clock Tower, Vithaldas Haridas Pavilion, the Coronation Park, and several schools. Approximately 90 percent of the total was devoted to African development.[40]

The later Madhvanis donated in their fathers' names. In 1958 Jayant set up the Muljibhai Foundation Trust and erected an impressive building for it in Kampala. At independence he donated the trust and building, valued at Shs. 4 million with an annual income of Shs. 400,000, to the new African government. In 1971 Nitin established the Jayant Madhvani Foundation with an initial endowment of Shs. 1 million. In his late father's honor he also provided for the preschool program "Sesame Street" to be shown on Uganda television for six months at a cost of £130,000.[41]

The Chandarias, a family of Jains from a farming background

near Jamnagar, deserve attention with the Aga Khans, Mehtas, and Madhvanis. Premchand Popat Chandaria, the first to immigrate, began work in 1914 as a shop-boy for a Nairobi importer. Three years later he formed with three Khimasia brothers a provisions firm (Premchand Popat & Co.). Joined by his own brothers and nephews, he soon expanded to Mombasa and combined with one Khimasia and several Shahs in the establishment of a retail trading firm (Premchand Raichand & Co.), which for the next fourteen years rapidly expanded into a variety of enterprises. Through the parent and subsidiary companies the Chandarias exported African produce, imported petroleum, quarried stone, ginned cotton, and manufactured aluminum ware, wattle extract, and pasta. As described in Chapter 3, some of the new ventures were undertaken in India.[42]

After 1948 the Chandaria interests were to be managed by Premchand's four very able sons, Devchand (known as D. P.), Ratilal (R. P.), Keshavlal (K. P.), and Manu, together with their uncle, Maganlal (M. P.), and their cousins, Kanti, Kapur, and Anil. The university degrees in engineering and commerce-banking obtained by K. P., Manu, Kanti, and Kapur in 1950 and 1951 and by Anil later greatly enhanced the family's capability.[43]

During the fifties the Chandarias began a rapid industrial expansion. They created a second aluminum plant, acquired a match factory, began two flour mills, and set up a rolling mill for sheet aluminum, the first in tropical Africa. After independence they registered ten new companies in Kenya to manufacture PVC pipe and molding, paper products, floor wax, paints, steel wire, casements, and metal fasteners. In Tanzania they added four factories for the production of stationery, garments, aluminum ware, stoves, and drawn steel, and in Uganda two steel and aluminum industries. They became, next to the Madhvanis and Mehtas, the third largest industrial concern in East Africa.[44] Not all the family's activities were confined to Kenya, Uganda, and Tanzania. As explained in Chapter 3, the Chandarias by the mid-seventies were putting most of their capital into other world areas where economic policies offered more opportunity.

The Chandarias are unusual in providing a detailed record of their donations. In 1955 in honor of Premchand's father, D. P. and

M. P. established the Popat Hira Chandaria Charitable Trust with a capital of Shs. 150,000. They were joined in this family endeavor by Mulchand S. Khimasia, their cousin, the son of Popat's sister. Between 1955 and 1983 the trust, which in 1964 was renamed the Chandaria Foundation, donated a total of Shs. 2,257,779 to charitable causes or organizations in East Africa. Bestowing close to one hundred grants each year, the trust spread its contributions over the following categories:

Health	Shs.	572,872
Education		566,253
Religion		112,297
Other		1,006,357

The total disbursed was only Shs. 3,543 the first year, but by 1963, the year of Kenya's independence, it had grown to Shs. 85,728. The high point was in 1974, when the donations totaled Shs. 417,008. As late as 1983 the annual total was still sizeable, Shs. 42,261.[45]

The Chandaria Foundation contributed to a wide variety of organizations and causes, whether primarily African, Arab, European, or Asian, and whether Christian, Muslim, Hindu, Sikh, or Jain. The gifts varied in amount from less than a hundred shillings to several thousand. A large number were devoted to the Chandarias' Oshwal community, and a considerable number went to other Asian organizations such as the Hindu Mandir of Kabale, the Arya Girls' School of Nairobi, and the Aga Khan Special School of Mombasa. The foundation, however, contributed to European organizations, including the Vasco da Gama Museum Fund, the Lady Crauford Charities, the Seventh-Day Adventist Church, and the Mombasa YWCA. Among the African and Arab beneficiaries were the Mombasa Institute of Muslim Education, the African Almoners' Fund, the Tanu Youth Settlement Farm, and the Mama Ngina Kenyatta Home.

In 1974, to increase the amount of its charitable contributions, especially in aid to Africans, the family formed the Supplementary Chandaria Foundation with an initial capital of Shs. 6,610,000.

From 1976 to 1983 the total donations of Shs. 3,520,511 were distributed as follows:

Health	Shs. 1,178,725
Education	1,112,569
Religion	140,171
Other	1,089,046

As is evident in these statistics, the annual donations of this second foundation were much larger. They averaged nearly a half million shillings each year, and in 1979, the peak year, they reached Shs. 636,613.[46]

Like the earlier organization, the Supplementary Chandaria Foundation distributed its funds among all the racial communities — African, Arab, and European as well as Asian — but it concentrated heavily on African welfare and development. It aided many African organizations, such as the Mutomu Church Building Fund, the Kakuswi Harambee Secondary School, the John Mukungar Limuru Boys Center, and the Unjiru Self-Help Dispensary. It also assisted many individual Africans in meeting the costs of their education. The scholarships and other financial assistance covered school fees, uniforms, books, and travel primarily in East Africa, but also in India and the United Kingdom.

The Kenya industrialist Meghji Pethraj Shah shared with the Chandarias the philanthropic leadership of the Oshwal community. In 1919, when fifteen years old, M. P. left the village of Dabasang near Jamnagar to work as a bookkeeper for a relative in Nairobi. After two years he joined his two brothers in forming a general store (Raichand Bros.), which soon established a branch in Mbale, added the manufacture of hair oil, and expanded into road transport. He then merged with the Chandaria-Khimasia-Shah group in forming Premchand Raichand & Co. and, like the Chandarias, became involved with many industries in East Africa and India. In 1943, when the company was dissolved, M. P. acquired the wattle-bark factory (Kenya Tanning Extract Co.), which proved extremely profitable. He subsequently undertook textile exportation, built three factories on a sisal plantation, and formed a financial concern.[47]

In 1953, when only forty-nine years old, M. P. Shah retired to devote the rest of his life to philanthropy. He then had a capital worth of £2.5 million and employed 3,000 Africans. Five years before retiring he had established two charitable organizations: the Meghjibhai Foundation in Nairobi for donations in Kenya; and the Meghji Pethraj Shah Charitable Trust in Jamnagar for contributions in India. He moved to Jamnagar, and it was India, as shown in Chapter 3, that received the major share of his philanthropic contribution. His donations to Kenya, however, totalled Shs. 5,625,000 by 1959, when he died, and were distributed in his or his wife Maniben's name as follows:[48]

Health centers throughout Kenya	Shs. 2,000,000
M. P. Shah Hospital, Nairobi	1,500,000
Scholarships (35) to Africans for higher education abroad	400,000
M. P. Shah High School, and Primary School, Thika	300,000
M. M. Shah Primary School, Mombasa	
Royal Technical College, Nairobi	200,000
Sonapuri Rath (3), Cutchi Gujarati Hindu Union, Nairobi	200,000
M. P. Shah Wing, Nurses' Home, Kenyatta National Hospital, Nairobi	200,000
M. M. Shah School, Kisumu	200,000
M. P. Shah Dispensary, Mombasa	200,000
Halari Visa Oshwal Mahajanwadi, Nairobi	125,000
Murang'a College of Technology	50,000

Devji Karamshi Hindocha, a pioneer in the sugar and cotton industries, was another major benefactor. After immigrating from Saurashtra in 1908 at age eighteen, he obtained employment in Kampala with Vithaldas Haridas & Co. and quickly rose to the position of partner. In 1946, when the firm was dissolved, Hindocha assumed the Kenya interests. A year later he purchased the Miwani Sugar Mills Ltd., which became the principal source of his fortune. It eventually included 15,000 acres of cane, employed 4,200 Africans, produced each year 20,000 tons of sugar, and represented an investment of £2,300,000.[49]

Hindocha is said to have been respected for many charities "without discrimination of colour, creed or class," and after his death his family founded in his name a trust that carried on the tradition. The contributions of the Devjibhai Hindocha Family Trust during a typical two-year period were the following:[50]

	1970	1971
Scholarships	£2,449	£1,800
YMCA, Kisumu	2,500	50
Gatundu Hospital	1,000	250
Port Victoria Self-Help Development	250	—
Onjiko Primary School	250	—
Wall clocks for schools	—	1,237
Blankets for the poor	—	798
Other	2,651	2,396
Totals	£9,100	£6,531

Among other well-known benefactors were Indar Singh Gill, Mohamedali Rattansi, Anant J. Pandya, and Jayantilal Keshavji Chande. Gill, a Kenya-Uganda industrialist and the principal Sikh philanthropist, would admit in 1973 only to have given £5,000 for a nursery school in 1947 and some Shs. 20,000 to various charities in Kenya during the three months since his expulsion from Uganda, but his overall contribution was much higher. Rattansi, who assumed a large share of the business interests of Allidina Visram, was said by his son to have frequently given money away even when he could ill afford to do so. After 1956 most of his donations were distributed by the Maniben and Mohamedali Rattansi Educational Trust Fund that he formed that year. Eventually administered by his son Hassan, the trust fund, as explained in chapter 5, provided an annual sum of from £10,000 to £20,000 for the education of Kenyans irrespective of race.[51]

Anant J. Pandya, the Mombasa barrister and political leader who succeeded his illustrious father in managing the family's retailing and import-export businesses, was involved, together with his uncle Ravishanker B. Pandya, in nearly every charitable endeavor sponsored in Mombasa during the three decades after World War II. Because of limited resources the Pandyas' monetary contributions were not large, but in common with their close associate A. B. Patel, what they could not give in money they made up for in service. In 1973, for instance, Anant was an active participant in all the following organizations:[52]

Allidina Visram High School, board of governors (member, former president)
Brahamali Samaj (member)
Coast Hockey Union (member, founder)
Coast Workshop, Mazeras (chairman)
Council of Commonwealth Societies in Kenya (member, founder)
Gandhi Memorial Society (secretary)
Higher Education Loans Board (member)
Kenya Business Aid Society, Mombasa Branch (chairman)
Kenya (Indian) Congress (president)
Maniben & Mohamedali Rattansi Education Trust Fund (director)
Mombasa Housing Society Ltd. (director)
Old Allidinians' Association (member, founder and former president)
Pandya Memorial Society, & Clinic, Executive Committee (chairman)
Rent Control Board, Coast (member)
Rotary International (member, former president of club, and district governor)
Saturday Club (member, founder and former president)
Saturday Club Charitable Trust (trustee)
Seif bin Salim Public Library, Governing Committee (member)
Social Service League (member)
Star of the Sea Secondary School, Board of Governors (member)
United Kenya Club of Mombasa (director, former president)

Like Pandya, J. K. Chande, who at the end of the colonial period was one of the wealthiest and most influential Asians in Tanganyika, was involved with an extraordinary number of social organizations. After 1959, when he succeeded his father as manager of Chande Industries Ltd., Chande merged his family interests with those of the Madhvanis through his marriage to Muljibhai's daughter. He became the principal representative in Tanzania of the Madhvani as well as the Chande enterprises, and when nationalization terminated his industrial activities, he was the director of twenty-five companies as well as an outstanding political and social leader. In 1970 his numerous service activities included these:[53]

Association of Round Tables in Eastern Africa (honorary life member)
Automobile Association of East Africa, Tanzania Management Committee (chairman)
College of Business Education, board of examiners (chairman)
Council of the Federation of Commonwealth Chambers of Commerce (member)
Dar es Salaam Round Table (honorary life member)
Dar es Salaam Secondary Education Society (president)
Gandhi Memorial Society (trustee)
Lohana (East Africa) Education Trust (trustee)
National Museum of Tanzania, board of trustees (chairman)
Rotary Club of Dar es Salaam (member, director 1972–73)
Rotary Club, Community Service Committee (member, chairman 1972–73)
Shaaban Robert Secondary School, board of governors (chairman)
Tanzania Red Cross Society (vice-president)
Tanzania Society for the Deaf (chairman)
Upanga Sports Club (trustee)
World Council of Young Men's Service Clubs (international president)
World Council, International Travel Fund Trustees (chairman)

Among the Asians there have been many individuals whose charitable activities have been extensive but not widely recognized. Zarina Patel, who, as will be explained, brought four African children into her home, is one of these. Though trained as a physiotherapist, she decided to devote her life to promoting the well-being of Africans. She began to work for the YWCA and the Lions Club in Mombasa in raising funds for various African projects, such as the construction of the children's park in Majengo. She soon joined the National Christian Council of Kenya and, though the only Asian member, became executive secretary of the Council's Home Industries Center. Established in 1965, the center was designed to train Africans in handicrafts, find markets for their products, and devote the proceeds to African education. Zarina also organized and became secretary of the council's Community Relations Workshop for promoting a meaningful association among Africans, Asians, and Europeans.[54]

Since almost all Asians contributed to charitable causes, it is difficult to single out more for special mention. The following are typical of many others. As subsequently explained, Lakhamshi R. Shah, director of the textile firm Hemraj Bharmal Ltd., aided many Africans personally in their education, but he also helped in numerous other ways. In 1945 he responded to a plea from James Gichuru, the Kikuyu political leader, for financial aid to his brother's wife, who had contracted tuberculosis. Shah told Gichuru to take the woman to the hospital, and for the next two years, until she was well, he met all the expenses. Premchand Vrajpal Shah, another influential member of the Oshwal community, devoted the last eight years of his life, 1953–61, to social work. He paid daily visits to hospitals, clinics, and schools and aided them as necessary with money from a family trust. Another member of the same community, Jeshand Punja Shah, retired to India in 1969 and on departure left 25 percent of his considerable property to African friends with whom he had had a long business relationship. Keshivji Tethabhai Chande, the Lohana merchant of Tanzania who made a fortune in trade and established a network of industries in the western area, is described by his son as "a great humanitarian" who "helped everyone, regardless of colour or creed." In 1938–39, when the Western Province suffered a severe famine, Chande organized a relief fund, pooled the resources of the Asian businessmen of the province, and placed them at the government's disposal. Sewa Haji Paroo, the Ismaili who in the 1880s and 1890s outfitted caravans for the Germans and from Bagamo set up a number of trading stations, was, like Allidina Visram, his counterpart in the British territories, a noted philanthropist. At his death in 1897 he bequeathed all his property to a Catholic mission for benefit of the indigenous people.[55]

The ways of Asian philanthropy were various. When the young Nairobi businessman Ratilal Vershi Malde died in an auto accident, his family donated Shs. 200,000 in his memory to the Duke of Gloucester School. They specified that the money go toward construction of the school swimming pool "as he was keenly interested in swimming."[56] The Nairobi lawyer M. M. Patel, before coming to Kenya in 1954, had organized two medical camps that offered free food, beds, and service for patients needing eye operations, dental work, or treatment for tuberculosis. Doctors donated their services, pharmacists contributed drugs, schoolgirls volunteered as nurses, wealthy townsmen gave food, and hospitals lent X-ray machines. One camp held four hundred patients, the other two hundred. Hoping to establish a similar camp in Kenya, Patel in work with the Oriental Art Circle and the Lions Club obtained promises from several Asian doctors and pharmacists for free service and drugs. He then approached Africans in government and offered to donate a farm he had in Ruiru for use as the camp. To his disappointment, no African would take charge of the project.[57]

Notes

1. Roger K. Tangri, "Early Asian Protest in E.A., 1900–18," *Afa. Quarterly* (New Delhi) 8, no. 2 (July–Sep 1967): 161. Shanti Pandit, ed., *Asians in E. and Cen. Afa.* (Nairobi: Panco, 1963), 93.
2. The associations appear frequently in the chronological files of correspondence of the congress (EAINC) records on microfilm at Syracuse Univ., film series 1929, reels 1–14. The records of the Nairobi Indian Association are together with those of the congress in film 1929, reels 1–36, and film 2087, reels 1–3. Others are on separate film: Mombasa, film 1926, reels 1–15; Kisumu, film 2232, reels 1–4; and Nakuru, film 2081, reels 24–29.
3. Taken from corresp. ibid.
4. For formation of the congress, see chronological file "1885–1915," EAINC records, film 1929, reel 1; and "Report of the First Session of the EAINC, 7–8 Mar. 1914," encl. Sir Henry Belfield (governor, E.A.P.) to sec. of st. for cols., 1 May 1914, C.O. 533/157.
5. Dana April Seidenberg, *Uhuru and the Kenya Asians: The Role of a Minority Community in Kenya Politics, 1939–63* (New Delhi: Vikas, 1983), 15–16. See also file "1920, Dec.," EAINC records, reel 1.
6. Seidenberg, *Uhuru,* 51–60, 73, 125–26.
7. Among the SU microfilms are the records of the Federation of Indian Chambers of Commerce and Industry in Eastern Africa and those of the Nairobi Indian Merchants' Chamber (film 1923, reels 1–3), the Mombasa Indian Merchants' Chamber (film 1922, reels 1–3), and the Nairobi Chamber of Commerce (film 1924, reels 1–6).
8. S. H. Jaffer intv. Z. Patel intv.
9. A. J. Pandya intv.
10. *Souvenir Brochure: Saturday Club, Momb., Silver Jubilee* (Momb.: Reliance Press, 1972), 17.
11. Ibid., 4.
12. Ibid., 18. For the club's donation to the Coast School for the Physically Handicapped, see 12.
13. R. M. Desai intv.
14. One of the flag days of the Mombasa Indian Women's Association raised

money for the Pandya Memorial Clinic. *Kenya Daily Mail* (Mombasa), 27
Feb. 1948, 6. Mrs. D. Kotecha intv. Mrs. U. Jhaveri intv. Nergis Dastur intv.
Letter by S. G. Hassan, *E. Afn. Chronicle* (Nairobi), 12 Oct. 1957. R. M. Desai
intv.
15. H. M. Kotak intv. Munawar-ud-Deen intv.
16. K. P. Shah intv.
17. Indar Singh Gill intv.
18. N. S. Thakur and Shanti Pandit, "Brief Hist. of the Devt. of Indian Settlement
in E.A.," in Pandit, *Asians,* 16.
19. Pandit, *Asians,* 161–62.
20. A. Y. A. Karimjee intv.
21. Pandit, *Asians,* 161.
22. Ibid., 67.
23. For a biography of Virjee, see B. G. Vaghela and J. M. Patel, eds., *E.A. To-day
(1958–1959): Comprehensive Directory of Brit. E.A. with Who's Who* (Bombay: Overseas Info. Pub., 1959), 154.
24. K. R. Paroo intv. Paroo's grandfather's brother was Sewa Haji. Paroo's father
worked for Visram. See also Pandit, *Asians,* 66–68.
25. Gregory discussed the demise with Visram's descendants in Nairobi.
26. Pandit, *Asians,* 68.
27. Ibid., 76–78.
28. A. Raishi intv. Raishi worked in Jeevanjee's main office during the twenties
and read his personal papers.
29. Pandit, *Asians,* 76–78. Pandit was assembling and indexing these papers
when they were suddenly burned by the Kenya government. Jeevanjee was
one of the few Asians who left a large collection of personal papers.
30. Ibid., 76–78.
31. *Combined Rept. of the Third Annual Meeting of the E. Afn. Muslim Welfare
Soc. . . . 10th and 11th Nov. 1944* (Momb.: EAMWS, 1949), Zafrud-Deen
Papers, SU microfilm 2174, reel 1.
32. Mehta is the only Asian who wrote a personal account of his business activities: *Dream Half Expressed: an Autobiog.* (Bombay: Vakils, Feffer & Simons,
1966).
33. Ibid., 156, 168–72, 179–82. D. N. Mehta (son) intv. K. N. K. Mehta (son)
intv. Pandit, *Asians,* 183–84, 359–60.
34. Mehta, *Dream,* 285. Pandit, *Asians,* 183, 359–60. D. N. Mehta intv.
35. Pandit, *Asians,* p. 184. Vaghela and Patel, *E.A. To-day (1958–1959),* 639. D.
N. Mehta intv.
36. Pandit, *Asians,* 79–80. H. P. Joshi, Bhanumati V. Kotecha, and J. V. Paun,
eds., *Jayant Muljibhai Madhvani* (Nairobi: Emco Glass Works, 1973), 61,
89, 313, 314. Surprisingly little has been written about Muljibhai Madhvani.
37. Paul Munyagwa-Nsibirwa, "Dynamic Industrialist," chap. 74 in Joshi, Kotecha, and Paun, *Jayant Muljibhai Madhvani,* 103. Clipping from *Econ.
Times,* n.d. [Aug. 1971], ibid., 314. "Speech of Mr. Jayant Madhvani on
behalf of Steel Corp. of E.A. Ltd. . . . 21st of April, 1961," chap. 347, ibid.,
347–48. Joseph Mubiru, "Econ. Colossus," chap. 12 in Robert Becker and
Nitin Jayant Madhvani, eds., *Jayant Madhvani* (London: pub. privately,
1973), 55–56. A. T. Lal intv. H. P. Joshi intv.
38. Joshi, Kotecha, and Paun, *Jayant Muljibhai Madhvani: In memorium,* 168–

69. Yash Tandon, "Pragmatic Industrialist," in Becker and Madhvani, *Jayant Madhvani,* caption, 14–155. Munyagwa-Nsibirwa, "Dynamic Industrialist," in Joshi, Kotecha, and Paun, *Jayant Muljibhai Madhvani,* 103.
39. Provided by H. P. Joshi during interview. Not shown in the statistics are Shs. 1,000,000 for endowment of the J. N. Muljibhai Madhvani Foundation in 1972.
40. Ibid. Pandit, *Asians,* 79–80.
41. Joshi, Kotecha, and Paun, *Jayant Muljibhai Madhvani* 315, 318–19. N. Madhvani intv.
42. G. D. Shah intv. K. P. Chandaria intv.
43. K. P. Chandaria intv.
44. Ibid. Robin Murray, "The Chandarias: The Devt. of a Kenyan Multinational," chap. 7 in *Readings on the Multinational Corp. in Kenya,* ed. Raphael Kaplinsky (Nairobi: Oxford Univ. P., 1978), 292. K. Shah intv.
45. "Chandaria Foundation, Chandaria Supplementary Foundation: Analysis of Donations," typescript submitted to Gregory by R. P. Chandaria, 16 Oct. 1984, London.
46. Ibid.
47. Marett, *Meghji Pethraj Shah,* chaps. 1–5.
48. Ibid., chaps. 6–9 and p. 133.
49. Pandit, *Asians,* 144–45.
50. "Miwani Sugar Mills Ltd.," typescript submitted to Bennett during interview with D. K. Hindocha.
51. I. S. Gill intv. H. Rattansi intv. Nairobi. V. D. Shah (trustee of the trust fund) intv.
52. Pandit, *Asians,* p. 203.
53. At the same time Chande was director (or former director) of twenty-five registered companies. Vita of J. K. Chande given to Honey in interview.
54. Z. Patel intv.
55. L. R. Shah intv. D. P. Shah (son) intv. J. P. Shah intv. "The Late Keshivji Jethabhai Chande," typescript given in J. K. Chande interview. A. Vellani intv.
56. Pandit, *Asians,* 82–83.
57. M. M. Patel intv.

3

Deployment of Earnings and Savings

*The modernisation of the nation will be
completed only if every person contributes, as
much as he can, to this end. Accordingly, I too,
am making a contribution according to my
means in order to fulfill my own obligation. By
making this contribution I am not obliging
anybody but I am simply doing my duty.*
—Meghji Pethraj Shah, 1955

Like peoples everywhere in a relatively free economic environment, the Asians found a variety of uses for the capital that they accumulated as wage earners, businessmen, craftsmen, farmers, industrialists, professionals, and money-lenders. Published statistics on the deployment of capital are few, and most Asians, for a number of reasons, did not keep detailed records of their financial activities. Because of the existence of some relevant information in writing and the oral testimony of numerous Asians, however, it is possible to provide a fairly comprehensive description. Beginning in the early years of settlement, Asians sent money overseas for the repayment of loans, support of relatives, children's education, and an eventual retirement overseas. As the community became more affluent, the Asians exported money for the establishment of foreign businesses. Near the end of the colonial period and into the era of independence, when investment in East Africa no longer appeared profitable and retention of their communal identity seemed uncertain, most Asians disposed of their business properties, withdrew their savings, and endeavored to send out all their capital. Throughout their stay in East Africa, the Asians also devoted a sizeable portion of their income to the support of philanthropic projects overseas.

Investment in East Africa

Until the closing years of the colonial era, business in East Africa in the form of retailing, wholesaling, importing, exporting, transporting, and money-lending proved to be the most attractive investment for the Asian community. As explained in Chapter 1, the earliest Asians, apparently even those associated with the coast centuries ago, were primarily traders engaged in exchanging South Asian manufactures for Africa's ivory, gold, hides, skins, shells, and timber. Most of their profits presumably were devoted to expanding their trading opportunities. After the expiration of their indentures, many of the Asians who had been employed in constructing the Uganda Railway served as the skilled artisans of East Africa, but in time they and their descendants, by means of their earnings, moved into contracting or some shopkeeping concerned with the materials of construction. Only a few of the Asian civil servants remained in government employment to the retirement age. Most quit after a few years to invest their savings in some business enterprise. The shopkeepers devoted their profits not only to expansion of their establishments, but also to the development of road transport. The professionals—the doctors, dentists, advocates, teachers, pharmacists, accountants, and architects—who were mostly among the later immigrants, also tended to put their earnings into some business enterprise. Increasingly after World War II, many from all these categories invested in some form of manufacturing or estate agriculture.

Although the statistical evidence is meager, the magnitude of the Asians' African investment is manifest. "All one has to do," as the Nairobi advocate Velji Devji Shah asserted, "is look at Nairobi." [1] East Africa's cities and towns were a result primarily of Asian enterprise. Most of the commercial edifices were established by Asians. Even the buildings belonging to Europeans, including Fort Jesus, were constructed largely by Asian contractors and artisans. As illustrated in succeeding chapters, many of the noncommercial buildings, such as temples and mosques, schools, hospitals, and libraries, and most of the public parks and much of the impressive statuary were also created by Asians. Nearly all the ginneries and sugar mills that produced Uganda's main export commodities were additional contributions chiefly from Asians. Throughout East Africa the network of roads represents mainly the governments' response to the Asians' development of road transport.[2]

Despite the lack of comprehensive information there are some revealing statistics. Between 1935 and 1946 the Kenya Asians invested £32,709,000 in private companies, £2,379,000 in urban commercial property, and £223,000 in agricultural estates.[3] In 1946 they paid an estimated £860,000 in import and excise duties on commodities.[4] By 1936 a total of 6,680 Kenya Asians, as compared with 3,451 Europeans, held deposits in the Post Office Savings Bank.[5] In Tanganyika 349 Asians by 1936 held 316,000 acres, 16 percent of the alienated agricultural and pastoral land.[6] In 1951 some 3,000 Tanganyika Asians were employing a total of 108,860 workers. A decade later 8,707 Tanganyika Asians were engaged in commerce, 1,999 in manufacturing, 1,953 in public services, 1,852 in transport, 898 in agriculture and forestry, 809 in construction, 540 in banking and insurance, 482 in teaching, and 149 in mining and quarrying.[7] In Uganda the Asians by 1933 had acquired 46 agricultural estates comprising 42,512 acres.[8] Three years later they were described as owning 105 of the 137 registered ginneries.[9] In Zanzibar 20 of the 22 licensed clove exporters in 1960 were Asians.[10] Many other statistics such as these attest to the magnitude of the Asian investment.

Exportation for Relatives, Education, Retirement, and Investment

Though probably inferior in amount to that invested locally, considerable Asian money was sent abroad. During the nineteenth century most Hindus who settled on Zanzibar and traded in the coastal cities of East Africa retained very close ties to India. They usually left their wives in India, partly to safeguard them from the hazards and hardships of life in East Africa, and partly to ensure a suitable education for their children in Indian schools. These Hindu businessmen thus made frequent trips to India, sent "home" a relatively large proportion of their profits, and anticipated an eventual retirement in the vicinities of their places of birth. The same pattern is discernible in the lives of sons or other relatives who succeeded them in the family businesses.[11]

The Muslims more easily severed the ties to India. Their religious affiliation was to the Kaaba in Mecca rather than to temples in the Gujarat or Punjab.[12] Although many Bohras retained a custom of returning to India to marry, nearly all the Ismailis and Ithnasheris selected wives from the local communities.[13] Those who could afford to do so might educate their children in India simply because adequate facilities in East Africa were lacking, but they did not for long support relatives in India, make trips to India, nor so often plan retirement there. Instead, they assisted their relatives to join them overseas. The Ismailis were foremost in this. "They left India," it is said, "with the idea of making their homes in East Africa." [14]

The indentured railway workers, who at the turn of the century were forerunners of a great wave of Asian immigrants, apparently remitted most of their earnings to India. Nearly 82 percent (32,583) of the indentured Asians employed in East Africa between 1895 and 1922 returned to India.[15] In 1906 large numbers of the Punjabi workers were described as "mailing away part of their monthly wages" at the Mombasa General Post Office. "To judge from their half-starved appearance," reported the East African Standard, '99 percent of their wages were being disposed of in this way." [16] Even the indentured Asians who opted to stay in Africa must have remitted a considerable amount of their wages to relatives in India. That the money earned by these workers should remain in East Africa, however, was never intended by the governments. Nor was there much money involved. The minimum monthly wage was only Rs. 15.[17]

Although the free immigrants of the twentieth century obviously invested most of their money in East Africa, many retained close ties and sent a portion of their earnings to India. This is especially true of the first-generation immigrants, who often had to reimburse relatives for passage costs and support wives, children, and others whom they had left behind. Two examples may be cited. Abdulla Fazal, a Bukoba wholesaler and manufacturer, earned after he arrived in 1910 only Shs. 25 per month, and of that he regularly sent

Shs. 10 to his mother in Kutch.[18] Hariprasad Bhatt, who in 1938 left Saurashtra to work in a Kampala motor parts company, supported his wife in India for nearly four years, and later three sons for several years during their education in India.[19]

For most Asians, whether first-, second-, or third-generation immigrants, the profits before 1945 were relatively small, and there was a pressing need for reinvestment in the local countries. Before 1930 most new immigrants were just beginning their business ventures, and during the depression years of the early thirties they were lucky to survive.[20] On the whole not much money could have been sent away. There were, of course, many exceptions. The Patel and Punjabi civil servants, it is said, went home on leave every three years, built additions to their homes, and, looking forward to retirement on their pensions, "poured money into India."[21] The Shahs spent a lot of money in frequent trips to the Gujarat because, as one remarked, the social life of their community was there. Perhaps more than any other community, they also sent money regularly to families in India.[22]

World War II was a turning point in the relations with South Asia. Although some continued to have difficulty in earning a living in East Africa, the Asians as a whole were prosperous. They had the means not only to send their children to India or Pakistan, but to the United Kingdom and even to the United States for secondary and higher education. Increasingly an education in Europe or America was recognized as more valuable and more prestigious. Moreover, as a greater proportion of the Asians were born locally, the retention of close ties to South Asia acquired less value. For many the mother land was no longer home.

Despite a growing cultural estrangement, the more affluent Asians looked first to South Asia when considering the investment of money overseas. During the late thirties, after his remarkable success in cotton ginning and sugar manufacture, Nanji Kalidas Mehta proposed to the Uganda government a cooperative venture in establishing a textile industry. When, to his disappointment, the government declined, he turned to his home area in Saurashtra. The maharana of Porbandar welcomed the project and offered full cooperation. In 1940, leaving family members in charge of his Uganda industries, Mehta moved to Porbandar to establish with

Uganda money the Maharana Mills Ltd., a huge textile and weaving concern, together with a smaller ancillary enterprise, the Porbandar Ginning and Pressing Factory Ltd. He also began a vegetable glue factory. Although the last proved unprofitable, the other two were very successful. In 1961 from the profits of these factories, he introduced another large complex in Porbandar, the Saurashtra Cement and Chemical Industries Ltd. According to Mehta's sons, Uganda money was used only to initiate the Saurashtra industries, and until 1965 most of the profits made in Uganda were invested in East Africa.[24]

During the same period, though not so successful as Mehta in their initial foreign investments, a group of Shahs undertook several financial ventures in India. In 1940, as previously explained, Meghji Pethraj Shah joined with Devchand Premchand Chandaria, Premchand Vrajpal Shah, and several others to manage jointly a total of eight enterprises in different centers of Kenya.[25] The next year they expanded into India. In Jamnagar they founded Premchand Popat & Co., which briefly preceded Mehta's textile factory as the first in Saurashtra. About the same time the organizers of this company, incorporating other Shahs, formed a large brokerage business in Jamnagar and dealt in futures of ground nuts, castor seed, cotton, and precious metals. They quickly acquired a monopoly of the delivery of silver to the entire area. As newcomers, however, they were resented by the established members of the Shah community in Jamnagar, who dubbed them the *Mahjan* (untouchables). The group soon adopted the epithet with pride. In 1942 under the leadership of Devchand's brother Rupilal, some of the Mahjan undertook another venture — the building of four dhows in Mangalore and the inauguration of a passenger service between Bombay and Mombasa. During the war years, when the Indian Ocean steamer traffic all but ceased, the dhows did a thriving business and made the voyage in as few as eight days.[26]

At the end of the war, for several reasons, the Shah experiment in India collapsed. When steamship travel resumed, the dhow service was no longer profitable. Moreover, despite the success of the other businesses, most members of the group were beginning to realize that East Africa offered a much greater opportunity for investment.

The independence of India in 1947 brought a sizeable increase in taxation; income taxes became much higher than in East Africa.[27] Also, after independence the government of India prohibited external banking accounts, with the result that money sent to India could not be taken out.[28] A crisis occurred in 1948 when the Mahjan overspeculated in silver futures and fell Rs. 3,500,000 in debt. Subsequently Premchand Popat & Co. was terminated, and all the Kenya members except P. V. Shah withdrew their investments and returned to East Africa. In India P. V. Shah began again in 1950 by forming a Jamnagar oil mill, Jam Oil Products, but all members of his family except a nephew, Gulabchand, left to renew their fortunes in East Africa. It was not profit from India but the proceeds of the family's new company in Kenya, Steel Africa Ltd., that within five years enabled P. V. and Gulabchand to become financially solvent.[29]

A number of other Asians invested in India during these postwar years. Though employing a greater percentage of his money in East Africa, Muljibhai Madhvani established a large factory in Bombay, the Mukesh Textile Mills (Private) Ltd., and with the proceeds expanded further in India.[30] In 1942 Jagannath B. Pandya, the Mombasa business leader, set up in Bombay a branch of his hardware firm, East African Hardwares Ltd., and formed in Bhavnagar with his wife's brother a trading concern, Pandya & Trivedi Inc. Later in the year when he was negotiating to purchase the Ahmedabad newspaper *Sandesh* (Message), all his investments were terminated by his untimely death.[31] As Pandya and the others illustrate, it was the wealthier Asians who experimented in these years with investment in India. The Goan civil servants were a possible exception. Though their savings were meager, the Goans were able to look forward to a comfortable retirement on government pensions, and many of them in anticipation built or purchased fine homes in Goa and Bombay.[32] There were also some businessmen in this category. During four decades in Uganda A. Kalidas Patel acquired nine ginneries and then diversified into insurance, breweries, paper production, agriculture, and housing rental. In the years preceding exchange controls he transferred about 25 percent of his profits to India for eventual retirement in Baroda.[33]

Exportation for Security

During the late fifties and early sixties a series of events in Africa created for Asians and Europeans alike a sense of insecurity and considerably augmented the move to transfer money to overseas countries. The "winds of change" in the wake of Mau Mau culminated in the Lancaster House Conferences of 1960 and 1962. Even before the second conference met, the transfer of power began as first Tanganyika, then Uganda, Zanzibar, and Kenya, were to gain independence. After 1962, following Belgium's precipitous withdrawal, the Congo rapidly fell into turmoil. Two years later Zanzibar erupted in violent revolution, and armies mutinied in Tanganyika, Kenya, and Uganda. Perhaps even more ominous was the fact that many Africans in East Africa were declaiming against the Asians' presence.[34]

As a safeguard many Asians began to send money out of East Africa. A considerable number who hoped to remain opened bank accounts and purchased securities in other countries, especially in the United Kingdom, Switzerland, and the United States. They turned to these countries not only because of the countries' relative economic and political stability, but also because most of the non-Western nations, including Pakistan as well as India, did not recognize external accounts. This does not mean that these Asians ceased investing in East Africa on a permanent basis. As the Chandarias illustrate, many of the wealthier Asians transferred their money into external accounts in foreign countries temporarily with the intention of reinvesting it in East Africa as opportunity arose.[37] There was nevertheless a sizeable drain from the economy by Europeans as well as Asians. After examining the records of savings withdrawals in Kenya during 1959–60, Donald Rothchild concluded, "Panicky Europeans and Asians in all walks of life sent very considerable sums of money to banks in Europe and Asia for safekeeping. Around 1959 some £4 million was withdrawn by non-Africans from building society deposits alone." [36]

The uncertainty that produced a transfer of savings also prompted investment of profits in other countries. The Chandaria family perhaps best illustrates this tendency to move outside East Africa. After withdrawing from the joint enterprise with the P. V.

Shah family, the Chandarias retained in India a financial interest only in the Halar Salt Works Co. of Jamnagar. During 1956–57, however, they opened in London a branch office of their parent company, Premchand Brothers Ltd., and acquired a controlling interest in a British holding company in steel, Preet & Co. Ltd. In 1951 they built an aluminum stamping-press plant in Bojumburu, Burundi, and in 1960 a similar factory in Bukavu, Congo. It was in 1962 that they began to have serious apprehensions about their African concentration. In that year Belgium abruptly abandoned the Congo, and Patrice Lumumba in a much-publicized speech denounced all foreign investment. The Chandarias contemplated leaving Africa entirely but on further reflection decided to spread their assets into more African countries. In Kenya they terminated their manufacture of hurricane lamps and all organizations except two wire-producing plants, which they amalgamated into East African Wire Industries Inc. Then, while retaining and expanding their operations in Burundi and Zaire, they established industries in Ethiopia, Malawi, Morocco, Mozambique, Nigeria, Rhodesia, and Zambia. For tax purposes they registered all the new organizations in Bermuda.[37]

Further difficulties with their African holdings prompted the Chandarias to move into Europe and Asia. In 1966, after unfavorable experiences in Malawi, Mozambique, and Rhodesia, they decided to diversify into western Europe, and within three years they had set up fifteen factories in seven countries. In these as in all the preceding, they built on their East African experience by manufacturing aluminum ware, galvanized roofing, metal doors and windows, plastic pipes, paper packaging, and steel wire. Turning to Asia in 1974, they quickly erected similar plants in Malaysia, Indonesia, Singapore, Australia, the Philippines, and Papua New Guinea. By 1978, although 50 percent of their holdings were still in Africa, they owned industries in at least twenty-two countries and, as mentioned, had acquired assets worth £40 million.[38]

Many other Asians were prompted by the uncertainties of the late fifties and early sixties to invest overseas. Beginning in 1965 with profits they had made from Steel Africa Inc., and its subsidiaries in East Africa and from Jam Oil Products in India, Gulabchand and his brothers Amichand and Hemraj established seven

industries in the Gujarat, and in 1971, two months before nationalization of the companies in Tanzania, they sold out of Steel
Africa. Since the purchaser of their shares was a foreign buyer, they
were able to invest the proceeds in India.[39] During the same years
the family of Rahamtulla Kassim Lakha, which built the Oceanic
Hotel in Mombasa and founded approximately fifty businesses,
mostly in Uganda, set up jute mills in Bangladesh and began to
invest in Canada and the United Kingdom.[40] In 1963, after founding a successful travel agency in Nairobi, Bhanubhai Acharya and
his son Mahendra shifted the headquarters of their Acharya Travelling Agency to Baroda. There they developed, in Bhanubhai's
words, "a fantastic business" with Indians traveling not to East
Africa, but to the United States. In 1971 with the profits from the
agency in Baroda, they bought three residential properties in London and opened an office there to offer tourist visits to East Africa.
Two years later they were in an ideal situation to provide about 150
charter flights for the Asians fleeing Uganda.[41]

Similar investments were undertaken by the industrialists Devjibhai Karamshi Hindocha, Chhotabhai Motibhai Patel, and
Gordhendas Vasanji. Early in the fifties, after buying the Miwani
Sugar Mills Ltd. in western Kenya, Hindocha founded and put his
son Laljibhai in charge of the Horizon Sugar Mills in Pondicherry.[42] In 1959 Patel, who had developed a widespread ginning,
marketing, and industrial complex of companies in Uganda, took
over the Khira Steel Works Ltd. in Bombay. The next year he
established Chandan Metal Products Ltd. to produce steel furni-
ture in Baroda.[43] In 1964 Vasanji, owner of a very successful Mombasa hosiery and garment factory, the Kenya Rayon Mills Ltd.,
opened a factory in West Africa, the Sierra Leone Knitting Mills
Ltd.[44]

Within this period the Shah community, fearing that their center
might have to be shifted from Nairobi, began to transfer money to
the United Kingdom.[45] Like many others, the Shahs also began to
buy houses in South Asia and Europe, especially in England, not
only for the purpose of future residence, but also to obtain a rental
income or hold for speculation. Much of the Asians' current rental
property in the London environs was acquired in these years.[46]

Beginning in the mid-sixties the Asians' fears for a viable future in East Africa began to be realized. The Africanization of the civil service, the increasing application of the "managed economy" with the growth of government agencies, parastatals, and cooperatives, the linkage of "citizenship" to the issuance of work permits and trade licenses, and the mounting popular agitation against the Asians generally were major causes of uncertainty in all the mainland countries. Moreover, even Kenya and Tanzania did not seem immune from the mass expulsions arising from the Zanzibar coup of 1964 and Amin's Uganda order of 1972.

In this situation most Asians naturally sought to transfer as large a portion of their assets as possible outside East Africa. As Sir Ernest Vasey, Kenya's former minister for economic planning, observed in 1973, the Asians "were desperate to get their money out." [47] An Asian leader in Tanzania agreed. "Even if a man could save only ten shillings per month," he remarked, "he would try to get six shillings of it to England." [48] Unfortunately for the Asians, the East African governments in 1965, acting apparently by common agreement, imposed exchange controls on the exportation of currency.

As a result of the 1965 legislation all Kenya residents were prohibited from removing currency except for personal travel, the education of children, or the support of dependents. The maximum travel allowance was £250 per year; permission for educational or dependent support required special application, and the amounts allowed were tightly constricted. Residents were forbidden to keep foreign currency or hold accounts in foreign banks. In time the initial controls were tightened, with the result that the Asians were permitted a maximum of only £200 for travel every two years. Moreover, the delays in processing applications became increasingly a more serious impediment. To encourage Asian emigration, however, the government permitted departing heads of families to take out Shs. 50,000 and to receive later installments of Shs. 25,000. [49]

In Tanzania and Uganda the initial currency restrictions were essentially the same as in Kenya. In Tanzania they eventually became the most restrictive. In 1970, for instance, the Tanzania Asians were prohibited from exporting money even for educational purposes. [50] In Uganda all the rules were changed during the exodus of 1973. The departing Asians were informed that they each could carry a maximum of Shs. 200 through customs. At the Entebbe airport, however, the officials in most instances took the money from them with an assurance that an equivalent amount in British pounds would be refunded to them on arrival in England. Later, as expected, the Asians found no refund at Heathrow.[51]

Through both open and devious means the Asians managed to send money overseas. A fortunate few, who at the invitation of the African governments had invested money from outside sources in the development of industry and other business, were permitted to withdraw a large percentage of the profits. In common with other expatriate investors the Chandarias, Madhvanis, and Mehtas were thus able to export legally from East Africa 30 percent of their profits.[52] The East African governments, like those of developing countries everywhere, had to make such a concession to attract foreign investment. Most local Asians, however, had no option but some illegal means.

The amount of money taken overseas in these years or earlier for the purpose of savings or investment is a matter of conjecture. The Asians themselves disagree widely in their estimates. Some assert that the community began to export money only after the imposition of exchange controls.[53] Most acknowledge, however, that the community regularly sent money out before then, and they think that the total was sizeable. One knowledgeable individual has estimated that nearly 50 percent of the Asians' profits left East Africa.[54] Another has observed that billions of shillings went solely for the support of relatives in India.[55] That simply is not true, still another has argued. Only paltry sums, he maintains, went to Indian relatives; more was sent out for the education of Asian children.[56] Others contend that the sums designated for education or family support were small compared to those that went for investment.[57]

Benevolence Overseas

A large portion of the money sent abroad by the Asians was designated for charitable purposes. Most of this philanthropic contribution went to India for relief occasioned by some natural disaster, but much was directed toward the construction of public buildings and the establishment of memorials. Some was given to support India's struggle for independence. Although India was the main recipient, South Africa, the Congo, and Saudi Arabia also were favored.

Beginning apparently in the 1930s as they emerged from the economic depression, the Asians began to organize in aid of suffering caused by the natural disasters that have periodically afflicted India and other parts of South Asia. In 1936, when a severe drought produced a famine in western India, the Shah community of Kenya held a series of meetings in which amounts as high as Shs. 50,000 were subscribed and then sent to India. The following year, as the famine continued, the community established a permanent Oshwal Education and Relief Board and appealed for new funds. By the end of 1937 the Shahs had forwarded a total of £20,000.[58] In 1943, when a similar famine occurred in Bengal, the Nairobi Asians, despite the fact that scarcely any came from Bengal, organized a relief fund and appealed widely for donations. Local Asians responded by quickly raising £12,286.[59] During the same year the Muslim Asians led by Shamsud-Deen initiated a Hejaz Famine Relief Fund for the aid of Arabs in the vicinity of Mecca.[60]

During the fifties the Asians collected money for three new disasters in South Asia. In 1950, when Assam was devastated by an earthquake, the East Africa Indian National Congress established an Assam Relief Fund and called for donations from Europeans as well as Asians. Within a few weeks it was able to send Shs. 86,291 to the government of India.[61] Three years later the Asians launched a drive for famine relief in Maharashtra, and in 1955 another for Indian flood victims. One Mombasa organization, the Shree Navnat Mahajan, which contributed Rs. 2,501, received praise from the local Indian Association for its "magnificent sum."[62]

The Asians responded to a disaster of another kind in 1962 when the Chinese invaded India's mountain passes. The donations to an Aid-India Fund were described by the president of the Nairobi Indian Merchants' Chamber, which sponsored the drive, as "overwhelming." More than a million shillings had been subscribed, he explained. "Money is pouring."[63]

Three years later as rival political factions threw the newly independent Congo into chaos, the Asians eagerly supported the Kenya government's plea for aid to the Congo refugees. The honorary secretary of the Nairobi Central Chambers of Commerce at once appealed to all members for contributions. "It is an imperative moral duty for us," he stated, "to join the Government in providing whatever aid is possible to the unfortunate refugees of the Congo, who . . . have been compelled to leave their sweet homes helplessly." In this instance the Asians donated food and clothing as well as money for shelter and medicine.[64]

While supporting such causes for disaster relief, the East Africa Asians also contributed to civil disobedience and passive resistance campaigns in India and South Africa. In 1923–24 and again in 1929, Mrs. Sarojini Naidu, Gandhi's associate in the Indian National Congress, visited East Africa and in cooperation with local Indian leaders established a Sarojini Congress Fund. Although a complete account of the drive is apparently no longer extant, there were at least 550 donors with contributions ranging from the Shs. 1,272 given by the Patel Brotherhood to Shs. 5 offered by several individuals.[65] In 1932 and 1933 during Gandhi's two historic fasts, Indian organizations in East Africa called for mass meetings and presumably collected funds in support of the Satyagraha movement.[66] There were similar collections in subsequent years. As late as 1949, two years after India's independence, the Hindu Union of Arusha prepared to sell one thousand flags for a "Free India Day." [67] Meanwhile in times of crisis, the Asians had contributed to a South African Passive Resistance Fund that had been in existence in India since 1909.[68] In 1948 the East Africa Indian National Congress was thanked by the Natal Indian Congress for its "unstinted financial assistance," and in 1952 the congress launched another appeal.[69]

The foremost fund-raiser in East Africa on behalf of India in these years was the Nairobi businessman Bachulal T. Gathani. Distinguished as the only individual who simultaneously was the president of both the East Africa Indian National Congress and the Federation of Chambers of Commerce and Industry in Eastern Africa, he made use of both offices to support philanthropic causes. For collecting more money for India than any Asian overseas, Gathani became known as the *Shere Hind* (Lion of India).[70]

Besides supporting disaster relief and resistance campaigns, the

Asians contributed to the construction in India of schools, temples, hospitals, and public halls, and to the establishment of memorials. The principal memorial, that to Gandhi's wife, was provided by the Kasturba Gandhi Memorial Fund in 1949. Largely through the effort of the Bhagini Samaj of Nairobi, the Asians raised Rs. 108,625.[71] Public edifices were supported most generously, as might be expected, by the two Uganda industrialists, N. K. Mehta and Muljibhai Madhvani, and their Kenya counterpart, M. P. Shah. Mehta and Shah were exceptional in that they donated more to India than to Africa. Three-fourths of Mehta's total charitable contribution of more than Rs. 24,000,000 is said to have gone to India, mostly to buildings in Porbandar, the city near his home village.[72] Among the buildings he established in Porbandar are the Arya Samaj Girls' School and College, the Rokadia Ahnuman Temple, the Arya Kanya Gurukul, the N. K. Mehta Hospital, and the N. K. Mehta Science College. He also restored the Porbandar house in which Gandhi was born and raised.[73]

Mehta's main contribution outside Porbandar was to the Shri Brihad Bharatiya Samaj in Bombay, a nonpolitical society designed for the promotion of the economic, social, educational, and cultural interests of Indians abroad. It is situated in a spacious, six-storied building, the N. K. Mehta International House, with a research wing, library, auditorium, hostel, and transit camp. Mehta was not the only donor for this building, which opened in 1963. There were literally thousands, and in fact the Asians of East Africa separately raised Rs. 250,000 in a special fund drive. Mehta's donation of Rs. 500,000, however, was by far the largest from any individual or organization and amounted to more than a fourth of the total cost.[74] Mehta also contributed to numerous other projects outside Porbandar, especially to those concerned with women's education. He subsidized, for example, a *gurukul* in Baroda and another at Choki.[75]

The overseas donations of M. P. Shah nearly equaled those of Mehta. As described in Chapter 2, Shah retired to Jamnagar in 1963, when he was forty-nine years old and had a capital worth of £2.5 million. Through the Meghji Pethraj Shah Charitable Trust that he had established for philanthropy in India, he initiated a ten-year plan for social welfare projects in Kathiawar (later Saurashtra). He designed the projects, directed the construction, and provided one-third to one-half the cost in towns and one-fourth to one-third in villages. The government contributed the remaining cost and assumed the administration on completion of construction.[76]

The projects continued beyond the ten years to M. P. Shah's death in 1964. By then the Jamnagar trust had expended more than Rs. 10 million, twice that of the Nairobi trust, which had been supporting similar projects in East Africa. In western India Shah had provided facilities for 34,000 primary and secondary pupils and 4,000 college students, hostels for 1,200 children, hospitals with 1,200 beds, and 800 village libraries. The more costly edifices were the M. P. Shah All India Talking Book Centre for the blind in Bombay (Shah's contribution: Rs. 1,800,000), the M. P. Shah Medical College in Jamnagar (Rs. 1,500,000), the Shrimati Maniben M. P. Shah Women's College and the M. P. Shah Junior College for women in Bombay (Rs. 700,000), and a glucose saline plant for the Gujarat Health Department (Rs. 600,000). Other buildings included a leprosy sanatorium in Bhavnagar, a cancer hospital in Ahmedabad, a college of commerce and law in Jamnagar, and a technical training center in Surendranagar. Shah spent the last seven years of his life in London, where he established two more trusts, for donations in England, and bought a commodities brokerage and organized two companies — Premchand Raichand London Ltd. and Oswal Investments Ltd. — to provide the capital. His subsequent donations in London, Leicester, and Jersey totaled $255,500.[77]

As the founding of the two British companies illustrates, a proportion of the cost of Shah's overseas philanthropy, like that of Mehta, was financed by money-making projects outside East Africa. Some of Shah's fortune had been acquired through Premchand Popat & Co. and the brokerage firm he had established in Jamnagar with the Chandarias and other Shahs in 1940. Four years later with his brothers and Chimanbhai U. Shah he had formed another Indian company, Raichand Brothers (India) Pvt. Ltd., which was soon purchasing from 80 to 90 percent of East Africa's wattle exports.[78]

Compared to those of Mehta and M. P. Shah, Madhvani's charitable donations overseas appear insignificant. Madhvani, unlike
the other two, never stayed for long in India and concentrated his
philanthropy on the development of East Africa. He did donate,
however, to numerous charitable causes in India. He provided the
library of the Shri Brihad Bharatiya Samaj, which includes a valuable collection of literature on Indians overseas. He also built a
school at Raval, near his birthplace in Saurashtra, and contributed
Rs. 30,000 to the Vallabh Kanya Vidyalaya.[79] Madhvani was probably able to finance all these contributions with the profits from his
Mukesh Textile Mills and other business ventures in India.

The other Asians who as individuals endowed public edifices in
India are relatively few, and their donations have not been widely
publicized. Lakhamshi R. Shah, the Nairobi businessman, endowed a hall at the National High School in Jamnagar, and Pi-
tamber A. Sachania, a Zanzibar building contractor, during a ten-
year stay in India, 1924–34, is described as having "built rest
houses, water fountains and donated generously at various places
and to various causes in Saurashtra." [80] The members of the Shah
community are said to have contributed to many social welfare
projects in their home villages around Jamnagar.[81]

Becoming increasingly sensitive to European charges that they
were exporting their profits, the Asians devised means to limit their
donations to India. In 1955 a resolution of the annual conference
expressly prohibited the Kenya Indian Congress and its affiliated
organizations from collecting funds for objects outside East Africa.
Later in 1955 when a delegation from India applied for congress aid
in collecting funds for the Shri Brihad Bharatiya Samaj, the congress agreed to extend the delegation "all courtesy," but not to
associate itself with the collection.[82] In subsequent years the Asian
organizations differed in their enforcement of the resolution. The
Mombasa Indian Association refused to patronize any appeal for a
charitable fund for the people of India, while the congress decided
to make an exception for disaster relief.[83]

How much money went to South Asia for charitable purposes is,
like that sent for investment, education, and support of relatives, a
moot question. Sums such as the Shs. 400,000 raised by the Oshwal

Education and Relief Board, the "more than a million" of the Aid-India Fund, and the Rs. 18 million and Rs. 10 million denoting Mehta's and M. P. Shah's philanthropy in India are impressive, but they represent the extremes. The average Asian probably made very little contribution to overseas charitable causes in comparison to his remittances abroad for other purposes. The total sent for philanthropy was probably the least among the various categories.

The Asians' charitable donations overseas present a pattern very similar to their exportations for investment, education, or support of relatives. Although they contributed generously in support of the needy overseas, their contributions were never sizeable during the seventy-year period in comparison to the amount invested in East Africa nor, it will be shown, to their donations to charitable causes in Kenya, Tanganyika, Uganda, and Zanzibar. As with investments, a few key individuals, the wealthy, contributed a large proportion of the money devoted to overseas charity, and much of what they gave came from the profits of the businesses they had established in India.

Notes

1. V. D. Shah intv.
2. The author is completing a volume on the Asians' economic and social history.
3. *Rept. of the Taxation Enquiry Committee, Kenya, 1947* (Nairobi: Govt. Ptr., 1947), 10–11.
4. Ibid., 79.
5. *Rept. of the Commission Apptd. to Enquire into and Rept. on the Fin. Position and System of Kenya,* Col. No. 116 (London: HMSO, 1936), 15.
6. *Kenya, Uganda—Tanganyika and Zanzibar Directory: Trade and Commercial Index,* 1936 (Nairobi: East African Directory Co., 1936), Tanganyika sec., 68.
7. Tang., *Stat. Abstract 1962* (Dar es Salaam: Govt. Ptr., 1962), 151. Ibid., *1938–1951* (pub. 1953), 45. The figure 3,000 for 1961 is estimated from a figure for 1957.
8. Britain, *Annual Rept. on the Soc. and Econ. Progress of the People of the Ug. Prot., 1933,* Col. Repts.—Annual, No. 1670 (London: HMSO, 1934), 27.
9. *Kenya, Uganda—Tanganyika and Zanzibar Directory,* 1959–60, Uganda sec., 55.
10. Ibid., *1959–60,* Zan. sec., 23.
11. Kashi Shah said this happened to her brother (intv.).
12. M. L. Shah intv.

13. In describing the tendency of Muslims to marry locally, Ali Mohamedjaffer, an Ithnasheri, made no distinction among Bohras, Ismailis, and Ithnasheris (intv.). Yusufali Pirbhai, a Bohra, asserted that his community was an exception (intv.).
14. S. Haji intv.
15. Gregory, *India and E.A.,* 53, 55, 61.
16. *E. Afn. Standard,* 15 Sep. 1906, 7.
17. Gregory, *India and E.A.,* 55.
18. Intv.
19. Intv.
20. Many knowledgeable Asians have testified to this, e.g., M. K. Lalji intv.
21. A. Raishi intv.
22. A. Raishi, while interpreting during interview of S. M. C. Shah. V. K. Shah intv.
23. D. N. Mehta intv. M. N. Mehta intv. See also Pandit, *Asians,* 184.
24. The eight were (1) Premchand Bros. & Co., Mombasa; (2) Premchand Raichand & Co., Nairobi; (3) Kenya Extract & Tanning Co., Thika; (4) Kenya Aluminium Co., Mombasa; (5) Limuru Tanning Co.; (6) Pure Food Products, Nairobi; (7) flour mills in Meru, Sangana, and elsewhere; and (8) a lumber factory, Limuru. K. P. Chandaria (brother of D. P.) intv.
25. Ibid. G. D. Shah (P. V. Shah's nephew) intv. D. P. Shah (P. V.'s son) intv.
26. M. K. Lalji intv.
27. L. R. Shah intv.
28. D. P. Shah intv.
29. K. P. Chandaria and G. D. Shah intvs.
30. C. P. Shah and L. V. Kakad intv. jointly. A. J. Pandya intv.
31. A. J. Pandya (son) intv. H. (Mrs. A. J.) Pandya intv.
32. F. A. de Souza intv. Jose Pio de Sousa has related how his brother, a physician, retired from Uganda to a large home he built in Bombay. Another brother, he said, retired to Britain to avoid the taxes he would have to pay in India on money he made in East Africa (intv.).
33. A. K. Patel intv.
34. India, Min. of Ext. Affairs, *Annual Report, 1964–65* (New Delhi: Govt. Ptr., 1965), 60.
35. A. J. Pandya intv.
36. Rothchild, *Racial Bargaining,* 134.
37. K. P. Chandaria intv.
38. Ibid. Murray, "The Chandarias," in Kaplinsky, *Readings on the Multinational Corporation in Kenya,* 298–300.
39. G. D. Shah intv.
40. A. R. Kassim Lakha (son) intv.
41. M. B. Acharya intv.
42. A. J. Pandya intv.
43. Pandit, *Asians,* 280–81, 296.
44. G. Vasanji intv.
45. A. Raishi intv.
46. A. J. Pandya intv.
47. Sir E. Vasey intv.
48. F. Kapadia intv.

49. V. B. Shah intv.
50. K. L. Vohora intv.
51. U. Patel intv.
52. K. P. Chandaria intv.
53. J. Mehta (high commr. for India to Tan.) intv.
54. M. J. Thakkar intv.
55. A. Raishi intv.
56. D. S. Trivedi intv.
57. S. D. Kothari intv.
58. L. R. Shah intv.
59. See three letters of appeal, *E. Afn. Standard,* 28 Oct. 1943, 4. For the Asian response, see ibid., 29 Oct. 1943, 10. For the collecting in Central Province, see "Hist. of Fort Hall from 1888–1944," file FH/43,DC/FH6/1, Central Prov. daily corresp., SU microfilm 4751, reel 24.
60. Letter by Shamsud-Deen, *E. Afn. Standard,* 6 Sep. 1943, 4.
61. Ibid., 19 Sep. 1950, 5; 27 Sep. 1950, 4; 23 Oct. 1950, 5.
62. P. N. Mehta (hon. sec., Ind. Assoc., Momb.) to hon. sec., Shree Navnat Vanik Mahajan, 26 Sep. 1955, Momb. Ind. Assoc. records, SU microfilm 1926, reel 4; and S. C. Gautama (hon. gen. sec., EAINC) to hon. sec., Ind. Assoc., Momb., 6 July 1953, ibid.
63. K. V. Shukla to hon'ble speaker, Lok Sabha, New Delhi, 4 Dec. 1962, Nairobi Central Chamb. of Commerce records, SU microfilm 1924, reel 6.
64. V. R. Shah (hon. sec., Central Cham. of Commerce, Nairobi) to all members, 19 Jan. 1965, ibid.
65. "List of Sarojini Congress Fund," n.d., and "List of Donours of the Sarojini Congress Fund with the names of donours and the respective amounts donated," n.d., file "Gen. Corresp. [n.d.], File One," EAINC records, SU microfilm 1929, reel 14.
66. R. M. Shah (hon. sec., Ind. Assoc., Momb.), "Rept. of the Ind. Assoc. for 1932," 19 Dec. 1932, Momb. Ind. Assoc. records, reel 11. Hon. jt. sec. (Ind. Assoc., Momb.) to DC, Momb., 28 May 1933, ibid.
67. President (Hindu Union, Arusha) to president, EAINC, 11 July 1949, EAINC records, reel 11.
68. Gregory, *India and E.A.,* 132.
69. Debi Singh (gen. sec., Natal Ind. Cong., Durban) to sec., EAINC, 3 June 1948, EAINC records, reel 11. K. P. Shah (organizer, EAINC) to hon. sec., Ind. Assoc., Momb., 27 Sep. 1952, Momb. Ind. Assoc. records, reel 4. Though supporting the resistance campaigns in India and South Africa with money, the Asian organizations refrained from assisting local Asians in attempts to join the movements. See the denial of a request in hon. jt. sec. (Ind. Assoc., Momb.) to Becharbhai G. Patel, Ind. Affairs Committee, Momb., 13 Mar. 1932, Momb. Ind. Assoc. records, reel 11.
70. B. T. Gathani intv. Others confirmed this.
71. President (Bhagini Samaj, Nairobi) to commr. for govt. of India in E.A., Nairobi, 2 Aug. 1949, EAINC records, reel 11.
72. D. N. Mehta intv.
73. Ibid. Pandit, *Asians,* 184.
74. *Shri Brihad Bharatiya Samaj: Inaugural Souvenir, Oct. 1963* (Bombay: Jaya Art Printers, 1963), 170.

75. Pandit, *Asians,* 184.
76. Marett, *Meghji Pethraj Shah,* 57–58.
77. Ibid., 57–79, 83–84, 104–5, 129–33.
78. Ibid., 45.
79. *Shri Brihad Bharatiya Samaj,* 171. Pandit, *Asians,* 80.
80. Pandit, *Asians,* 93. L. R. Shah intv.
81. N. T. Karia intv. The author looked for such evidence during a tour of the Gujarat and Goa during the summer of 1973.
82. President (Kenya Cong.) to hon. sec., Ind. Assoc., Momb., 25 May 1955, Momb. Ind. Assoc. records, reel 4. The congress resolution was no. 12 of the 22nd session.
83. Hon. sec. (Ind. Assoc., Momb.) to hon. sec. Momb. Surat Dist. Assoc., 28 Sep. 1959, ibid.

4

Creation of Religious, Social, Medical, and Library Facilities

Humanity is the greatest religion.
—Mombasa Social Service League, 1923

Partly because of the need to preserve and practice the tenets of their culture and partly because of the colonial governments' concentration on providing social services for the Europeans and Africans, the Asians, as explained in Chapter 1, were constrained to establish religious, social, medical, library, and educational facilities. The means was philanthropy; individuals contributed a sizeable portion of their earnings to the common welfare. In the early years of settlement, each religious community attended mainly to its own needs. Somewhat later, because of the advantages in merging their communal interests and because of a growing sense of a collective identity as Asians, the various religious communities shared in the creation of intercommunal facilities. Some of these facilities were founded without restrictions of race or creed and so provided services to peoples other than Asians, and some were created specifically for Africans.[1]

Mosques, Temples, and Shrines

One of the foremost Asian charitable endeavors was the raising of money for the construction of religious edifices. Since the government, unlike its practices with educational institutions, provided no financial aid, the Asians had to rely entirely on their own resources in erecting communal halls and temples, mosques, and shrines. In each of the major towns Muslims, Hindus, Sikhs, Jains, and Christians contributed to the construction and maintenance of their separate religious buildings.

Support for these structures was, in each instance, a communal enterprise with most families contributing according to their means. Because of the Muslims' emphasis on architecture, their contribution is the most evident. Every urban center in East Africa is graced by one or more impressive communal halls and mosques representing various sects of Islam. On the Indian Ocean littoral, as the ruins of Gedi illustrate, the Arab, Persian, and Indian Muslims constructed such edifices centuries before the advent of European colonialism. During the colonial period as the Muslims moved into the interior, increased in population, and acquired affluence, the Islamic structures greatly grew in number, size, and ornamentation. Among the Asians the outstanding donor was the Aga Khan. The East African Muslim Welfare Society, which he founded in 1945, provided most of the funds for most mosques built after that date, and by 1957 it had been the principal donor to 150 mosques. The Grand Kabuli Mosque of Kampala, which the Muslim Welfare Society initiated and which Prince Aly Khan opened in 1951, is perhaps the foremost example, and it illustrates, as most of these Muslim edifices do, a cooperative effort between Asians and Africans. Towards the cost of this mosque the non-Africans, of whom Ismailis were the main donors, provided Shs. 34,000, and the Africans Shs. 19,900.[2]

Among the Muslim contributors to religious edifices there were a number of influential philanthropists other than the Aga Khan. The brothers Madatali and Hussein Suleman Verjee in 1920 donated Shs. 1,140,000, most of the money, for the historic Khoja Mosque in Nairobi. Mohamedali Sheriff, an Ithnasheri of Moshi, during the 1950s before losing his money in a futile contest for a legislative seat, subsidized the construction of several Sunni mosques in Tanganyika.[3]

Though less visible in such donations, the non-Muslims also supported the establishment of many religious institutions. In urban centers throughout East Africa the various Hindu sects usually combined in contributions to a common Hindu temple, but as with the Muslims there was often an individual or family that provided the initiative and most of the cost. The foremost Hindu contributor was the wealthy Uganda merchant, planter, and industrialist Nanji Kalidas Mehta, who supported many religious endeavors and especially those of the Arya Samaj. Mehta and many other Hindus, exhibiting an extraordinary appreciation for differing faiths, frequently gave to African churches and mosques. Like the Hindus, the Sikhs established their temples all over East Africa. One of the first was the Nairobi temple, which was built in 1910 at an estimated cost of Rs. 4,000. The Shahs, concentrated in Nairobi, incorporated their religious shrine in their communal center and maintained it after 1952 with the tax of Shs. 100 levied on every Shah businessman.[4]

The Goans as Roman Catholics were exceptional among the non-Muslims. Between 1906 and 1908 they built their first communal center, the Goan Institute in Nairobi, at a cost of Rs. 8,000 by soliciting a contribution of Rs. 50 from every member of the community. They themselves did not initiate their religious edifices, which were designed by the church, but, as a leading Goan has testified, they "kept the Catholic Church and its charities going." [5] One of the principal Goan benefactors was Francis Anthony de Souza, an accountant in the Kenya Civil Service who from 1957 to 1963 was secretary of the Nairobi branch of St. Vincent de Paul's Society. For his work in raising funds for the Nairobi Cathedral and other charitable activity, he was awarded the *Pro Ecclesia et Pontifica.*[6]

While the Goans channeled much of their philanthropy through the St. Vincent de Paul's Society, the other Asians formed their own charitable organizations. Every Asian community, as one Asian has observed, "had its own social service organization," and each was designed to administer to the needy members of the particular community.[7] The Ismailis and the Shahs were probably foremost in their many communal services. They provided not only religious, medical, and educational facilities and support, but even sponsored programs for young people, prenatal and postnatal care, cultural improvement, employment, housing, insurance, and investment. The Ismailis' East African Muslim Welfare Society was unique in that it was designed primarily for the conversion of

Africans to Islam. Although this conversion effort was disappointing in that less than one hundred Africans became Ismailis, more than £400,000 was collected in the early years, branches of the society were formed in sixteen centers, and many mosques with attached Muslim schools were built.[8]

Social Service Leagues

The Asians' most important charitable organizations were those produced by a combined effort of their communities. Among such organizations were the Social Service Leagues, which, like the communal halls and religious edifices, were established without any contribution from the governments and were maintained with only token grants from the municipal councils. The first Social Service League, which as conceived in 1917–18 was to serve East Africa as a whole, was organized mainly by the Nairobi advocate V. V. Phadke with financial support largely from Allidina Visram, Suleman Verjee & Sons, Ali & Son, and Walji Hirji & Sons, all of whom were designated as the "patrons." The Nairobi Indian Association was entrusted with the collection of funds, and Asian Hindus, Muslims, and Sikhs all subscribed. In 1923 when the league was formally launched, it was centered in Mombasa rather than Nairobi, and in succeeding years it was regarded as a Mombasa organization. All members of the league donated their services without pay. The league was financed mainly by membership subscriptions, dispensary fees, donations from Asian individuals, companies, and foundations, and a small annual grant from the Mombasa Municipal Board.[9] It also received gifts of property from numerous individuals, and the rent from these helped to meet the many expenses.

Taking the motto "Humanity is the greatest religion," the league defined its objects: "(1) to offer every possible help to the distressed, poor, disabled and destitute persons; (2) to make efforts for preserving health and sanitation; (3) to make efforts for spreading knowledge and education among the people; (4) to render prompt help in case of epidemics and accidents; (5) to make efforts for removing social defects and to promote unity and moral uplift." [10]

In pursuit of these objects the league offered many services. It set up a dispensary and a library and reading room. It assisted impoverished Asian immigrants in repatriation to India, distributed food rations to poor and distressed families in Mombasa, and donated to local schools and student fees. It provided medical services at modest cost to those able to pay and free to those who were destitute. The library charged small fees for borrowing books, but the reading room was free to everyone. Until 1967, when by constitutional amendment it was opened to all without distinction of race or creed, the league restricted its membership to Asians. In its activities, however, the league from the beginning served Africans and Arabs as well as Asians. In fact the influential coastal Arab Sir Ali bin Salim was so favorably impressed with the league's charitable endeavors that in 1929 he donated a spacious building, valued at Shs. 123,000, to serve as the league's new office and library.[11]

The league's charitable activities are impressive. During 1968 it operated three dispensaries, which ministered to a total of 92,169 patients. Among the patients were 42,934 Africans and 29,492 Arabs in contrast to only 19,743 Asians. During the year the library housed 7,562 books and subscribed to 54 newspapers and periodicals variously printed in English, Gujarati, Hindi, and Swahili. A total of 2,250 of the books were borrowed by 93 readers, and the reading room was in everyday use by Africans and Arabs as well as Asians. The league served 33,084 rations at a cost of Shs. 35,084 to 90 families, gave Shs. 2,251 in school fees, books, and scholarships, and provided lodging amounting to Shs. 1,576 for 42 needy persons returning to India.[12]

Separate Social Service Leagues formed subsequently in Nairobi, Kampala, and Dar es Salaam engaged in similar activities. Of these Nairobi's was by far the most important. Its origin can be traced to 1931 when four Hindus—C. R. Patel, Bagwan Dass, Shambu Shankar Vyas, and Dharamshibhai Patel—decided to help destitute Asian families at a time when the railway was releasing employees in blocks of one to two hundred. The four collected money from wealthier Asians and made up food parcels for the needy families. The next year they combined with Tulsiram Dosaj and B. L. Menon in forming an organization, the Samaj Seva, for setting up a dispensary for the Asians. In 1933, renaming their organization the Social Service League, Nairobi, they collected Shs.

10,000 and purchased a well-equipped dispensary from a departing European physician. In 1942 with a grant of Shs. 20,000 from the Dinshaw Byramjee family, the league moved the dispensary to a new site and renamed it in honor of its benefactor.[13]

Throughout its history the Nairobi league retained a medical emphasis. In a 1948 statement of purpose it set as its first object the administration of "Nursing Homes, Hospitals, Dispensaries, Clinics, Sanitoria, Medical Schools, Operating Theatres, Nurses' Homes, Institutions, Mental Hospitals and Asylums."[14] In 1951, largely through the generosity of Dr. Vimal Arya, it added a clinic for women. Four years later, in 1956, the league took over the Lady Grigg Maternity Hospital, which the government had closed because of an insanitary kitchen, and then at a cost of £40,000 it built a new wing in the name of its principal donor, Seth Dharamshi Pancha Shah. In 1958, as will be explained, the league assumed control of the Parklands Nursing Home and fashioned it into the M. P. Shah Hospital.[15]

The Nairobi league, in common with many other Asian charitable organizations, was instituted because of a pressing need within the Asian community, but in time, like most of the other organizations, it extended its services to Africans. In its constitution the league differed from its Mombasa counterpart by being nonracial from the outset. The first of its stipulated "aims and objects" was "to prevent and alleviate human suffering amongst communities in Nairobi, without distinction of caste, creed or colour." Also, its membership was open to anyone on payment of the annual subscription of Shs. 6, and its trustees included Europeans and Goans.[16]

The league's total medical service, which after independence was enjoyed increasingly by Africans, is revealed in the following statistics for 1971. The dispensary administered to 32,553 patients, the clinical laboratory conducted 26,414 investigations, the maternity hospital had 1,301 admissions, and the M. P. Shah Hospital served 7,310 patients and performed 1,213 major operations. In addition, the league's General Purposes Committee distributed to the "poor and needy" Shs. 2,301/50, which it had collected on a flag day. Patients in the M. P. Shah Hospital were about 25 percent African and 75 percent Asian with only a few Europeans, all Italians. In the other institutions the Africans and Asians were approximately equal in numbers. Although the hospital had a Shs. 20 fee per day for inpatients, those unable to pay were aided by the league's Samaritans' Fund, which had been organized in the early thirties for destitute Asians and after 1942 became available to all races.[17]

Hospitals, Dispensaries, and Clinics

Medical facilities represent in themselves another form of charitable endeavor. The efforts of Jamshed Dinshaw Byramjee, a Parsi schoolteacher and clothing merchant, in creating the M. P. Shah Hospital well illustrate this form of Asian philanthropy. Becoming interested in the Nairobi Social Service League about 1936, Byramjee was instrumental in endowing the league's dispensary with a sizeable donation from the family inheritance of his late father. Afterward he moved into management of the league. As vice-president in 1942 and president in 1943, Byramjee set as his goal the creation of a hospital for Asians. The only medical facility available to Asians of East Africa at that time was a thirty-six-bed wing of the Native Civil Hospital (formerly the King's African Rifles Hospital) in Mombasa. The hospital had no maternity ward, with the result that all babies were delivered in Asian homes with or without untrained midwives. There were no trained Asian nurses anywhere in East Africa, and Nairobi, the leading city, had only two practicing Asian doctors.[18] Byramjee thus had ample reason to appeal to the Kenya government for assistance. He asked for a grant of land and, on assurance that the league would raise the building costs, was given 5.25 acres in Parklands.

Byramjee then set to work to collect funds. He obtained from a wealthy, retired Goan, V. F. Saldanha, an agreement to donate £4,000. Saldanha had had a very unpleasant experience as a patient in the Native Civil Hospital. Byramjee campaigned in the Nairobi bazaar for the rest of the building cost, an estimated £20,000. At that time Ismail Rahimtulla Walji Hirji, an Ismaili who had inherited a fortune, committed suicide and left a will providing for the creation of two rest-houses and the donation of £60,000 to a hospital charity. At Byramjee's initiative the league asked for the £60,000 but was refused because of a stipulation in the will that the government had to build the hospital. The Walji Hirji bequest subsequently went toward the addition of an Asian wing for the Native City Hospital (later Kenyatta Hospital) in Nairobi. Undaunted, Byramjee and a team then returned to soliciting money from the Asian community at large, going house to house, and they raised, with Saldanha's pledge, a total of £25,000. Hearing that the government had matched £200,000 raised by the European community for the new Princess Elizabeth Hospital, Byramjee undertook to raise an additional £100,000 and succeeded in persuading twenty wealthy Asians each to promise £5,000.[19]

At that time it was not at all certain that the government would match the Asian money. Two new hospitals had just risen in Nairobi—the Aga Khan Hospital and the Parklands Nursing Home—and in opening the latter, Governor Sir Evelyn Baring had remarked that there were now enough Asian hospitals.[20]

Byramjee nevertheless was successful in his approach to the government. His building plans, drawn inexpensively by an Asian architect, were approved with some modification, and the government pledged matching funds of £100,000. The cornerstone was laid in 1953, and construction began. Suddenly without warning, after the Asians had spent nearly £8,000, the government decided against the building design and demanded that a new plan be drafted by the European architect A. D. Connel. A year's delay ensued. In the end the Asians were faced with not only a much higher architectural fee, but also a much more expensive building that seemed beyond the league's means. Then a fortunate circumstance occurred. The Parklands Nursing Home, which a few Asian doctors and merchants had built as a profit-making venture, asked the league to take over its building and enlarge it. Byramjee called a meeting of all the prospective donors—about 150—and it was decided that the league would accept the offer and add a wing. The government permitted the league to sell the 5.25 acres, which brought £22,000, and to apply the proceeds to the cost of construction. In the end the Asians took over the Parklands Nursing Home for approximately £75,000 and, with a matching grant and later additional government funds, built a new wing. When the hospital opened in 1958, the existing building was named after Saldanha, and the wing in honor of the principal donor, M. P. Shah. The structure as a whole became the Social Service League M. P. Shah Hospital.[21]

The other hospital representing a combined philanthropic effort was the Pandya Memorial Clinic in Mombasa. After the sudden death in 1942 of Jagannath B. Pandya, the Mombasa businessman who had founded the Federation of Indian Chambers of Commerce and Industry in Eastern Africa and won recognition as one of the foremost Asian leaders, Asians everywhere talked of raising a memorial in his memory. In November 1942 the executives of the Federation and the East Africa Indian National Congress jointly appointed a Pandya Memorial Committee under the chairmanship of the Mombasa advocate and legislative councillor Ambalal Bhailalbhai Patel. During the many meetings of this committee, the Asian physician Dr. Shankar Dhondo Karve argued for the establishment of an Asian hospital. Karve, who had practiced medicine for two decades in Kenya, was acutely aware of the pressing need for a better facility than that offered by the government's Native Civil Hospital. Offering to surrender his lucrative private practice to devote a free and full-time service to the proposed hospital, he was persuasive. The Pandya family decided to donate Shs. 250,000 as half the estimated cost with the expectation that it would be matched by contributions from others within the Asian community. Before the end of 1942 the committee formally recommended the creation in Mombasa of a hospital to be named, as Karve suggested from the famous Mayo model, the Pandya Memorial Clinic.[22]

The plans for the hospital were successfully implemented between 1942 and 1951. Because of the world war the fund drive had to be postponed until 1946, and in that year, just after a Pandya Memorial Society was formed to collect funds, the government offered the society a building for a nominal rental. The Fleet Club, as it was called, was a spacious three-winged edifice that had been erected during the war by the Royal Navy. Although dedicated to constructing a hospital, Karve, the Pandyas, and other promoters seized the opportunity to begin a medical service without delay. They quickly remodeled the interior, replaced the thatch roofing with tile, and set up equipment purchased at minimal cost from a defunct military hospital. In its Fleet Club building the Pandya

Memorial Clinic opened its doors in February 1947. Karve was joined by a European surgeon from Uganda and a subassistant surgeon from India, and during the first six months the hospital accommodated 269 patients in its eighteen beds. Meanwhile the society continued with its drive for a permanent edifice. In 1950 after collecting Shs. 611,940, it laid the foundation stone at a five-acre site leased from the government.[23]

The new building, which was completed in December 1951, cost Shs. 1.3 million and was described at the time as "the best planned institution of its kind in East Africa." [24] Two stories high, with side wings and adjacent buildings of concrete and stone, it had twenty-six single wards and two three-bed wards — thirty-two beds in all — an operating theater, a maternity ward, an X-ray room, a section for outpatients, staff quarters, and all the facilities that a modern hospital required. An unusual feature was that each room had an extra bed for a person who stayed with the patient, and two lavatories, one Indian style, the other European.[25]

Although the government provided matching funds, the new hospital was clearly a result of Asian initiative and philanthropy. By the time of its opening, the Pandya family had given Shs. 350,000, and Asian individuals, trusts, and business concerns, more than two hundred in all, had donated Shs. 251,940. From a single European, the late J. M. Battersby, a personal friend of J. B. Pandya, had come Shs. 10,000. The government's matching contribution was pledged only after the hospital was built. As a non-profit institution the hospital was dependent for its upkeep on patients' fees and voluntary contributions. By 1963 further Asian donations and a matching government grant had enabled Shs. 1.4 million of additions and alterations.[26]

Like the league's M. P. Shah Hospital, the Pandya Memorial Clinic was designed primarily for Asian welfare but in time increasingly served Africans. The following statement in the inaugural brochure well describes the initial conception: "It would be run and staffed by Indians for Indians giving its users, mainly Indians, all the modern medical facilities with sympathetic and loving care that can only be given to the patients and their relatives by their own countrymen." [27] From the beginning, however, the hospital was open to all races irrespective of caste or creed. It was in fact the first nonracial hospital in East Africa. The 269 patients treated in the first six months in the Fleet Club building included 120 Hindus, 96 Muslim Asians, 16 Goans, 13 Arabs, 7 Seychellese, 6 non-Goan Christian Asians, 5 Parsis, 4 Chinese, and 2 Europeans. Africans, notably absent in this initial list, then preferred the Mombasa Native Civil Hospital because of the Pandya Memorial Clinic's inpatient Shs. 15 fee. In time, however, Africans began to use the clinic, and after independence, despite a rise in the fee, they became the most numerous. Those who could not pay the fee were aided by the clinic's Almoners' Fund. During 1971, when the number of beds had been increased to sixty, the hospital admitted 4,071 patients, treated 5,503 others as outpatients, performed 1,890 operations, gave 1,858 X-rays, and completed 5,966 laboratory tests. The executive committee, under the chairmanship of Anant J. Pandya, then included two Africans and an Arab as well as seven Asians.[28]

Although the M. P. Shah Hospital and the Pandya Memorial Clinic are significant examples of Asian philanthropy, there were many other medical institutions founded by the Asians. Foremost among them were the Aga Khan Hospitals established during the fifties in Nairobi, Dar es Salaam, and Kampala. They were large hospitals furnished with the latest medical equipment and staffed by well-trained Ismaili doctors and nurses. Initiated by the Aga Khan and funded by matching sums from the local Ismailis and the governments, they were designed primarily for the various Ismaili communities. Though open to all peoples, they remained comparatively unattractive to Africans because of their high fees.[29]

In addition to these Ismaili hospitals, there were a number of smaller, well-equipped institutions founded or generously supported by Asians. As noted in Chapter 2, Tayabali Hassanali A. Karimjee donated the Hassanali Karimjee General Hospital at Zanzibar. A well-run hospital was also founded in Nairobi by the Oshwal community. Small hospitals were established in Zanzibar and Dar es Salaam by R. H. Paroo, in Mombasa by Dr. A. U. Sheth, another in Mombasa by the Ismail Rahimtulla Waljee Trust, in Thika by a group of Shahs, and in Kisii by the resident Asian community. At Gatundu, Kenyatta's birthplace, the hospital established in his name was supported by large annual grants — Shs. 20,000 in 1970, for instance — from the Hindocha family. At ginnery sites and sugar plantations, hospitals were also built by the Mehtas, Madhvanis, Hindochas, and Kotechas. The Mehtas' hospital at Miwani had eighty-one beds and four qualified doctors as well as several medical assistants, nurses, and midwives. Except for the Aga Khan Hospital, the Asian hospitals in Uganda, unlike most of those in Kenya, were designed primarily for Africans. The Asians claim that they ran all the Uganda hospitals and dispensaries before independence.[30]

Dispensaries and clinics represent another facet of Asian philanthropy. As early as 1927 the Ismailis opened a dispensary in Mombasa. Beginning about 1950 the Chandaria family subsidized many clinics for Africans in rural areas of Kenya.[31] In the early sixties Dr. Gunvantri Jayantilal Bhatt, describing himself as a "bush doctor," founded rural dispensaries "throughout the Fort Portal area" of Uganda and visited them regularly.[32] Dispensaries were also established in Dar es Salaam by the wealthy Jain importer T. B. Sheth, and in Mombasa by the Rahimtulla trust. In Kampala the Indian Women's Association, which began in 1948, opened its doors to African women and their children for free medical treatment. The association arranged for Asian doctors to give free service there and for Asian chemists to donate free medicines.[33]

Asians were also instrumental in establishing a national program of medical insurance. In the early fifties the Kenya government, at the request of European leaders, required every European with an income of £800 or more to pay a hospital tax for medical insurance. J. D. Byramjee solicited the aid of John M. Nazareth, leader of the Indian Elected Members' Organization of the Legislative Council, in urging the government to establish a similar tax for Asians and Arabs. In response the government in 1959 created an Asian-Arab Hospital Fund Authority, which in turn appointed a five-man committee. There were two Asian committee members — Byramjee and Dr. Karve. Under the chairmanship of Byramjee for the next five years, the committee devised a plan whereby all Asians and Arabs earning £800 or more paid Shs. 240 annually for government medical insurance. The plan was subsequently extended to Africans and institutionalized as the National Hospital Insurance Fund.[34]

Libraries

As they had to found their own hospitals and dispensaries to receive adequate medical care, and their own schools to gain an education, the Asians had to establish libraries to promote and serve the reading interests of their community. The Europeans' libraries, such as the McMillan in Nairobi, were closed to Asians as well as to Arabs and Africans. When the Asians first arrived in East Africa, they had scarcely any reading material. In 1918 the Shahs of Nairobi, realizing that there were only two books in their entire community, opened a library in the back of one of their shops. A decade earlier the Patels set up the first library in Dar es Salaam, the Daya Punu Library. In 1905 the Ismailis, with a donation from V. Nazerali, established a library in Zanzibar, and subsequently they built libraries wherever they formed a sizeable community. In 1951, to popularize a plan for augmenting their library resources, they proclaimed an Ismaili Library Week.[35] As in so many other ways each Asian community tended to think initially only of attending to its own needs.

The next step was the formation of libraries designed to serve the entire Asian community. Apparently, the first institution of this kind was the Library and Free Reading Room established in 1921 by the Mombasa Social Service League. Its counterpart in Nairobi was the Desai Memorial Library, which opened in 1944. Each year following the death in 1926 of the revered Asian political leader M. A. Desai, the Asians in the larger urban centers held a flag day and a mass meeting to commemorate Desai and raise funds for a memorial.[36] More than a decade elapsed, however, before the Asians rallied under the leadership of the Goan physician Dr. A. C. L. de Souza to raise the necessary money.

The funding of the Desai Memorial Library is a unique instance of a shrewd Asian philanthropy. During 1931 – 32 the Kenya government was remodeling Thika by demolishing the old buildings and selling new business plots by public auction. Many Asians, including a large number from Nairobi, participated in the first auction and elevated the prices by actively bidding against one another. With typical Asian acumen, Isher Dass, the radical Nairobi politician, organized the Asians into a Thika Syndicate for the next auction with a view to submitting only a single, very low Asian bid on each plot and then auctioning the land at competitive and much higher prices among themselves. The money collected in the Asians' auction would be devoted to some charity of their choice. The scheme was very successful, and the Asians raised not only most of the money needed for the library, but also enough to build a new Thika school. The library fund was subsequently augmented by contributions from individuals. Next to the Thika Syndicate the foremost donor was N. K. Mehta, who was given the privilege of laying the foundation stone.[37]

The library and reading room, and the Desai Memorial Hall in which they were housed, were restricted initially to Asians, but during the fifties they were opened to all peoples, and Africans became the main participants. In 1962 the library had about one thousand active members. Approximately eight hundred borrowed books each week, and many others perused the numerous newspapers and periodicals in the reading room.[38]

Most other libraries representing a combined effort by the Asians began with service to a single community. Among them were the T. B. Sheth Hindu Public Library in Mombasa, the Ismail Rahimtullah Library in Mombasa, and the Abdullah Shah Library in Nairobi. The last was not confined to Asians, but was designed solely for Muslims.[39]

A striking exception to this pattern of restriction is the Seif bin Salim Public Library of Mombasa. Founded in 1903 as the Mombasa Public Library, it has been described as not only "the oldest library" but also the oldest "inter-racial cultural institution in East Africa."[40] From the beginning it was open to peoples of all races and creeds. Endowed chiefly by two influential Asians, Jaffer Dewji and Allidina Visram, the library was administered during its first ten years by Cowasjee Manekji Dalal. By 1919 it had ninety-nine members who, during the year, borrowed 4,364 books — significant numbers in view of the fact that Mombasa then had probably little more than one hundred literate adults. During the twenties, when still dependent entirely on private donations, the library suffered from lack of effective leadership and survived only because of the beneficence of a few Asian donors, notably the

Alibhai Esmailjee and Suleman Verji families and Allidina Visram's son, Abdul Rasul. Beginning in 1929, when A. B. Patel became its president, the library steadily improved. Patel attracted more support, including an annual municipal grant of £100, and in 1939 moved the library into a more spacious building shared with the Mombasa Indian Association. In that year the Arab Sir Ali bin Salim pledged an annual grant of £100, and the library was renamed in honor of his brother, Seif bin Salim.[41]

During the mid-fifties under the presidency of Ramanbhai Becharbhai Patel, the library launched a fund drive for a new building. By then the municipality had raised its grant to £250 and the Kenya government had begun an annual subsidy of £150, but it was clear that the money for a building suited to the needs of the rapidly growing public library—the only such library in Mombasa—would have to come from the Asian community. In 1956, when less than half the £15,750 necessary for the building had been raised, A. B. Patel and the Arab coastal leader Sheikh Mbarak Ali Hinawy personally guaranteed a loan of £10,000 so that construction could begin. Apparently, the Asians eventually raised all the money. The four main donors were the Aga Khan, the Sheth Yusufali Charitable Trust, the M. P. Shah Charitable Trust, and Bawa Singh Birdi, the building contractor, each of whom gave Shs. 10,000. N. K. Mehta and Pandya & Co., the other two chief contributors, each bequeathed Shs. 2,500. As customary, the benefactors were divided into categories—in this case donors, patrons, and life-members—depending on their contributions. The magnitude of the Asian interest is apparent in the fact that besides the 4 donors, there were 35 patrons and 193 life-members. In these numbers were four Arabs, and it was an Arab who gave the land. Surprisingly, there were no European contributions to Mombasa's multiracial public library, which opened its doors in 1957.[42]

Although none had such an early beginning, there were a few other Asian-initiated libraries not restricted by race. Preeminent among these was the University of Nairobi's Gandhi Memorial Library, which became the largest and most important in East Africa. The intensive campaign that led to its founding is described in Chapter 6. Another important institution, the Tanzania National Library, which is the main public library in Dar es Salaam, was established with an award of £65,000 by A. Y. A. Karimjee and a matching grant from the government. The Public Library in Jinja and the Mehta Library at Lugazi were endowed by N. K. Mehta, and the Kampala Public Library and the Makerere University Library largely by the Madhvanis. The Zanzibar Books Library, one of the oldest in East Africa, was founded early in the century by Asians and, like those begun by Karimjee, Mehta, and the Madhvanis, was used by Africans and Arabs as well as Asians. After World War II Faiz Hassan, a Dar es Salaam advocate and big-game hunter, built up a library in his home that, according to one Asian, was the best private library in East Africa.[43]

Notes

1. Educational facilities are described in subsequent chapters.
2. *E. Afn. Standard,* 3 Mar. 1951, 2.
3. The gift was in florins (570,000), which had twice the value of the shilling. A. Raishi intv. B. R. S. (Jimmy) Verjee intv. Y. Sheriff intv.
4. D. N. Mehta intv. H. P. Joshi intv. A. Raishi intv. *E. Afn. Standard,* 29 Jan. 1910, 9.
5. Dr. A. Ribeiro intv. *E. Afn. Standard,* 1 Aug. 1908, 12; 22 Dec. 1906, 14.
6. F. A. De Souza intv.
7. Z. Patel intv.
8. K. R. Paroo intv. For a description of the Ismaili organization, see G. M. Wilson, "Welfare Orgs. & Services in Momb.," chap. 15, in Wilson, *Mombasa Social Survey,* 440–44, SU microfilm 2081, reel 12.
9. "Patrons" each donated Rs. 300 or more with Visram at the top with Rs. 555. "Life members" each donated Rs. 75, and "Ordinary Members" Rs. 9. List enclosed in Duni Chand (for promoters, Soc. Serv. League, Nairobi) to Hon. Sec., Nairobi Ind. Assoc., 10 Apr. 1918, EAINC records, SU microfilm 1929, reel 1. See also M. A. Desai (Hon. Sec., Nairobi Ind. Assoc.) to "Those whose subscriptions are not-yet paid," 20 May 1918, ibid. In 1967 the main individual donor was Maganlal Gokul. The leading company was Messrs. Assanand & Sons. Foundations included the M. J. Doshi Charitable Trust (most generous), the R. B. Patel Charitable Trust, the Premchand Charitable Trust, and the Chandaria Trust Foundation. C. I. Patel (pres., Mng. Committee) intv. *Momb. Soc. Serv. League, Momb.: The 47th Annual Rept. and Account of the League* (Momb.: Reliance Press, 1968).
10. 'Rules and Reguls. of the Soc. Serv. League, P.O. Box 36, Momb.', Momb. Ind. Assoc. records, film 1926, reel 4.
11. *Soc. Serv. League, Momb.: The 48th Annual Report and Account of the League* (Momb: Reliance Press, 1973), 4–6.
12. Ibid.
13. J. D. Byramjee intv.

14. Ibid. "Memo. of Assoc. of the Soc. Serv. League," 1948 draft, EAINC records, film 1929, reel 11.
15. *E. Afn. Standard*, 5 Feb. 1951, 2. J. D. Byramjee intv.
16. *Soc. Serv. League, Nairobi: Rules and Reguls., Revised 1939* (Nairobi: Regal Press, 1939). "Soc. Serv. League, Nairobi: 34th Annual Rept. for the Years 1971 and 1972" (typescript, Nairobi, 5 Oct. 1972). J. D. Byramjee intv. with personal tour, 5 Feb. 1973, Nairobi.
17. J. D. Byramjee intv.
18. Ibid.
19. Ibid.
20. Ibid.
21. Ibid.
22. Other committee members were Dr. Shankar Dhondo Karve (hon. sec.), K. R. Paroo (hon. treas.), Abdulhussein H. Kaderbhoy, and Dr. Amritlal Ujamsi Sheth. Dr. S. D. Karve, "Origin and Growth of the Pandya Memorial Clinic," in *Pandya Memorial Clinic: Sixteenth Anniversary Brochure, 1947–63* (Momb.: Momb. Times Ltd., 1963), 10–15.
23. P. D. Master, "Pandya Memorial Clinic," ibid., 7–8.
24. Ibid.
25. Ibid.
26. Donors and gifts are listed in ibid., 11–12. Battersby, with the largest donation, was named a patron. Vice-patrons were Maharashtra Amateurs (Shs. 4,350) and the Jain Youth League of Thika (Shs. 4,310). There were 56 donors (Shs. 2,000–3,500), 45 life members (Shs. 1,000–2,000), over 100 members (Shs. 250–1,000), and many others with lesser amounts. See speech by Ernest A. Vasey (memb. for educ., health, and govt.) at the opening ceremony, *Pandya Memorial Clinic Inaugural*, 17, 19. Among the main Asian donors in the ensuing two decades were the Maida Charitable Trust, the Popatlal Karman family, Kashibai Joshi, Dr. I. S. Patel, and B. G. Patel.
27. Master, "Pandya Memorial Clinic," 7.
28. "Pandya Memorial Hospital," *Coastweek* (Momb.), 20–26 July 1984, 8. J. Lyon, "Sixteen Years of Progress," in *Pandya Memorial Clinic*, 5, 15, 22–23, and inside cover. See also A. H. Nurmohamed, "Foreword," in ibid., 2.
29. Wilson, "Welfare Orgs. & Services in Momb.", in Wilson, *Mombasa Social Survey, part 1*, 440–44.
30. K. N. Shah intv. A. Vellani intv. G. D. Shah intv. Z. K. Shah intv. Dr. P. R. Puram intv. D. N. Mehta and H. P. Joshi intvs. "Miwani Sugar Mills Ltd., 20 Apr. 1973," typescript obtained by Bennett from the mills. The Kotechas' hospitals were in Molo and Nagongera, the sites of their ginneries in Bukedi District.
31. *Kenya Daily Mail*, 2 Sep. 1927, 2. H. P. Joshi intv.
32. G. J. Bhatt intv.
33. A. T. B. Sheth intv. Mrs. K. R. Paroo (ex-wife of Abdulla Rahimtulla Walji Hirji) intv. G. J. Bhatt intv.
34. J. D. Byramjee intv.
35. A. Raishi intv. L. R. Shah intv. A. T. B. Sheth intv. A. Vellani intv.
36. Hon. sec., Desai Memorial Committee, Nairobi, to hon. sec., Momb. Ind. Assoc., 6 July 1933; R. M. Shah (hon. sec., Momb. Ind. Assoc.), "Rept. of the Ind. Assoc. for 1932," 19 Dec. 1932; and Shah to A. M. Amin (hon. sec.,

Desai Memorial Committee), 22 Aug. 1932, Momb. Ind. Assoc. records, film 1926, reel 11.
37. A. Raishi intv. Frustrated in its attempt to raise revenue, the government at later auctions required all bidding to be by tender in sealed envelopes.
38. Hon. sec., Desai Memorial Committee, to sec., Kenya Ind. Congress, 28 Nov. 1956, EAINC records, film 1929, reel 14.
39. Sheth had donated Shs. 25,000 (intv.). Munawar-ud-Deen intv.
40. Sir Paul Sinker (dir.-gen., Brit. Council, London) in anon. brochure, *Seif bin Salim Public Library and Free Reading Room, Momb.* (Momb.: Reliance Press, 1957), 13.
41. Ibid., 17–20.
42. See list in ibid., 27–30.
43. A. Y. A. Karimjee intv. J. Sondhi intv. D. N. Mehta intv. H. P. Joshi intv. Abdulla Amour Suleiman was one of many Africans using the Zanzibar Books Library in the 1930s (intv.).

5

Provision of Schools

*One of the principal anxieties of Indians of
every community in East Africa had always
been the education of their children.*
—H. S. Morris, 1968

Foremost among the Asians' philanthropic endeavors was their contribution to education. As with their charitable pursuits generally, the Asians began with a preoccupation with the needs of their particular ethnic groups, then expanded to a concern for the entire Asian community, and finally in the later colonial years acquired a humanitarian interest in the educational needs of the Africans. Like the Africans and Europeans, the Asians placed a high value on education and were willing to sacrifice in the extreme to achieve the best possible instruction for their children. As the various castes and sects, which divided the Asians in the early years, merged their interests in economic expansion and in the political struggle for racial equality, the Asians acquired a sense of community, one expression of which was the development of a common system of education. Not until most of their own educational needs were met, and when their financial resources permitted, did many Asians seriously consider the needs of the larger, multiracial society. There are, of course, many exceptions to these generalizations. Some Asians, for instance, were motivated by humanitarian concerns from the beginning of their stay in East Africa.

The Asians' educational needs were affected by the changing circumstances of the colonial society. During the early years of the British and German administrations, the education of the Africans was entrusted to missionaries, and the education of the Asians, Europeans, and Arabs was left to the initiatives and resources of the separate communities. In this situation only the Goans, whose children were able to attend the Roman Catholic mission schools, benefited.[1] The earliest Asian schools were the Muslim Koranic institutions, which were housed within the mosques, admitted only boys, and offered only traditional religious instruction. The non-Muslims, and the Muslims who valued secular as well as religious training, had to make their own educational provisions. For many years the secular education of most Asians was very informal: Boys learned the family trade or business from their fathers, and girls the domestic arts from their mothers; this training was enhanced by associations within the extended families and basic communities. With the opening of the African interior, as the governments expanded and trade and business thrived, there arose a need for many new skills and a broader knowledge. Society was in a state of rapid and radical transformation. There was not only a great economic opportunity, but also, because of the increased intermingling of cultures, a threat to ethnic identity. The Asians began to perceive the need for a new system of education that would enhance their economic opportunities and, at the same time, foster the preservation of their traditional cultures.

Asian Communal and Common Schools

The Asians responded to these circumstances in various ways. Many who immigrated to East Africa left their wives in India, or sent them there when the first children reached school age, to care for the children as they attended Indian schools. Some entrusted their school-age children to close relatives in India, and others sent them to Indian boarding schools. The great majority, however, sought a solution in East Africa. In nearly every urban center as families gathered and organized for religious, economic, and social reasons, most ethnic groups eventually founded their own schools. The first schools of each Asian community in Kenya, shown in Table 5.1, present a pattern that was typical for East Africa as a whole.[2]

These schools usually had informal beginnings. In most cases

TABLE 5.1

Initial Asian Communal Schools in Kenya, 1890–1951

	Year	Place	Type
Muslims			
Bohras	1890	Mombasa	boys' primary
Ithnasheris	1904	Mombasa	boys' primary
Ismailis	1918	{ Mombasa	boys' primary
		Nairobi	girls' primary
Memons	1922	Mombasa	boys' primary
Sunnis	1929	Kisumu	girls' primary
Hindus			
Arya Samaj	1910	Nairobi	girls' primary
Shree Sanatan Dharam Sabha	1918	Nairobi	girls' primary
Cutch Gujarati Hindu Union	1926	Nairobi	girls' primary
Gujarati Balmandir	1930	Nairobi	mixed primary/ kindergarten
Ardasha Vidyalaya	1933	Nairobi	Mixed elementary
Gujarati	1937	Kisumu	girls' primary
Jains (Visa Oshwal)	1951	Nairobi	mixed primary
Sikh	1907	Nairobi	girls' primary
Goans	1928	Nairobi	mixed primary

they began, if Muslim, in the local mosque or, if Hindu or other denomination, in the home of the teacher.[3] In some instances teachers were recruited in India, but most of the early schools relied on local, dedicated women or men who offered their services to the community without remuneration.[4] Though initially offering instruction only in the first few standards, the schools added classes as they proved successful and, with standard VIII, became fully primary.

Most schools soon moved out of the mosques and private homes into buildings usually constructed specially for the purpose, and some eventually added secondary classes culminating with the sixth form. Among the communal primary schools in Kenya that advanced to the secondary level were the Ismaili boys' school in Mombasa, the Sunnis' girls' school in Nairobi, the Sikhs' Nairobi and Nakuru girls' schools, the Shree Sanatan Dharam School in

Nairobi, and the Dr. Ribeiro Goan School in Nairobi.[5] Some schools were established primarily as secondary schools. Those in Kenya included the Allidina Visram High School (1923), the Mombasa Institute of Muslim Education (1947), the Arya Girls' Senior School in Parklands (1961), the Siri Guru Singh Secondary School in Kisumu (1969), the Aga Khan Kenya Secondary School in Mombasa (1967), and the Aga Khan Academy in Nairobi (1970).[6]

In a few instances because of unusual circumstances, Asians of different religions combined to educate their children. Throughout East Africa, usually in the small settlements where they were not sufficiently numerous to support communal schools, Asians formed common schools. To enlist government aid and ensure adequate enrollment, the Zanzibar Asians, for example, joined in 1890 to form the island's first Asian primary school, the Sir Euan Smith Madrasah. For similar reasons the Asians of Lamu and of Mombasa each established their own common schools in 1899.[7] In Kisii the Ismailis, Hindus, and Goans together formed a primary school in 1936.[8] A few common schools were formed to serve special educational needs. In 1905, for instance, a school was opened in Nairobi by the Muslim leader Shamsud-Deen for the children of Asian railway workers.[9] Unfortunately, because of dispute over instruction concerning religion and language, some of these common schools—the Kisii school is an example—were short-lived. The effort to form such schools, however, was aided by the fact that some Asian groups, notably the Parsis, Patels, and until the 1950s the Shahs, did not form their own communal schools and attended those of others.[10]

All the initial communal and common schools were formed through voluntary contribution. Apart from business the Asians' principal expenditure was on education. Cast in an inferior context and suffering from discrimination, the Asians regarded education not only as a determinant for economic progress, but also as an essential for political participation and social improvement. For the education of their children most Asians were willing to forego luxuries, comfort, and even health and security. Thus they donated liberally to the establishment of local schools in both urban and rural areas. Since the financial resources for the establishment of adequate schools were much superior in the larger urban centers to those in the smaller towns and the villages, the Asians with school-age children tended to gravitate to the cities. Education, like business, was a key factor in Asian urbanization.

The contribution to schools took many forms. Usually when a community decided to found a school, a fund drive was held with each household contributing according to its means. There were often lotteries, fetes, dances, and other social forms of fund-raising. One of the most affluent members of the local community, or a family company, would frequently open the drive with a large donation, sometimes equal to half the anticipated cost, with the expectation that others in the community would provide matching funds.

The leading benefactors are well known. They were men of considerable wealth, those described in Chapter 2, who contributed to many kinds of charitable causes. The foremost include Nanji Kalidas Mehta and Jayant Madhvani in Uganda; Meghji Pethraj Shah, Indar Singh Gill, and Devji Kamalshi Hindocha in Kenya; Abdulkarim Y. A. Karimjee in Tanganyika; Sir Yusufali A. Karimjee and Sir Tayabali Karimjee of Zanzibar; and though not a resident of East Africa, the Aga Khan. Most of these men donated throughout East Africa, not only in one territory.

There are many others who in proportion to their more modest financial circumstances gave very generously to education; unfortunately, only a few can be mentioned here. Devshi Mepa Shah, a pioneer merchant-industrialist who made the local Asian school his pet project, became known as the "father of education in Thika." [11] For aid to the Nyeri schools, Meghji Rupshi Shah, a merchant in building materials, gained a similar reputation. [12] Premchand Vrajpal Shah, leader of the well-known Nairobi firm Premchand Raichand Ltd., assisted Jomo Kenyatta in establishing the Technical Training College, which, though proscribed during Mau Mau, developed into Kenyatta University College. [13] Suleman Verjee gave Rs. 100,000 towards the cost of the Ismaili boys' school in Mombasa. Dr. R. A. Ribeiro financed the Goans' school in Nairobi. Alibhai Panju contributed £7,500 for the Ithnasheri primary school in Mombasa, and Lalchand Moolchand & Bros. donated £5,000 for the Shree Sanatan Dharam school in Nairobi. [14] In

1905 three businessmen — V. Nazerali, Alnoor Kassum, and Patalai Vellani — pooled their resources to build the first Ismaili school and library in Zanzibar.[15]

Among the various ethnic communities the Ismailis and the Shahs were the most organized in financing their communal education. Both placed a great emphasis on educating their children in the local environments, and both, unlike most other Asian communities, provided equally for the education of boys and girls.

The Ismailis established schools in nearly every center where their people gathered, even where there were as few as ten children. The classes were first held in the home of a voluntary teacher. As enrollment increased, the community at its own expense erected a building and, if resources permitted, hired teachers from India. The Ismailis, as noted, opened their first school in 1905 in Zanzibar and their first schools on the mainland — a boys' school in Mombasa and a girls' school in Nairobi — in 1918. By 1970 in Kenya alone they had established thirty schools, which offered collectively instruction from the nursery to the advanced secondary level. In Tanganyika they developed a similar system including, as in Kenya, several hostels in the major centers. In 1970, disappointed in the government's provision for secretarial education, they organized in Dar es Salaam a secretarial college to ensure a high quality of training each year for approximately 120 Asian and African girls.[16]

The Ismaili schools were usually initiated by the local communities, but the Aga Khan played a key role. In the early years he contributed the major share of the expenses for beginning a school, but in time, as the community became more affluent, he expected the local people to match his grants and to maintain their schools by paying whatever fees were necessary. If a school were unable to meet its maintenance costs, he personally paid for the expenditure to ensure a continuing high standard. The Aga Khan also initiated a bursary system to provide for the education of the more needy children and to subsidize Ismaili higher education abroad. Beginning in 1918 at his direction the community established Ismaili provincial boards that administered the schools and were directly responsible to him. The result was a very well educated community with an extraordinarily high percentage of doctors, lawyers, teachers, and other professional people.[17]

The Aga Khan's educational contribution is evident in the Ismaili schools that carry his name. In Kenya by 1972 there were four Aga Khan secondary schools, two in Nairobi and two in Mombasa, including the prestigious Aga Khan Academy in Parklands. There were also the girls' school and the boys' school in Mombasa, two coeducational primary schools in Nairobi, nursery schools in Nairobi, Mombasa, Kisumu, and Eldoret, and student hostels in Nairobi and Mombasa. In Tanzania the Aga Khan institutions included the Dar es Salaam School of Commerce, primary schools in Arusha, Mbeya, Moshi, and Musoma, a nursery school and boys' and girls' hostels in Dar es Salaam, and a boys' boarding house in Iringa.[18]

Though very late in developing their program, the Shahs, comprising the Visa Oshwal community, eventually rivaled and perhaps even surpassed the Ismailis in educational attainment. In 1918 they opened a small communal library in the back of a Nairobi shop, and in 1927 they formed a general donation fund for assisting in the payment of school fees. In 1934 with the government's assistance they established their first school, the Balmandir Institution in Mombasa, a "school for little children," which served about eighty boys and girls from ages three to ten. Except for this one endeavor, however, the Shahs lacked the resources to found schools and had to send their children to institutions founded by other communities. Before World War II only one Shah, Amritlal Raishi, graduated from secondary school. As Kenya emerged from the depression, however, the Shahs began to prosper. In 1937, organizing an Oshwal Education and Relief Board to help alleviate the famine in India, they were able to raise Shs. 400,000. Encouraged by this success, the Shahs within the next four years formally organized their social institutions, built an impressive communal center in Nairobi, and began to emphasize education. Through the Education and Relief Board, they easily raised another Shs. 400,000. They then decided to forego any form of government aid. In 1952 they began to impose an annual tax of Shs. 100 on each of their licensed merchants, and during the two ensuing decades, by this means alone they collected more than Shs. 4 million.[19]

Between 1951 and 1972, with their own money, the Shahs financed eight Nairobi schools extending, in all, from the nursery to the highest secondary level and accommodating 3,400 pupils.

Some of these were boarding schools designed for children in areas where facilities were lacking. One of the schools, which evolved into a regular secondary school, was unique in that it began as "a school for failures" to enable the "late developers," who had failed the entrance examinations for government schools, to continue their education.[20]

The Shahs claim that by 1972 they had become the most highly educated community in the world. They were then spending nearly Shs. 40 million annually on higher education alone, a world record, they said, for any community in proportion to its members. Among their 16,000 people in East Africa, at least 4,500 were studying at the secondary or higher levels, and approximately 500 were graduating each year in higher education. The money for this achievement came not only from the Shah merchants, but from special fund drives, sizeable donations from the wealthy, and rental of their spacious communal hall, which could provide food and seating for as many as ten thousand people. From the hall alone, where Asians and eventually Africans of many communities celebrated annually about one hundred marriages, the Shahs netted each year approximately £12,000 for education. They also financed some of their educational ventures with interest-free loans. Shah merchants, for instance, advanced in 1962 the £35,000 needed to build the Visa Oshwal Girls' School in Nairobi. They lent the money without interest and were fully reimbursed by the community within four years. Since money was not a problem, the quality of education in the Shah schools was very high. Among the teachers were often a number of volunteers who had recently completed their higher education and were awaiting professional employment.[21]

Government Aid

Not all Asians were as fortunate as the Shahs in ability to finance their educational needs, and nearly all, including the Ismailis, relied on some assistance from the reluctant colonial governments. In 1906, when Shamsud-Deen was unable to continue the school he had opened in Mombasa, the Uganda Railway converted it into a school for Asian railway employees. Assuming control of this

TABLE 5.2

Government Aid to Asian Schools, 1938 and 1960

	Government	Aided	Unaided	Total
1938				
Kenya	13	55	8	76
Tanganyika	3	47	11	61
Uganda	2	50	—	52
1960				
Kenya	44	99	17	160
Tanganyika	12	130	2	144
Uganda	25	105	—	130

school in 1912, the government separated it from the railway and opened it to Asians generally. It had taken over a similar school for Europeans in 1907, and in 1913 it was to open its first school for Africans. After establishing a Department of Education in 1911, the government also began to confer grants-in-aid on European and African private schools. Not until 1925, after prolonged urging from the Asian community, however, did the Kenya government extend its grants-in-aid to Asian schools. Zanzibar had taken the same step in 1924, and Uganda followed in 1925 and Tanganyika in 1929.[22] Each territory set up an advisory council on Asian education and, with the community's consent, levied a special tax on the Asians to support the increased educational expenditure. Eventually three types of Asian schools emerged in East Africa: the government schools, the private schools enjoying a government subsidy, and the private schools without aid. As shown in Table 5.2, Asian schools greatly increased after World War II.[23]

Government subsidies to Asian education conferred a mixed blessing. The schools taken over by the governments were situated in the large urban centers and were open to all Asians regardless of caste or creed. Though emphasizing instruction in English and a Western-oriented curriculum, they maintained relatively high standards of admission and instruction. They benefited especially the poorer Asians whose communities were unable to provide adequate schools, but they were appreciated by nearly all the Asians.

The government schools and the aided private schools, however, lost a degree of control that the Asians valued. Even the aided schools were required to admit all qualified Asian applicants regardless of religion or caste; they were subject to frequent inspection, and their teachers had to be approved in each territory by the director of education. The aided schools also felt a pressure to convert to English as the medium of instruction and to mold their curricula to those of the government schools. There was always the threat that nonconformity to the government interest would be met with a diminished subsidy or, in the extreme, a termination of all aid.[24]

The Asians deeply resented the governments' discriminatory conferral of aid. Throughout East Africa the governments allocated far more expenditure per student to the European community than to the Asian, Arab, or African. In 1939, for instance, Kenya spent £51,881 on the Europeans' education compared to £45,602 for Asians, £7,414 for Arabs, and £81,869 for Africans.[25] In proportion to population this meant that the Europeans received 2.5 times the amount accorded Asians, 4.7 times that for Arabs, and 94.6 times that for Africans. Even in Uganda, where discrimination was least evident, the government in 1938 was averaging £22 for each European student's education and only £19 for an Asian's.[26] To the Asians in rural areas, however, where few had much money and population was small, government aid often meant the difference between a school and no school.

Despite the value of this aid, the Asian schools were built and maintained largely with Asian money. Almost all the schools were initiated by the Asians and financed by communal contributions. Eventually the governments assumed control of a few and provided subsidies for most of the rest. The money used by the governments, however, was that obtained from the Asian education cess, and in nearly all instances the governments' overall contribution was considerably less than the Asians' private support. The Burhaniya Bohra School in Mombasa is an example. Begun in 1890 entirely with Bohra money, the school was rebuilt in 1939 through a donation of Shs. 125,000 from A. M. Kaderbhai. Not until 1956, when a new building was contemplated, did the government contribute a

sum matching the £25,000 donated by Tayabali Hassanali A. Karimjee.[27]

The other form of official support, the annual grant-in-aid, was
also inferior to the Asian contribution. Again, one institution, the
Naivasha Indian School, can be described as typical. The school
was established in 1919 by the Ismailis, and two years later, after
agreeing to change its name, admit children of all faiths, and appoint a representative governing committee, it began to receive a
government monthly subsidy of Shs. 75. The amount was raised to
Shs. 383 by 1928, then, because of the depression, was decreased to
Shs. 105 in 1931, and raised to Shs. 170 by 1937. Citing the inade-
quacies of recent years, the school principal complained in 1934
that the grant-in-aid provided less than half the monthly expenditure of Shs. 440. Despite fees of Shs. 4 per month for each of its
twenty-seven boys—the thirteen girls were admitted free, as was
often the custom in Asian schools—and sizeable donations from
individuals in the community, the school had begun the year with a
deficit of Shs. 2,000. The principal pleaded in vain for the government to take over the school.[28]

As the financial strait of the Naivasha school illustrates, the
Asian educational institutions often lacked essential resources. The
teachers taught English as a second language. In many schools the
teachers had no formal training, carried too heavy a work load, and
were poorly paid. Students of various ages and at several educational levels were taught simultaneously in a single classroom. The
buildings were not designed as schools, and playgrounds and laboratory equipment were nonexistent. Such conditions frequently
prevailed during a school's initial years, and they were characteris-
tic of many schools before World War II.[29]

In many other schools the conditions essential for a significant
achievement in education were quite adequate. The government
schools maintained high standards, and the official requirements
for grants-in-aid and the system of close supervision were important inducements to the pursuit of quality in the aided schools.
More important, however, was the Asians' zeal for education.
Their children's needs very often required severe sacrifice. In the
early years of settlement the relatively few wealthy Asians such as

Allidina Visram, A. M. Jeevanjee, and the Aga Khan gave generously to education, but the schools, once handsomely begun, had difficulties in continuing. After World War II, when the community as a whole could provide substantial financial support, the number of well-endowed schools greatly increased. Two of these schools — the Allidina Visram High School and the Mombasa Institute of Muslim Education — deserve description as outstanding examples of Asian educational philanthropy.

The Extraordinary Secondary Schools

The Allidina Visram High School, which opened in 1923, was to become one of East Africa's preeminent secondary schools. In 1917, the year after his father's death, Abdul Rasul Visram approached the government with a view to erecting a magnificent memorial to East Africa's foremost businessman. He was aware that the Mombasa Indian School, which the local Asians had recently established and which the government administered, lacked a suitable building. Nearly four hundred of the town's six to seven hundred Asian boys, he pointed out, were unable to obtain an education. Requesting a plot of land, Abdul Rassul offered to construct a much larger building and to finance its administration for the first three years. The school would be named after his father and would be fully maintained by the government after the three years.[30] The site selected, three and one-half acres on the high headland separating the eastern shore of Mombasa Island from the mainland, was spectacular in its situation and view of the ocean, Old Town, and the Port of Mombasa. In constructing the school, Abdul Rasul, despite the collapse during the war of his father's far-flung financial empire, spared no expense. Hiring an architect from India and importing the gray stone and other materials from India, he erected a splendid two-story building of intricate design with columns, balconies, gargoyles, and floors inlaid with mosaic.[31]

Although Abdul Rasul was to die only eight months after the opening in 1923 and was never to see its development, the Allidina Visram High School proved a fitting memorial to his illustrious father. Open to Asian boys of all creeds and castes, the school enrolled 400 pupils its opening year. At first entirely primary like its predecessor, it gradually added secondary courses with the result that its students sat for the London Matriculation Examinations beginning in 1929, the Cambridge School Certificate Examinations in 1948, and the Higher School Certificate Examinations in 1958. Though closed and occupied by the military during World War II, the school was flourishing again in 1945 with 892 pupils. With this number, however, it was seriously overcrowded. In 1957 it eliminated the primary classes and dropped its enrollment to a more manageable 374 students.[32]

Throughout its history, despite large enrollments, the school retained a general excellence. A relatively high percentage of those who took the examinations passed. In 1968 fifty-nine Allidina candidates achieved First Division Certificates in the East Africa examinations, a higher total than that of any other school, and in 1972 one student, Sanjay Chotai, gained eight distinctions in eight subjects with a total of six points in his best six subjects.[33] Although it began with a large donation from an Ismaili, the school differed from the Ismaili institutions in being independent from the Aga Khan and having a governing committee representative mainly of non-Muslims. Before independence four of the nine successive headmasters and nearly all the staff were Asians, and Asians dominated the governing committee. A. B. Patel, J. B. Pandya, and later Pandya's son Anant, Mombasa's three leading Asian political figures, presided over the committee and provided an essential communal direction including the management of many fund drives to supplement the government's financial contribution.

While emphasizing academic achievement, the school encouraged sports and other extracurricular activities. Students competed with those from other schools primarily in hockey, cricket, and football, but also in volleyball, table tennis, badminton, and softball. Within the school there was an annual sports day for all. The students could participate in as many as thirty-two club or societal activities ranging from literature of various types to Boy Scouts, science, farming, band, chess, music, film, and animal protection. They wore a school badge and tie, recited a special prayer, and had a code of ethics. There was great pride in becoming an "Allidina boy," and among the members of the Old Allidinians' Association there have been many distinguished doctors, lawyers, politicians, businessmen, and scientists.[34] Obviously, the school made a significant contribution to the professional development of East Africa.

Like the Allidina Visram High School, the Mombasa Institute of Muslim Education was a boys' secondary school and, as its name denotes, largely a product of Muslim philanthropy. The initiative was taken early in 1948 by the Aga Khan who, after consulting the sultan of Zanzibar, approached the Kenya governor, Sir Phillip Mitchell. The governor in turn conferred with the British Resident at Zanzibar and a British expert on Arab affairs, and then, in a despatch to the secretary of state for the colonies, proposed the establishment of the institute. The aim was to raise the educational and economic standards of Muslims on Zanzibar and along its coastal strip in Kenya and Tanganyika by providing technical and vocational training as opposed to commercial education. The commercial professions, it was thought, were overcrowded, and there was a need for development of practical skills. Courses would be offered, following standard VI, in marine and electrical engineering, navigation and seamanship, agriculture and foresty, human and veterinary medicine, and boat-building, masonry, and other manual skills. Addressing the public by radio in June 1948, Mitchell explained that the institute would serve primarily the Arabs and followers of the Aga Khan. In his despatch to the secretary of state, he had stated that it would also meet the educational needs of the Somalis.[35] In time other fundamentals of the institute became apparent. Instruction would be solely in English, classes would be entirely secondary, and, though open to Africans as well as Arabs and Asians, only Muslims would be admitted.

As with many of the later schools, the institute was established as a joint venture between the public and private sectors. An Arab sheikh, Khamius bin Mohomed bin Juma, leased a site of thirty-four acres for the institute. The Aga Khan contributed £100,000, the Bohra community £50,000, and various individuals £20,000, a total of £170,000 toward the initial costs of construction, equipping, and staffing. The imperial government, through its Colonial Development and Welfare Fund, provided £100,000 in the name of the sultan of Zanzibar, and the Kenya government gave £50,000. After opening, the institute was to be maintained by annual grants-in-aid from the governments of Kenya, Tanganyika, Uganda, and Zanzibar as well as school fees and continuing private donations.[36]

The institute was established as planned. Differing markedly from the Allidina school in its architecture, it adhered to a plain, but imposing, traditional Arab style. The initial buildings were completed early in 1951 at a cost of £253,000. The sultan presided over the opening ceremony in April 1951, and by the end of the year 103 students had been admitted. By 1953 there were 161 students, who came from British Somaliland and Uganda as well as Zanzibar, Kenya, and Tanganyika. A few were Africans. The 59 Kenya students were taking technical courses in general engineering, electricians' and radio mechanics, building and woodworking, motor-vehicle mechanics, and seamanship. They also were studying the theory and practice of Islam, a compulsory subject for all. In 1955, when enrollment reached 190, the principal was optimistically planning the addition of many new courses leading to City and Guilds Intermediate Examinations, East Africa certificates, and diplomas.[37]

Some of the high expectations were not realized, and independence brought significant changes. In the late fifties the institute had difficulty in placing its students in employment, with the result that it enrolled no new students in 1959 and in 1960 offered courses only in mechanical and electrical engineering.[38] To allay criticism of religious discrimination, the institute also began to admit a token number of non-Muslims. Meanwhile it had become solely a Kenya school. In 1958 the Kenya government assumed full responsibility for the grant-in-aid, which previously had been contributed by all the East African territories. In 1964, the year following the independence of Kenya, an important education commission, which was chaired by Prof. Simeon H. Ominde and recommended sweeping changes in the nation's educational system, advised that the institute "become the technical college for the Coast Region and Eastern Kenya." [39] Following the commission's report, the institute in common with all other educational institutions in Kenya was opened to all qualified students regardless of race or creed. By 1972, when its enrollment was 961, it admitted girls as well as boys, and most of the students were Africans.[40]

The Asians helped to found a number of other secondary schools. Among them are the Aga Khan Academy of Nairobi and the Shaaban Robert Secondary School of Upanga, which from the beginning have been open to students without distinction of race or religion and are renowned for the quality of their instruction.

Notes

1. There were some exceptions. In 1894 the CMS, Mombasa, opened a school for Asian and Arab boys. In the early 1900s the Roman Catholic Mission School, Zanzibar, admitted Parsi as well as Goans. Gregory, *India and E.A.,* 406.
2. Elsa Abreau, *Role of Self-Help in the Devt. of Educ. in Kenya, 1900–73* (Nairobi: Kenya Lit. Bureau, 1982), chaps. 3, 4, 5 passim. The history of Asian education in East Africa to 1947 is briefly described in A. A. Kazimi, *Enquiry into Indian Educ. in E.A.* (Nairobi: Govt. Ptr., 1947).
3. The Arya Samaj school for girls in Nairobi, e.g., was first held in the home of Mathura Dass Arya. Ibid., 97.
4. The Ismaili boys' school at Mombasa was one of those that recruited teachers from India. Ibid., 57, 109–10.
5. Ibid., 57, 78–79, 111, 118, 132–33, 159.
6. Ibid., 61, 63, 83–84, 100, 116–17.
7. Gregory, *India and E.A.,* 406. J. S. Mangat gives the date 1891: *Hist. of the Asians,* 133. So does Abreau, *Role of Self-Help,* 133. See also Francis Naronha, *Fifty Years: A Hist. of Allidina Visram High School, 1923–72* (Mombasa: Huseini Packaging & Ptg., 1972), 1.
8. Abreau, *Role of Self-Help,* 66–67.
9. Ibid., 34.
10. Ibid., 121, 133.
11. K. N. Shah intv.
12. M. M. R. Shah intv.
13. V. D. Shah intv.
14. Abreau, *Role of Self-Help,* 57, 72, 131, 155–56.
15. S. G. Mehta intv.
16. Several Ismaili leaders contributed to this description. The most informative was Lutof Ali Bhatia, administrator of the Aga Khan Educ. Board, Dar es Salaam (intv.). Abreau, *Role of Self-Help,* 121–22.
17. Ibid.
18. Taken from the 1972 Kenya and Tanzania telephone directories.
19. Mrs. K. J. Shah intv. Abreau, *Role of Self-Help,* 124.
20. A. Raishi intv.
21. Ibid. L. R. Shah intv. I. S. Patel intv. V. D. Shah and Mrs. K. J. Shah intvs. Abreau, *Role of Self-Help,* 121–22.
22. O. W. Furley and T. Watson, *Hist. of Educ. in E.A. (N.Y.: NOK, 1978),* 82. Mangat, *Hist. of the Asians,* 134. Abreau, *Role of Self-Help,* 34, 36.
23. Compiled from the annual *Stat. Abstracts* of the three territories. Government control of a school often resulted in several changes of name. The

Indian Boys' School, Nairobi, became successively the Government Indian High School, the Government Asian High School, the Duke of Gloucester High School, and finally Jamhuri High School.

24. For Asian dissatisfaction in Uganda with the government schools, see Morris, *Indians in Ug.,* 150–53.
25. "Kenya Educ. Dept. Annual Rept., 1939," typescript, p. 3, C.O. 544/56.
26. Gregory, *India and E.A.,* 490.
27. Abreau, *Role of Self-Help,* 74–75.
28. G. G. Desai (prin., Naivasha Ind. School) to H. O. V. Hodge (DC, Nakuru), 23 Feb. 1934 and 23 Aug. 1934, file NKU-2/12/2/II, "Educ.: Pvt. Schools; Asian Schools (Naivasha School), 1933–39," Rift Valley Province daily corresp., SU microfilm 4752, reel 35.
29. For a description of Asian school inadequacy resulting from shortage of funds, see Kenya, *Rept. of the Select Committee on Indian Educ.* (Nairobi: Govt. Ptr., 1949), 3–4.
30. Abdul Rasul Allidina Visram, statement, *Evidence of the Educ. Commission of the E.A.P., 1919* (Nairobi: Swift, 1920), quoted in Abreau, *Role of Self-Help,* 25.
31. Naronha, *Fifty Years,* 7–11.
32. Instruction was in Gujarati in the lower classes and in English in the higher. Ibid., 16, 23–29, 117, 120, 125.
33. Ibid., 51, 125.
34. Ibid., 40–41, 44, and chap. 6.
35. Abreau, *Role of Self-Help,* 83.
36. Ibid., 84. *Kenya Daily Mail* (Momb.), 10 June 1948, 1. *E. Afn. Standard,* 7 Dec. 1951, 5.
37. Prin., Momb. Inst. of Mus. Educ., to Ind. Assoc., Momb., Sep. 1955, Coast Prov. daily corresp., SU microfilm 1926, reel 4. *Kenya Daily Mail,* 18 June 1948, 8. Kenya, *Educ. Dept. Annual Rept. 1953* (Nairobi: Govt. Ptr., 1955), 45–46; *1950,* 24–25; *1954,* 34. Furley and Watson, *Hist. of Educ.,* 217.
38. Furley and Watson, *Hist. of Educ.,* 217.
39. *Kenya Educ. Commission Rept., part 1* (Nairobi: Govt. Ptr., 1964), 96.
40. Abreau, *Role of Self-Help,* 84.

6

Establishment of a Gandhi Memorial

> We should go in for a scheme of East African
> University to commemorate the name of
> Mahatma Gandhi. . . . There could be no
> discrimination. Indians, Africans, Arabs,
> Europeans and in fact any person who calls
> himself or herself an East African citizen should
> have full freedom to avail of this facility.
> —Nanji Kalidas Mehta, 1949

Among the philanthropic contributions of the Asian community the most important by far was the University of Nairobi. The university was not entirely an Asian contribution. In the long run the governments in East Africa and Britain donated far more money to its development. The concept, however, of creating in Kenya an institution similar to Makerere in Uganda, with a full academic curriculum incorporating the humanities, social sciences, physical sciences, mathematics, commerce, and applied arts—this was primarily an Asian contribution. Moreover, in the beginning most of the impetus and most of the funding essential to implementation of this ideal were provided not by the local and imperial governments, but by the Asians. Their drive for contributions was the most successful of all fund drives by any people in East Africa. It was the most widespread, extending through all four British territories, and it involved the greatest number of individuals and raised the most money.

The project was conceived primarily as a response to Mohandas K. Gandhi's assassination on 30 January 1948. Through his achievements with passive resistance in South Africa and civil dis-

127

obedience in India, Gandhi had shown Indians throughout the world a unique and successful means of liberation from colonial oppression. In addition, his dedication to the principles of nonviolence, self-sacrifice, spirituality, and the brotherhood of all peoples had made Gandhi a symbol of the ideal man, a model to be emulated by Indians everywhere. He was truly a *Mahatma,* a great soul. In East Africa the Asians of all creeds and sects — Hindus, Muslims, Jains, Sikhs, and Goans — had closely followed Gandhi's work in India and donated generously to his campaigns.

There was universal sorrow at the news of Gandhi's death. On 31 January when the news arrived, hundreds of Asians in Nairobi gathered in the Desai Memorial Hall to mourn. The next day, on instructions from the Indian Chamber of Commerce, Asians of all sects closed their shops, and following a directive from the Aga Khan Ismailia Provincial Council, all the Ismaili schools in Kenya closed. The Daudi Bohra Community expressed "its profound sense of shock and horror." [1] The Goan Institute, the Sikh Union Club, and the Nairobi Central Muslim Association were among many Asian organizations that sent telegrams of condolence to India — to Prime Minister Nehru, the governor-general, and Gandhi's relatives. Others sending telegrams included Kenya's governor Sir Philip Mitchell and the principal African political organization, the Kenya African Union. In the afternoon an orderly procession of mourners, about eight thousand in all, filed solemnly through the streets. Then, gathering in a mass meeting under the auspices of the East Africa Indian National Congress, the throng endorsed a resolution expressing "profound sorrow" and "the deepest horror and indignation." "In an hour of desperation," the resolution continued, "India has lost her most devoted servant and the world its greatest apostle of peace." [2]

In other urban centers throughout East Africa there was a similar reaction, and as the congress president, Devi Dass Puri, observed, "all communities and races joined together in paying tribute to this great Son of India." Some Africans composed poems and essays in Swahili and sent them to the press. [3]

The demonstrations of respect for Gandhi continued beyond February 1948. An urn bearing a portion of *Bapuji's Asthi* (Gandhi's ashes) was brought from India to East Africa in June by

Sorabji Rustamji, Gandhi's old co-worker in South Africa. In Mombasa and Nairobi the urn was displayed, and thousands of people filed by — in Nairobi in rows six deep — to pay their respect in what the Indians called a *darshana*.[4] A few days later the urn was again put aboard ship and displayed successively in Dar es Salaam, Beira, and Durban. The ashes were then to be immersed in the Indian Ocean. In East Africa, however, suggestions came from many Asians that the ashes should also be immersed in Lake Victoria, the heart of the continent that was so important to Gandhi. The Asian leaders successfully submitted a request, with the result that, after some of the ashes were scattered in the waters off Durban, the urn was returned to Mombasa and thence Nairobi. It was again displayed not only in these centers, but also in Thika, Naivasha, Gilgil, Nakuru, Kericho, Eldoret, Kakamega, and Kisumu — and thence into Uganda at Mbale, Kampala, and Jinja. In a solemn ceremony, 14 August, the ashes were immersed in Lake Victoria.[5] Meanwhile the congress had prepared for its annual session a resolution extolling Gandhi and exhorting "all Indians in East Africa to dedicate themselves to the work for which he stood and to honour him by following in his footsteps." [6] In subsequent years the date of Gandhi's assassination was to be observed as a day of mourning, and the date of his birth as a day of celebration.[7]

Asian Plans for a Liberal Arts College

Despite the fact that all Asian groups mourned for Gandhi, any meaningful association between the Muslims and non-Muslims in East Africa in establishing a memorial had become virtually impossible by January 1948. The estrangement that had been developing between the two communities since the early thirties had been augmented by events in India culminating in the partition. At the time of Gandhi's assassination the Muslims of East Africa were calling for separate electorates and separate seats in the territorial legislatures, and in June they were to resign from the congress.[8] Since the creation of Pakistan, their aversion to the name "Indian" had been leading, as mentioned previously, to the coinage of the term "Asian" to designate the collective immigrants from South Asia. Another factor that militated against the Muslims' joining with non-Muslims in forming a memorial is that by 1948 they were involved in a philanthropic enterprise of their own. The Ismailis, Bohras, Ithnasheris, and other Muslims, in combination with the Arabs, were then busily engaged in establishing the Mombasa Institute of Muslim Education.[9] It was thus the non-Muslims—the Hindus, Sikhs, Shahs, and Goans—who decided to establish a memorial to Gandhi.

During 1948, while the Gandhi Smarak Nidhi at Ahmedabad coordinated the raising of funds for a memorial in India, there was a diversity of effort in East Africa. In Mwanza a prominent Uganda cotton industrialist and businessman, Chaturbhai Khushalbhai Patel, endowed a Mahatma Gandhi Memorial Hall. In Mombasa a group of concerned Asians led by Purshottamdas Dhanjibhai Master formed a Gandhi Society to propagate the Mahatma's ideals and consider a memorial. In Thika the Jain Youth League decided to hold a lottery throughout East Africa to raise funds for a memorial, and it requested aid from the congress in obtaining permission from the territorial governments for the sale of tickets. When the Zanzibar Asians pointed out, however, that a lottery was "highly repugnant and obnoxious" as contrary to Gandhi's principles, the congress withdrew its support, and the project was abandoned.[10]

The establishment of the Gandhi memorial that led to the University of Nairobi can be traced to a meeting of the standing committee of the Congress on 5–6 February 1948 when a decision was made to erect an appropriate memorial.[11] In June at a public meeting in Nairobi, called by the congress, a large gathering of Hindus, Jains, Sikhs, and Goans enthusiastically endorsed a proposal to undertake an intensive campaign for funds throughout East Africa. The coordination of the campaign and nature of the memorial were entrusted to a provisional committee chaired by the Nairobi advocate Shivabhai Gordhanbhai Amin.[12] In August while attending the immersion ceremony at Jinja, Amin took the opportunity to confer with Asian leaders from the other territories. All agreed that a memorial should be erected, but they differed on whether there should be several memorials, sited at various places, or just one for the whole of East Africa. Some among those favoring a single memorial suggested a college of higher education. In September on his return to Nairobi, Amin summoned the provisional committee, which then resolved:

1. There should be a central memorial for the whole of East Africa.
2. The memorial should be an institution for higher education capable of making a permanent contribution to the cultural development of the people of East Africa.
3. It should include a chair for the study of the life of Mahatmaji and his teachings.
4. As a first step a permanent committee consisting of equal members from each territory should be formed.[13]

The permanent committee that resulted from this meeting was representative of Asians in all East Africa. Entitled the Mahatma Gandhi Memorial Committee, it had forty members—twelve each from Kenya, Tanganyika, and Uganda, and four from Zanzibar. At its inaugural meeting in September 1949 in Kampala, this memorial committee reaffirmed the decisions of the provisional committee and elected the Mombasa barrister and politician Ambalal Bhailalbhai Patel as its president. At that time Patel was chairman of the Mombasa Gandhi Society and a member of the Kenya Legislative and Executive Councils. Enjoying the confidence of the government, he was the most influential and respected of all Asian political leaders not only in Kenya, but in East Africa.[14]

Patel's first step as president was to inform Governor Mitchell of the Asians' intention. Patel was aware that at a recent ceremony inaugurating the Mombasa Institute of Muslim Education, the governor had invited similar educational ventures and offered to match, pound for pound, with a grant from Britain's Colonial Development and Welfare Fund, any money raised privately. Patel also knew that since 1947 the imperial government had been contemplating the establishment in Kenya of a technical institute to provide middle-level training in the highly skilled trades. In May 1947 Mitchell's deputy had appointed a special committee, chaired by a prominent educator, G. P. Willoughby, to draft a detailed scheme. Reporting in March 1949, the Willoughby committee had recommended the establishment of a multiracial Kenya Technical and Commercial Institute, which would provide instruction and workshop experience in joinery and cabinet-making, building, smithery, plumbing, fitting, electrical work, and auto mechanics and repairs. On a higher technical level the institute would also offer training in mechanical engineering. Mitchell had forwarded this report to the secretary of state for the colonies, who had referred it to his Advisory Committee for Colonial Colleges of Arts, Science, and Technology.[15]

It was while the Willoughby report was being considered in London that Patel met with the governor. According to Patel, Mitchell expressed "great pleasure" with the Asian scheme, agreed to grant a charter and provide "a site of 150 acres in or about Nairobi," and offered to recommend assistance on a matching basis up to £100,000.[16]

The Government's Assumption of Control

Patel's next step, after receiving this important pledge from the governor, was to enlist the support of the newly appointed high commissioner for the government of India in East and Central Africa, Apa B. Pant. Delighted with the prospect of a memorial, Pant invited Professor Humayun Kabir, educational adviser to the government of India, and another Indian educator, Professor Nirmal Kumar Sidhanta, to visit East Africa and advise on the nature of the Gandhi institution. In December 1949 the two visitors met with Kenya Asian leaders, expressed thanks to the governor, and toured East Africa to ascertain the potential support. Four months later they reported in favor of establishing a Gandhi Memorial College that would include instruction in agriculture, engineering, and medicine as well as the arts, science, and commerce. Though strongly endorsing the idea that the college should serve Africans, Europeans, and Arabs as well as Asians, the professors argued, with surprising conservatism, that the Asians, by convention, should be accorded about 50 percent of the enrollment. Because of the necessity to have instruction in English, they recommended that the college be affiliated, not to an institution in India as some had proposed, but to the University of London. They also suggested that the fund goal be raised to £250,000.[17]

In May 1950 at a meeting in Kampala attended by sixteen of its forty members, the memorial committee provisionally adopted the professors' report and appointed a subcommittee to study the financial implications. It also authorized A. B. Patel and the Uganda industrialist M. P. Shah to compile quickly a list of about sixty donors who could be counted on to contribute half the contemplated £250,000.[18]

Shortly after this meeting the Asians received further encouragement from the governor. Mitchell informed Patel that he was leaving for Britain in September to confer with the secretary of state, and he expressed hope that the imperial government's matching contribution would be as high as £200,000.[19] At this time apparently neither the governor nor the Asian leaders had thought of combining the technical institute and the Gandhi Memorial College.

In London Mitchell found the Colonial Office anxious to receive the Asian money but staunchly opposed to a separate Asian educational institution. In August Philip Rogers, assistant secretary in the Colonial Office, had written to administrators in Kenya, Tanganyika, and Uganda, "While we are naturally in favour of anything which would collect more money for higher education in East Africa . . . we must do everything possible to prevent a separate College being set up." [20] In reply Robert Scott, administrator of the East Africa High Commission, had denounced the Kabir-Sidhanta report as "a very specious document" with "completely phony" estimates. "Personally, I regard the formulation of this scheme as an attempt to capitalize in the political interest of India the desire of Indians in East Africa for greater facilities for higher education; and as a part of the build-up of a 'coloured' front united against 'colonialism.' " [21] Scott's opinion was endorsed by Colin H. Thornley, Kenya's deputy chief secretary, who was heading the government in Mitchell's absence.[22] Bernard De Bunsen, principal of Makerere University, warned against the creation of an Asian institution, which, he asserted, "could not escape from being through its sponsorship a racial College," and Sir James F. Duff, vice-chancellor of

Durham University, who had recently served on higher education commissions in West Africa and India, informed the Colonial Office that he "was horrified by the proposal." [23]

Such was the climate of opinion when Mitchell arrived at the Colonial Office for a meeting with Andrew B. Cohen, assistant undersecretary of State, and Walter Adams, secretary of the Inter-University Council on Higher Education in the Colonies. Apparently at Mitchell's urging, a decision was made to try to persuade the Asians to combine their memorial with the proposed technical college. [24] All were anxious not to lose the Asians' potential monetary donation. "One of the original objects of the scheme," noted a colonial official later, "was to persuade the Indians to make a financial contribution." [25] Writing to Patel in September 1950, Mitchell proposed that the two institutions be combined: [26]

> If you care to join with the Government of Kenya (which has set aside £120,000 for the purpose) in the project to establish an institution designed to develop into either a Polytechnic or the Faculty of Technology for a future East African University . . . an amount of £150,000 from the Treasury could be obtained. Indeed, I would almost feel justified in saying that it *would* be obtained if you and your associates could raise the same sum. . . .
>
> I do not think there would be any difficulty in arranging that a specific part of the Institute should be in effect the Memorial that you desire.

The combination proposed by the governor and the Colonial Office was quite different from what the Asians had envisaged. The Asians had in mind an academic college similar to Makerere, not a technical school, and they intended above all to honor Gandhi, whose name was to be prominent. Moreover, they had been led to believe that the imperial government's contribution would not be limited to £150,000, but would fully match their own. Mitchell informed the Colonial Office that Patel had responded negatively. "The withdrawal of Mr. Patel and the funds earmarked for the Gandhi Memorial," confided an official, "is a blow and means that the finances for the first stage are a bit shaky." [27]

To persuade the Asians and also to see if the Tanganyika and Uganda governments would assume some financial responsibility, the Colonial Office in November 1950 had despatched its adviser on technical education, Dr. Frederick J. Harlow, to East Africa. In addition to conferring with government personnel, Harlow spent several weeks in consultation with Asian committee members and others in Nairobi and Kampala, and finally in January he met with the entire memorial committee in Commissioner Pant's Nairobi residence.[28]

At this meeting after prolonged discussion, an essential compromise was reached. The Asians and the Kenya government would combine in the development of a single institution, a Royal Technical College, which would be open to all qualified applicants and offer diplomas in both academic and technical subjects. The Gandhi memorial would consist of the academic core, with its precise nature dependent on how much money the Asians raised. Harlow anticipated a grant of £200,000 from the Colonial Development and Welfare Fund and hoped that the Asians would be able to match it.[29]

On the basis of Harlow's favorable report, the government quickly proceeded with plans for the Royal Technical College. In November, before Harlow's visit, Mitchell in addressing the East African Association of Engineers had proposed a technical institute, and in December, while Harlow was in East Africa, he had appointed a siting and building committee with Willoughby as chairman.[30] In May 1951 the secretary of state, James Griffiths, visited East Africa and at a Nairobi luncheon announced that the imperial government would contribute £150,000 to the Royal Technical College. Kenya would give a five-acre site and £120,000, and Uganda £100,000. It was subsequently revealed that Tanganyika would donate £50,000.[31] Mitchell then let contracts for the foundation of the main building and a workshop and appointed the college's governing council with Willoughby as chairman. Holding its first meeting in November, the council was predominantly European in membership but included two Asians—a Muslim and a Sikh—who, incidentally, were not members of the Mahatma Gandhi Memorial Committee. Mitchell meanwhile had granted the college a charter, and in April 1952 he laid the foundation stone. At this ceremony and on each of the previous occasions, however, nothing was said about a Gandhi memorial or Asian participation.[32]

Unlike the Kenya government's, the Asian drive after the negotiations with Harlow lost its momentum. Patel and Shah visited India in hope of securing a sizeable grant from the Gandhi Smarak Nidhi (Gandhi Memorial Society), but they were unsuccessful. Before their arrival Nehru had issued a statement deprecating moves by individuals and societies in India to erect memorials, which, he said, would savor of mere idolatry and displease Gandhi. Moreover, the Nidhi decided that it would be unfair to its donors to send its funds outside India.[33] In East Africa the forty-member memorial committee was proving an unwieldy administrative body as differences of opinion arose over its function and power. Also, the goal of an institution of higher education began to be questioned. Some argued that primary education was more important, others that the real need was for an excellent public school, and still others favored hospitals and model interracial townships.[34] Nanji Kalidas Mehta, the Uganda industrialist who was highly respected throughout East Africa, endeavored to rally the group toward the goal of the Harlow agreement, and he pledged £15,000 as a first contribution. No one, however, followed his example, and as time wore on he considered withdrawing his offer.[35]

A meeting of the memorial committee in Nairobi in September 1951 illustrates the confusion of the time. Only nine of the forty members attended. Patel, as chairman, related the events of his fruitless trip to India and his difficulties in obtaining contributions in East Africa. Some members questioned the goal of establishing a college, and there was uncertainty as to the government's intentions. Finally it was resolved that Patel would be empowered to appoint a more manageable seven-member committee for initiating the scheme.[36] This resolution, however, produced no apparent change as the Asian drive continued to languish.

The Fund Drive and the Great Celebration

It was Mehta who eventually provided the impetus for change. In mid-1952 on a visit to India he arranged for one of India's most outstanding educational leaders, Dr. Ramanlal Kanaiyalal Yajnik, to be released from his duties in India in order to coordinate the drive in East Africa. At that time the director of education for Saurashtra, Yajnik had been hailed for selfless service in the cause of education as the *Malaviyaji* of Saurashtra. Accomplished, scholarly, energetic, tactful, and dissociated from the politics of East Africa, he had the necessary qualifications for leadership. At the formal request of Apa Pant, Yajnik sailed to Kenya in August 1952. Two days after Yajnik's arrival Pant invited the principal Asian leaders to a tea party. The meeting proved decisive. At a suggestion from M. P. Shah the group decided to dispense with the unwieldy memorial committee and form a small provisional committee of those most supportive of the Harlow agreement. A week later, meeting in Shah's home, the new provisional committee of eight members elected Shah as honorary treasurer, A. B. Patel as president, and Yajnik as secretary and executive officer.[37] Then Yajnik proposed a plan for a fund drive. Donors, he explained, would be classified according to the size of their contributions as patrons, vice-patrons, benefactors, donors, associate members, life members, or ordinary members. There would be an intensive collection of money during the seventeen days between Gandhi's Indian birthdate and his English birthdate. The target would be £125,000, half the eventual total they hoped to realize.[38]

The fund drive, held as proposed from 15 September to 2 October 1952, was successful. Yajnik enlisted the aid of the congress in collecting money and distributed "An Appeal for the Gandhi Memorial College," a two-page memorandum, throughout East Africa.[39] Mehta raised his contribution to £20,000, the largest donation. Muljibhai Madhvani, who shared Mehta's position of prestige and influence among Uganda Asians, gave £10,000, and so did M. P. Shah. Several others donated £6,250 each. With the contributions coming from the wealthier members of the community, mainly from Uganda, the goal of £125,000 was easily attained.[40]

Immediately after these seventeen days the Asians organized to raise an equal amount from those who were less affluent and those who lived in more remote areas. They formed subcommittees at strategic locations throughout the four territories and sent deputations from the main centers to coordinate their activities. The subcommittees worked with local Indian Associations and chambers of commerce to solicit contributions from Asian business concerns, families, and individuals. Every few weeks the provisional committee in Nairobi issued a bulletin detailing the funds received. Mathusudn Jethalal Thakkar, who was employed as an accountant at Lugazi, gave 10 percent of his annual salary, and, he recalled, that was not unusual.[41] Kanjee Naranjee, the wealthy Nairobi landlord, toured East Africa by car and is said to have personally collected £40,000. According to one estimate, as many as forty thousand Asian families and two hundred thousand individuals contributed.[42] Much of the success must be attributed to Yajnik. In touring East Africa, he combined lecturing on cultural and literary topics with soliciting money. In his fifth bulletin he raised the target to £500,000, and in the sixth he announced that the committee would give the government the first installment of £200,000 by early January 1954.[43]

When confident that the goal would be reached, the Asians renewed negotiations with the Kenya government. In September 1953 Yajnik discussed with Major-General Colin Bullard, newly appointed principal of the college, how the Gandhi memorial would be incorporated within the larger organization. In October Patel met with R. G. Turnbull, acting minister for education, Michael Blundell, leader of the European community, and Willoughby, chairman of the college's governing council. In these discussions it was decided that the Asians' organization would be entitled the Gandhi Memorial Academy. Tentative agreement was reached on the nature of the buildings, the land on which they would be built, the size of the government's financial contribution, the Asians' role in selecting faculty, and their long-range place in the governance of the college.[44] While these negotiations were proceeding, representatives of the East African governments met in Nairobi in an Interterritorial Conference on Higher Education to coordinate financial responsibilities.[45]

As a result of the negotiations the Asians created a permanent organization to represent their interests in the Royal Technical College. In September, shortly after the discussions began, the provisional committee called a general meeting in Nairobi to consider the main points and initiate a Gandhi Memorial Academy Society comprised of all the donors. The constitution of the society, drafted by the barristers J. M. Nazareth and Babulal Tulsidas Modi, was adopted at a second meeting in January 1954 and was then registered with the Kenya government. An administrative body for the society, composed of twenty-one members — five from each mainland territory, two from Zanzibar, and four co-opted for special functions — was elected, and again Patel was chosen president. The draft agreement with the college was also amended in a few particulars. Patel, Yajnik, and Nazareth were authorized to negotiate and sign a final version without further referral to the society.[46]

In December 1953, while the agreement was still in preparation, the Asians received a promise of Rs. 1,500,000 from the Gandhi Smarak Nidhi. The gift was a surprise in view of the firm rejection earlier. In mid-1953 Yajnik had approached Nehru and, with help from Pant, persuaded him to reverse his opinion and recommend the award. At subsequent meetings involving Yajnik, trustees of the Nidhi, and President of India Dr. Rajendra Prasad, the donation was arranged. With this money, which when sent to East Africa amounted to £97,893, the society established a trust, the Gandhi Smarak Nidhi Fund, and empowered it to provide student bursaries and scholarships "irrespective of race or creed," promote cottage and home industries, and endow two chairs, one of race relations and the other of comparative religion and philosophy. The fund was given to the college and was to be administered by four trustees — two from the college and two from the society.[47]

On 9 April 1954, after assurance that the college had received this Fund and an additional £150,000 from the society, the Central Legislative Assembly of the East Africa High Commission unanimously enacted the Royal Technical College of East Africa Bill. With this act the administration of the College, which until then had been undertaken by Kenya alone, was assumed by all four East African governments, and the scope of the college was thus extended to East Africa as a whole. The act vested the administration of the College in a governing council of seventeen members, two of whom were to be appointed by the Gandhi Memorial Academy Society. It stipulated that the faculties of arts, science, and commerce, the library, and certain hostels and staff housing would be known collectively as the Gandhi Memorial Academy and would be incorporated within the college. The act also created a permanent Gandhi Memorial Board to advise the governing council on the erection and management of the academy's buildings and "all matters" relating to its faculties. The seven-person board was to consist of a chairman and two other members appointed by the council from its members and of four others appointed by the society.[48]

Despite the progress in reaching the agreement and the enabling legislation, some Asians were dissatisfied. They felt that the society had made too many concessions, with the result that the Asians had lost control of their memorial. The foremost critic was Dr. Amritlal Ujamsi Sheth, M.B.E. and former president of the Mombasa Indian Association and legislative councillor. Since 1931 when he led a radical congress political faction, Sheth had been a rival of A. B. Patel in Kenya politics.[49]

In February 1954, after publication of the Royal Technical College Bill, Sheth circulated a satirical report in which he accused the society of handing over, after five years of fund-raising, its project and its money, more than £400,000, to the Kenya government. "As was predicted by many," Sheth claimed, the Gandhi memorial committee "found it impossible to establish or run" a college based on Gandhi's principles. He pointed out that the only real representation the Asians would have in the college would be the four members whom the society would appoint to the Gandhi Memorial Board. The other three members of that board, including the chairman, would be representatives of the governing council and presumably all European. Moreover, on the governing council the Asians were guaranteed only one representative, who would be an appointee of the board. Whereas the board had power only to advise, the governing council was empowered to appoint administrators and faculty and determine the curriculum. "It is without doubt," Sheth concluded, "that this Governing Council will have a great majority of Europeans — Kenya Europeans — on whom the Indian public has to rely for propagating the Gandhian Philosophy, Ideals and Teachings!"[50]

It was criticism such as this that had led the society to revise the draft agreement at its public meeting in January 1954. In negotiations with the government the provisional committee had been able to raise the Asian representatives in the governing council to four and to have them appointed, not by the Gandhi Memorial Board, but by the society. On the floor of the Central Legislative Assembly, however, European protest overrode Asian and African support and led to a reduction of this representation to two members before the bill was enacted.[51]

After enactment of the bill, while Yajnik and the college principal proceeded to Britain and India to recruit prospective staff, the board became involved with the design and construction of buildings, and the society expanded its drive to collect funds. The campaign was soon extended beyond the British East Africa territories as Indian Associations in the Belgian Congo, Northern and Southern Rhodesia, Nyasaland, and other neighboring territories were brought into the search for money. The society even tried to solicit funds in Portuguese Mozambique and the Union of South Africa but, in each, was refused permission. By far the greater proportion of the money collected came from eastern Africa, but some sizeable contributions were obtained from individuals and business firms in India.[52] By April 1955 the total money raised in Africa had risen to £250,000.

At that time Patel, as president of the society, submitted a formal application to the East Africa High Commission for a matching grant. In view of the previous assurances from Governor Mitchell and Colonial Office adviser Harlow, Patel had reason to anticipate an official donation from the Colonial Development and Welfare Fund as high as £200,000 and indeed, by the most optimistic interpretation, perhaps the full equivalent of £250,000.[53] Instead Patel modestly, or perhaps realistically, requested only £100,000. The money, he explained, would be added to whatever the society collected and donated to the Royal Technical College for whatever use the governing council might decide. He predicted that the Asians would raise eventually a total of £300,000 from East Africa, which when augmented by the £98,000 from India and £100,000 from the imperial government would raise the total Asian contribution to approximately £500,000. In July, while his application was being considered, Patel flew to Britain to present his case in person to the secretary of state for the colonies.[54]

To the profound disappointment of Patel and other Asian leaders, the imperial government did not contribute to the Gandhi Memorial Academy. Instead it awarded a grant of £107,000 from the Colonial Development and Welfare Fund directly to the Royal Technical College. Moreover, the money was designated for the completion of the assembly hall and workshops, buildings that were not a part of the academy.[55] Despite all the previous assurances, the governments thus gave nothing substantive, apart from the building site, directly or even indirectly to the Academy. From Britain there was only the statement, made by a local Kenya official announcing the award, that the secretary of state "had taken into account the generous contribution made by the Gandhi Memorial Academy Society towards establishing the College. He took the opportunity of expressing his own appreciation for their help."[56]

Besides this expression of thanks, the only consolation was that during the negotiations in London the secretary of state had confirmed an agreement that had been made locally whereby the title of the academy would be coupled to that of the college. Henceforth the new institution would bear the official title "The Royal Technical College of East Africa incorporating the Gandhi Memorial Academy." [57]

Early in 1955, during the culmination of the fund drive and the approach to the Colonial Office, the society had decided to erect a bronze statue to Gandhi. It initially had contemplated a bas-relief carved in wood as a decoration for the main hall, but the realization that Gandhi was himself a bronze color and that an art object of metal "would last for thousands of years" led to the conception of a bronze statue.[58] V. P. Karmakar, a famous Bombay sculptor, had just completed a marble bust of J. B. Pandya, the late Mombasa business and political leader, for the foyer of the Pandya Memorial Clinic, and at the suggestion of Pandya's son Anant, the governing council decided to hire Karmakar for the Gandhi statue. M. P. Shah offered to provide the estimated cost of Rs. 30,000. Then a plastic model of the statue, portraying Gandhi as greater than life-size in late age, clad in a simple dhoti, and striding in his customary way with staff in hand, was prepared in Bombay. After approval there by Yajnik, a representative of the governing council, and three officers of the Scindia Steam Navigation Company representing the society, the statue was cast in bronze, shipped to Kenya, and placed in the Gandhi wing on the second floor of the main building.[59]

On 12 July 1956 the unveiling of the statue and the formal opening of the Gandhi Memorial Academy were combined in a grand ceremony presided over by India's revered philosopher-statesman Dr. Sarvapalli Radhakrishnan, vice-president of India.[60] At the request of the society, Radhakrishnan had been invited by Mitchell's successor, Governor Sir Evelyn Baring. During the week preceding the ceremony in Nairobi, Radhakrishnan visited Salisbury, Blantyre, Dar es Salaam, Zanzibar, and Mombasa. At every appearance he was hailed and garlanded by crowds of thousands — seven thousand at one site in Dar es Salaam, five thousand at another in Zanzibar — and many Asians traveled hundreds of miles for a glimpse of him. The many photographs of his tour attesting to the numbers show on nearly all occasions a cluster of Europeans in the foreground, a mass of Asians behind them, and in the distant background, looking on wistfully, a surprisingly large number of Africans. In Nairobi during the cavalcade of honor — as the vice-president and the governor proceeded in an open car — some fifty thousand people, with all the races intermingled, lined the streets. That night all the shops of Nairobi were illuminated, a sight never seen before, and people were described as literally wild with joy.[61]

For three days the festivities in Nairobi continued. On the third day the unveiling and opening ceremony took place at the college. The grounds, filled with three thousand chairs, and an imposing dais were gaily decorated. The leaders sat at the dais, and the favored occupied the chairs, but thousands of others stood as Patel, Baring, and Yajnik as well as Radhakrishnan spoke. After the formalities those present filed through the open doors of the Gandhi wing to pass the floodlit statue of the Mahatma. The next day Radhakrishnan went to Jinja, and then to Kampala, and finally back to Nairobi and on to India. The spectacle was repeated at each stop of the fourteen-day tour. Never had East Africa had so large or so splendid a celebration as the commemoration of the Gandhi memorial.[62]

Notes

1. Quoted, *E. Afn. Standard* (Nairobi), 31 Jan. 1948, 1.
2. Ibid., 2 Feb. 1948, 1–3; 3 Feb. 1948, 1.
3. E.g., *Kenya Daily Mail,* 13 Feb. 1948, 12. Also, ibid., supplement, 20 Aug. 1948, 1.
4. Ibid., 19 June 1948, 1; 21 June 1948, 1; 22 June 1948, 2; 2 July 1948, 3.
5. Ibid., 27 June 1948, 2; 13 Aug. 1948, 8; 20 Aug. 1948, 4. S. G. Amin (pres., EAINC, Nairobi) to Ind. Assoc., Nairobi, teleg., 21 June 1948; hon. gen. sec., EAINC, to editor, *E. Afn. Standard,* 21 June 1948; Sangat Singh (ind. trade commr., Momb.) to sec., Immersion Committee, EAINC, 10 Aug. 1948 — EAINC papers, SU microfilm 1929, reel 11. See also Gandhi Memorial Academy Society, *Souvenir Volume* (Nairobi: GMAS, 1956), 1:45.
6. EAINC proposed resolution, "Condolence to Mahatma Gandhi," n.d., EAINC papers, reel 11.
7. E.g., *Kenya Daily Mail,* 31 Jan. 1949, 1; and R. C. Gautama (hon. sec., EAINC) to Ind. Assocs. in Kenya Colony, 20 Sep. 1948 and 20 Jan. 1949, EAINC papers, reel 11.
8. *Kenya Daily Mail,* 16 Jan. 1948, 8; 13 Feb. 1948, 12; 16 June 1948, 1; 18 June 1948, 2.
9. Abreau, *Role of Self-Help,* 83–84.
10. GMAS, *Souvenir Volume,* 1:32, 50. D. S. Trivedi (Momb.) to hon. sec., EAINC, Nairobi, 6 Mar. 1948; K. C. Shah (hon. sec., Jain Youth League, Thika) to hon. gen. sec., EAINC, 6 Apr. 1948; hon. sec., Ind. Natl. Assoc., Zan., to hon. gen. sec., EAINC, 30 June 1948; sec., EAINC, to Jain Youth League, 3 July 1948 and 5 July 1948 — EAINC papers, reel 11.
11. *Kenya Daily Mail,* 20 Feb. 1948, 7.
12. The meeting was called by J. D. Byramjee in convener, Gandhi Memorial Sub-Committee, EAINC to "Dear Sir or Madam," 24 June 1948, EAINC papers, reel 11. Other members of the committee were Byramjee, Makhan Singh, Trilock Nath, Gopal Singh, and K. V. Adalja. Members of the provisional committee and of an important subcommittee are listed in Chanan Singh, *Gandhi Memorial Academy Society: a Short Hist.* (pamphlet, Nairobi: Prudential, c. 1962), App. A, 32.
13. "Minutes of the third meeting of the Provisional Committee for Mahatma Gandhi Memorial held at Desai Memorial Hall on 20th Sep. 1948," ibid.
14. GMAS, *Souvenir Volume,* 1:45–46.
15. Kenya, *Rept. of the Technical Inst. Committee* (Nairobi: Govt. Ptr., 1949), esp. 3.
16. Recounted in Patel to aministrator, EAHC, Nairobi, 2 Apr. 1955, ptd. as App. 6, GMAS, *Souvenir Volume,* 1:71–72. See also *E. Afn. Standard,* 27 Nov. 1950, 1.
17. GMAS, *Souvenir Volume,* 1:46–47. For the Kenya government's reaction to the Kabir-Sidhanta report, see J. C. Leyden (Nairobi) to Philip (Mitchell), 7

July 1950; and "Extract from rept. submitted by Profs. Humayun Kabir and Sidhanta on the 13th March 1950," confid.—file "Indians in E.A.: Educ.: Mahatma Gandhi Memorial College Project, 1950," C.O. 822/143/6.

18. GMAS, *Souvenir Volume,* 1:7–8, 47.
19. Related in Patel to admin., EAHC, 2 Apr. 1955.
20. Rogers to Scott, 15 Aug. 1950, file "Indians in E.A.: Educ.: Mahatma Gandhi Memorial College Project, 1950," C.O. 822/143/6.
21. Scott to Rogers, 1 Sep. 1950, secret, ibid.
22. Thornley to Rogers, 13 Sep. 1950, ibid.
23. "Extract from a letter from Mr. de Bunsen, Prin. of Makerere College, to Mr. Walter Adams dated 16th Aug., 1950," ibid. Cohen to Scott, 7 Oct. 1950, secret, ibid.
24. The discussion is summarized in Cohen to Scott, 7 Oct. 1950 (see note 23).
25. Note by Gorell Barnes to Sir H. Poynton, 16 April 1951, file "Technical College for E.A. at Nairobi: C.D.W. Grant, 1950–51," C.O. 533/567/13.
26. Quoted, GMAS, *Souvenir Volume,* 1:47–48. Italics added.
27. Mitchell to James Griffiths (sec. of state), 20 Feb. 1951, file "Tech. College for E.A. at Nairobi." Note by R. W. Newman, 26 Feb. 1951, ibid.
28. Roy. Tech. College, *Calendar 1958–59,* 4–7.
29. F. J. Harlow, "Memo. on the Proposal to Estab. a Tech. College at Nairobi," 7 Feb. 1951, file "Tech. College for E.A. at Nairobi." GMAS, *Souvenir Volume,* 1:48.
30. *E. Afn. Standard,* 27 Nov. 1950, 1; Roy. Tech. College, *Calendar 1958–59,* 5–6.
31. *E. Afn. Standard,* 23 May 1951, 1; 7 Dec. 1951, 1. For the Colonial Office contribution, see file "Financial Assis. for Roy. Tech. College, Nairobi, 31/7/51-23/6/54," C.O. 822/627.
32. *E. Afn. Standard,* 12 July 1951, 5. In April 1952 Mitchell laid the foundation stone. Ibid., 26 Apr. 1952, 1. For the Roy. Tech. College constitution, see "Charter Made at Govt. House, Nairobi, in the Col. of Kenya the 7th Day of Sep., 1951, by Sir Philip Mitchell," file "Constitution of the Roy. Tech. College, Nairobi, 10/9/51-10/3/53," C.O. 822/628.
33. *Kenya Daily Mail,* 5 Mar. 1948, 10. "Minutes of a meeting of the Gandhi Memorial Committee," 30 Sep. 1951, Nairobi, EAINC papers, reel 12.
34. GMAS, *Souvenir Volume,* 1:48. For requests for schools, see *E. Afn. Standard,* 14 July 1950, 10; and 4 Aug. 1950, 10.
35. GMAS, *Souvenir Volume,* 1:48.
36. "Minutes . . . 30 Sep. 1951."
37. Other committee members were Kanjee Naranjee, C. K. Patel, Indar Singh Gill, D. M. Anjaria, and J. D. Shah.
38. GMAS, *Souvenir Volume,* 1:49.
39. R. K. Yajnik to sec., EAINC, 15 Aug. 1952; R. K. Yajnik, "An Appeal for the Gandhi Memorial College," 9 Sep. 1952—EAINC papers, reel 12.
40. GMAS, *Souvenir Volume,* 1:49.
41. M. J. Thakkar intv.
42. D. K. Naranji (son) intv. Dr. V. R. Patel intv.
43. V. R. Patel intv. R. K. Yajnik, "Gandhi Memorial College (Fifth Bulletin)," 18 May 1953; "Sixth Bulletin," 30 Oct. 1953—Momb. Ind. Assoc. papers, SU microfilm 1926, reel 4.

44. GMAS, *Souvenir Volume,* 1:50. See also Yajnik, "Gandhi Memorial College (Sixth Bulletin)," 30 Oct. 1953.
45. "Minutes of the Interter. Conf. on Higher Educ. Held in the Railway Conf. Room, Nairobi on 20th Oct., 1953," file "Roy. Tech. College Bill, 21/11/53-30/12/53," C.O. 822/624.
46. "Gandhi Memorial Academy Society Constitution," GMAS, *Souvenir Volume,* 1:58–63. See also ibid., 50–51; and R. K. Yajnik, "Notice," 1 Nov. 1953, regarding the const. meeting 10 Jan. 1954, Momb. Ind. Assoc. papers, reel 4.
47. GMAS, *Souvenir Volume,* 1:51, 68–70.
48. "An Act to make provision for the Govt., Control and Admin. of the Roy. Tech. College of E.A.," *Off. Gazette of the EAHC* 6, no. 12 (30 Nov. 1953): 119–43. For important excerpts from the critical debate in the Cen. Leg. Assembly, see Charles D. Newbold, "Roy. Tech. College of E.A.," *E.A. and Rhodesia* (London), 29 Apr. 1954, 1092–3.
49. Gregory, *India and E.A.,* 370–71.
50. A. U. Sheth, *Memo. on the Gandhi Memorial in E.A.* (Momb.: Modern Ptrs., 8 Feb. 1954), pp. 11–14, EAINC papers, reel 13.
51. *E. Afn. Standard,* 7 Apr. 1954, 1; 8 Apr. 1954, 1, 5. *E.A. and Rhodesia* (London), 20 Apr. 1954, 1093.
52. Sir Dorabji Tata and Sir Ratan Tata, the Bank of Baroda, and the Bank of India, e.g., were among the major donors. GMAS, *Souvenir Volume,* 1:28. J. M. Nazareth (hon. sec.) and R. K. Yajnik, "Gandhi Memorial Academy Society (Eighth Bulletin)," 16 Feb. 1955, Momb. Ind. Assoc. papers, reel 4.
53. Nazareth and Yajnik, e.g., stated in the "Eighth Bulletin," "We expect handsome contributions on a £ to £ basis to this Endowment Fund from the E. Afn. Govts."
54. Patel to administrator, EAHC, 2 Apr. 1955. See also GMAS, *Souvenir Volume,* 1:53.
55. GMAS, *Souvenir Volume* 1:54.
56. Quoted, ibid.
57. Ibid.
58. Ibid. See also "Eighth Bulletin," 16 Feb. 1955.
59. H. Pandya (Anant's wife) intv. GMAS, *Souvenir Volume,* 1:54.
60. *E. Afn. Standard,* 23 July 1956, 1.
61. GMAS, *Souvenir Volume,* 2:8, 13. This volume describes Radhakrishnan's tour.
62. Ibid.

7

From Royal Technical College to University of Nairobi

In Africa, as elsewhere, the basis of the social framework must be one which gives equal rights to all and which promotes the friendly co-operation of the various constituent elements of a nation. The Gandhi Memorial Academy, which is incorporated with the Royal Technical College of East Africa, has this ideal. I hope it will progressively succeed in realising its objectives.

—Jawaharlal Nehru, 1956

In one sense Nehru's hope, shared fervently by the Asians, was not to be realized. The Gandhi Memorial Academy was only a subdivision of the Royal Technical College, and the nature of the overall institution was to be determined by the college rather than the academy. From the outset Gandhi's ideals of truth, love, brotherhood, and nonviolence, constituting the foundation of the academy, were obscured, and as the college evolved into a university, Gandhi's principles and inspiration were lost and forgotten. In another sense, however, an institution of higher education without distinction of race or creed had been created, and through the succeeding years it continued to serve the interests of the East African peoples. Though quite different from the institution envisaged by the Asians, the college, and ultimately the university, made an important and enduring contribution.

Despite their extraordinary display of enthusiasm at the opening

147

ceremony, the Asians in 1956 had considerable reason for disappointment. The fact that the government did not honor its assurances of a pound-for-pound matching grant and, in the end, actually gave no monetary assistance to the Asian effort was but one of the unfulfilled expectations. The initial vision of a unique institution of higher learning, a Gandhi Memorial College, had not been realized. The institution that arose from their efforts was entitled the Royal Technical College, and the Asian contribution, the Gandhi Memorial Academy, was made to appear only an insignificant part of it. This was to become increasingly evident in time.

The selection of staff was an additional cause for concern. After the show of sending Yajnik and Principal Bullard to India to confer with the chancellors of Indian universities regarding suitable administrative and teaching personnel, the governing council selected nearly all Europeans. The initial heads of departments were Europeans recruited from institutions in Britain and British Africa. Not one was brought from India.[1] In 1957–58, the year following the opening of the college, the council included one Asian among its twenty members, and the faculty had only four Asians among the total of forty-three.[2]

The Asians were also misled as to the offering of diplomas. When it opened in April 1956, the college offered two-year courses in the faculties of arts, science, and commerce, but three-year courses in the faculties of engineering, architecture, and domestic science. At that time and for the ensuing three years the college developed no degree programs and offered, at most, courses leading to the Advanced General Certificate.[3] As its name denoted, the college appeared to be viewed by the governments as little more than an institute serving the needs of East Africa for practical training.

Even the campus was a reason for disappointment. Instead of 150 acres outside Nairobi, which Mitchell had told the Asians the government would provide, the Royal Technical College had only 18. Moreover, the site chosen, opposite the old settler haven, the Norfolk Hotel, was the police compound so notorious in Kenya history—the site where many Africans had lost their lives in protest over the arrest of Harry Thuku.[4]

Numerous Asians were disappointed with the memorial. Some,

like Dr. Sheth, either refused to donate or failed to pay money promised.[5] Among these was Indar Singh Gill, the Sikh industrialist who had been one of the early leaders in promoting a memorial. One political leader, N. S. Mangat, who was eventually to become an embarrassment to the community in his militant defense of Asian interests, criticized the Royal Technical College for admitting too few Asian students and demanded publicly that the college be disbanded.[6] In response to Asian criticism the chairman of the governing council invited the leaders of Asian political organizations to visit the college. "The Royal Technical College," he said, "has been the object of some controversy, and I think some misunderstanding. . . . I feel that the criticism we have received has only come about because of lack of knowledge."[7] Clearly, the chairman himself did not understand.

Distortion of the Memorial

Because of the changing political climate in East Africa and Britain, the government's narrow conception of the new college could not endure. One of the main thrusts of the British administration in East Africa after World War II was the move toward regional federation. The creation of the East Africa High Commission was the principal manifestation of this move, but there were several others, including the establishment of a common university. The first Working Party on Higher Education in East Africa, appointed in June 1955, was designed to further this aim. Led by Sir Alexander Carr-Saunders, the party described an urgent need for an increase in higher education facilities and recommended a close association among all recognized institutions of university college status in East Africa.[8] In March 1958 the four British dependencies issued a joint white paper, *Higher Education in East Africa,* in which they affirmed the recommendations of the working party and suggested that all institutions of college status be closely associated "within a single University of East Africa." The governments also asked the secretary of state to appoint another working party to examine the feasibility of the proposals.[9]

Much to the surprise of the Asians, the report of the first working party and the white paper recommended the creation of a new university college in Nairobi that would preclude the Royal Technical College from an integral place in the contemplated University of East Africa. They based this recommendation on the fact that the universities of the British Commonwealth affiliated to the University of London were purely academic institutions. There was no provision in the system for a college that would offer university degrees in combination with technical and professional training.[10]

The Asians began a concerted protest. In January 1958 the Gandhi Memorial Academy Society called a general meeting for consultation with the Kenya minister for education, Walter F. Coutts. The Asians vigorously protested when Coutts informed them that the conclusions in the report of the working party and in the white paper had been affirmed in two full-scale conferences in London, and that the University of London was insisting on the exclusion of the Royal Technical College. The Asians rejected an offer by Coutts to permit the transfer of their academy, including Gandhi's statue, to the new college.[11] Subsequently Nazareth, who had replaced Patel as president of the society, and N. K. Mehta met privately with local administrators and University of London personnel, including Dame Lillian Penson, to explain the commitments. At the society's urging, Yajnik returned to East Africa to assist in pleading the Asians' case.[12]

On this occasion the Asians prevailed. In November 1958, after an extensive investigation of conditions and opinion in all four territories, the second working party not only supported the idea of a University of East Africa, but also admonished the Kenya government for not upholding its promises to the Asians. Chaired by Dr. J. F. Lockwood, vice-chancellor of the University of London, the party had included six distinguished British educators, among them Dame Lillian. During its five-week tour it had met with leaders of all major communities in all four territories. Among the Asians were Yajnik, Prem Krishnan (Pant's replacement as commissioner from India), Nazareth, and other representatives from the society. The party also had received written statements from the society, the Indian Associations of Nairobi and Mombasa, and some individual Asians including Jayant Madhvani and J. J. Singh. In support of the Asians the working party argued that the Royal Technical College, "with the due honouring of the pledge given to the Gandhi Memorial Academy Society," should provide courses leading to university degrees in academic subjects. It recommended that the college, after expanding its campus and facilities, be transformed into "the second inter-territorial university in East Africa" and be renamed the Royal College, Nairobi.[13]

The report of the second working party marked a turning point for both the college and the academy. In 1960, to implement the report, the Kenya government appointed a British architect, A. M. Chitty, to advise on the development of an expanded site for the college. Later the same year Tanganyika and Uganda combined with Kenya in appointing a Quinquennial Advisory Committee, chaired by E. B. David, to work out a phased five-year program of implementation of the working party's report.[14] During 1961, the first year of the phased program, the college prepared degree courses in all the faculties and arranged for affiliation to the University of London.

In June 1961 the Royal Technical College was officially transformed into the Royal College, Nairobi, of the University of East Africa. As before, "Incorporating the Gandhi Memorial Academy" was appended to the name.[15] The college, with Asian financial assistance, soon acquired an additional sixty-two acres — the Chiromo campus — one mile distant from the initial site. It also erected many new buildings, one of the principal of which was a new library. With the society's consent, the building was renamed the Gandhi Library, and Gandhi's statue was moved to stand just inside its entrance. In May 1964 the Royal College became the University College, Nairobi, and in December 1970, with the disintegration of all vestiges of federation, it acquired a separate and autonomous status as the University of Nairobi.[16]

During the fifteen years of transformation, as the Royal Technical College developed into a university, the Asians agitated for reform. They expressed their dissatisfaction not only to the working parties, but also to government officials and the college administrators. The Asian political and economic organizations were intensely interested in the operation of the college. The Federation of Indian Chambers of Commerce and Industry in Eastern Africa, for instance, monitored the development of course offerings in the Faculty of Commerce. When the college adopted two new courses leading to the Bachelor of Science degree, Chanan Singh, a representative of the federation and a member of the Gandhi Memorial Board, expressed serious doubt as to the quality of the courses. He advised the federation to consult the East African governments, railways, post office, customs, income tax department, oil companies, banks, and important industrial and commercial firms to see if they would consider hiring anyone who obtained a degree based on such courses. In addition to investigating courses, the federation pressed for increased Asian representation on the governing council.[17]

Within the fifteen years and subsequently the Asians had valid reasons for protest. Their financial contribution was increasingly belittled or ignored. In 1958 an important East African committee on higher education indicated mistakenly in its report that the Asians had contributed only the second floor of one building.[18] In 1967–68 the college *Calendar* carried the name of the college — by then renamed University College, Nairobi — in large, bold, capital letters across its cover. Underneath this name in lowercase and much smaller type, and enclosed within parentheses, was the phrase "Incorporating the Gandhi Memorial Academy." Within the *Calendar* in a section on historical development was a paragraph on the academy, but the narration did not reveal the significance of the Asians' contribution in comparison with that of Kenya and the other governments.[19] After independence the Asians' role was quickly forgotten. By 1984–85 the *Calendar* included no reference to the Gandhi Memorial Academy on its cover or title page. It contained in the prefatory "Short History of the University" little more than the erroneous statement that the academy had been a 1954 addition to the Royal Technical College begun by the government in 1951.[20]

Perhaps even more distressing was the fact that there was no provision in the 1984–85 *Calendar,* either in personnel, courses, or extracurricular activities, for recognition and dissemination of

Gandhi's philosophy. Thus the key feature of the memorial envisaged by the Asians had been lost.

There was also continuing reason for dissatisfaction with the site and size of the campus, the nature of the courses offered, and the lack of any significant Asian representation on the governing council or among the administrative and teaching personnel. Unfortunately, no significant changes in any of these matters were realized after Kenya's independence.

The Asian Contribution

Despite their disappointment, the Asians in the long run had reason to be very proud of the institution they had done so much to create. They had made a substantial contribution. In September 1950, when the merger between the Kenya government and the Asian community was first seriously contemplated, it appeared that the government would contribute initially only the site and £120,000, in comparison to at least £150,000 from the Asians. By April 1952, when the foundation stone was laid and the Asians had set a target of £250,000, the Kenya government had raised its monetary contribution to £150,000, Britain had agreed to contribute £150,000, and the governments of Tanganyika and Uganda had pledged £50,000 and £100,000 respectively.[21] By December 1953, when the £98,000 was obtained from the Gandhi Smarak Nidhi, it was apparent that the total Asian contribution would be at least £400,000 and that of the colonial and imperial governments combined £460,000. By 1960 the funds raised by the Asians appeared as follows:[22]

£300,000 — Total cash raised by the society in its fund drive in Africa and India
97,894 — Contribution of the Gandhi Smarak Nidhi
39,940 — Donation from the Gandhi Memorial Trust toward purchase of the Chiromo campus; the remaining £20,000 was donated by the Colonial Development and Welfare Fund
£437,834 — Total Asian donation

As the college grew into a university, the non-Asian contribution, of course, far exceeded that of the Asians. By 1959, for instance, the college had received £409,500 from the Colonial Development and Welfare Fund and a total of £358,000 from the governments of Kenya, Tanganyika, and Uganda.[23] In subsequent years additional funds from Britain and grants from the United States government and private foundations such as Rockefeller, Carnegie, and Ford considerably augmented the non-Asian contribution.[24]

The comparative contribution of the Asians is revealed in the statistics. Although the governments gave more in the long run, the prospective initial contribution of the Asians far exceeded that of the Kenya government and obviously was a key factor in stimulating the colonial and imperial governments to expand their concept of a technical training institute into the plan for a university college. It is apparent too that this was a combined Asian and government venture. Among the various ethnic communities of East Africa only the Asians contributed. The lack of a direct African or Arab contribution is understandable, but one would expect a substantial European donation to this multiracial institution. There was none.

The funds donated by the Asians were used in a variety of ways. Approximately half the Asian donation was devoted to construction of the principal building, known as the main tuition block, and to men's and women's residence halls. Nearly £98,000, as already noted, was designated for the Gandhi Smarak Nidhi Fund. The rest was devoted to a Gandhi Memorial Endowment Fund, the interest of which was to be used for "the purposes of the College." [25] The main construction provided by the Asians, together with the names of those who specially contributed, was as follows:

Commerce Wing	— Nanji Kalidas Mehta
Library Hall	— Nanji Prabhudas Madhvani
Geography Laboratory	— Kanjee Naranjee
Chemistry Laboratory	— Dayal Madanji Vadera
Physics Laboratory	— Vithaldas Haridas & Co.
Chemistry Laboratory	— Sir Chinu Madhowlal
Biology Laboratory	— Naran P. Patel
Geology Laboratory	— Sir Dorabji Tata and Sir Ratan Tata
Men's residential unit	— Mulji Prabhudas Madhvani

Men's residential unit   — Meghji Pethraj Shah
Men's residential unit   — C. Parekh & Co.
Men's residential unit   — Narandas Rajaram & Co. (Africa) Ltd.
Women's residential unit — Devji Karamshi Hindocha
Women's residential unit — Santokhben Nanji Mehta

There was also the statue of Gandhi, one of the most impressive art works in East Africa, contributed by M. P. Shah.[26]

After the opening of the Gandhi Memorial Academy the Asians continued to donate and take an active interest in the new institution. By 1985 the annual official university prizes included (1) the Gandhi Smarak Prize of Shs. 3,000 to the best final-year student in each faculty, (2) the Gandhi Smarak Gold Medal to the best overall student in the University, (3) the Dr. A. C. L. de Souza Memorial Prize of Shs. 250 to the best first-year student, (4) the Kamala Memorial Gold Award of Shs. 1,200 to the best final-year student in medicine, and (5) three Asian Commercial Community Academic Awards totaling Shs. 5,000 to the best continuing students in commerce.[27] By then M. P. Shah's Meghjibhai Foundation had donated £200 to enable college personnel to attend courses on management training, and Ahamed Bros. Ltd. had given a sizeable sum to student sports facilities.[28] With accumulated interest from the Gandhi Smarak Nidhi Fund the Asians had also provided for five annual lecture series on subjects related to education, development, and international justice. Among the five distinguished lecturers was Nazareth, who was then chairman of both the fund and the society.[29]

The Asians' contribution must be weighed not only in terms of money, but also in respect to their emphasis on a multiracial, multiethnic institution offering degrees in academic subjects. The technical institute planned by the government when the Asians first became involved would probably have evolved into a university. Looking back in the light of educational developments throughout Africa, it seems inevitable that each of the three countries arising from British East Africa would have established its own university. That the Royal Technical College began, however, with an academic as well as a technological curriculum and that its successor, the Royal College, developed the academic part into a degree program and was not created as a separate institution — this must be credited largely to the Asians. It perhaps is no exaggeration to hold that the Asians were mainly responsible for the University of Nairobi. Although it bears Gandhi's name, if at all, only in a very insignificant way, the university may rightly be viewed as his memorial.

The Gandhi memorial is a striking example of philanthropy. It is the foremost instance of philanthropy in East Africa not only for the Asians, but also for the Europeans and Africans. For the Asians it was their greatest philanthropic effort, but not all their community participated. The memorial was created solely by Hindus, Jains, Sikhs, and Goans, apparently without any contribution from Muslim organizations or individuals. That in the circumstances the Gandhi Memorial Academy was designed from the outset as an institution without ethnic restriction, open to peoples of all races, sects, and creeds, even to the Muslims, attests to the impact of Gandhi's philosophy. From the beginning, in practice as in theory, the college was truly multiracial and multiethnic. In 1957–58, the first full year of operation, it admitted 104 Africans, 100 Asians, and 10 Europeans.[30] In 1962–63 the enrollment consisted of 115 Africans, 104 Asians, 23 Europeans, and 4 Arabs. In 1964, the year in which the first B.A. and B.Sc. degrees were awarded, there were Muslims as well as Hindus, Jains, Sikhs, and Goans among the Asian graduates. Eventually, although Africans became the main recipients, more Muslims than Hindus were awarded bursaries and loans from the Gandhi Smarak Nidhi Fund.[31]

The creation of the memorial cannot be ascribed chiefly to any individual, and since so many were involved and in so many different ways, it is almost impossible to accord a deserved recognition to each. A. B. Patel, Dr. R. K. Yajnik, Apa Pant, M. P. Shah, and N. K. Mehta seem to have provided the primary leadership. A large number of others, including J. M. Nazareth, Anant J. Pandya, Indar Singh Gill, and Narshidas Mathuradas Mehta, provided valuable service. Through 1956 the donors of the society consisted of 3,328 individuals and organizations. Heading this list are the patrons, each contributing £5,000 and over, and the vice-patrons, giving £2,500 to £5,000. With few exceptions the individuals among them may be regarded as the principal philanthropists among the Asians of their generation.[32]

Patrons

1. Nanji Kalidas Mehta (patron-in-chief), Lugazi. Pioneer merchant; industrialist in cotton, sugar, tea, oils, cement.
2. Santokben N. K. Mehta, Lugazi. Mehta's wife.
3. Muljibhai Prabhudas Madhvani, Jinja. Businessman; industrialist in sugar, tea, oils, confectionery. Donation shared by his wife, the late Parvatiben.
4. Meghji Pethraj Shah, Nairobi. Business magnate, retired to India; M.P. in India. Donation shared by his wife, Maniben.
5. C. Parekh & Co., Kampala. Cotton-textile firm co-directed by Chandulal P. Parekh and Chimanlal B. Parikh.
6. Narandas Rajaram & Co. (Africa) Ltd., Kampala. Chairman, Sir Purshotamdas Thakurdas of Bombay.
7. Devji Karamshi Hindocha, Kisumu. Sugar industrialist. Donation shared by his wife, Zaverben.
8. Nanjibhai Prabhudas Madhvani, Mombasa. Merchant. Donation by his widow, Santokhben.
9. Dayalbhai Madanji Vadera, Jinja. Industrialist in cotton, oil; planter of sugar, tea.
10. Vithaldas Haridas & Co. Ltd., Jinja. Pioneer business firm in Uganda.
11. Sir Chinubhai Madhowlal, Bart., Kampala. Merchant industrialist of India.
12. Naranbhai P. Patel Ltd., Jinja. Donation in honor of Patel, late businessman in cotton, coffee, oils, hardware.
13. Kanjee Naranjee, Nairobi. Merchant-industrialist, landlord, and sisal planter.
14. Sir Dorabji Tata and Sir Ratan Tata, Bombay. Late pioneers of India's iron and steel industry. Donation by their trust funds.

Vice-Patrons

1. Dhirendrakumar Nanjibhai Mehta, Lugazi. Son of N. K. Mehta; industrialist in sugar, tea, textiles.
2. Mahendrakumar Nanjibhai Mehta, Lugazi. Son of N. K. Mehta; textile industrialist.
3. Chandulal Kalidas Patel, Jinja. Barrister, legislative councillor, cotton industrialist.
4. Chhota Moti Patel, Kampala. Cotton and steel industrialist.
5. Ishverbhai V. Patel, Kampala. Cotton industrialist in Uganda and Tanganyika.

6. Bhagwanji Sunderji & Co. Ltd., Jinja. In honor of B. S. Nathwaani, late merchant and cotton planter.
7. Chhotabhai S. Patel, Bombay. Late cotton industrialist and magistrate.
8. Pandya & Co. Ltd., Mombasa. In honor of J. B. Pandya, late merchant-importer, legislative councillor, founder, Federation of Chambers of Commerce and Industry in Eastern Africa.
9. Premchand Bros. Ltd., Mombasa. Trading, industrial firm managed by Devchand Premchand Chandaria.
10. Bank of Baroda Ltd., Nairobi. Chairman, Tusidas Kilachand; M.P. in India.
11. Prahlad Singh Grewal, Bukoba. Businessman, timber producer, cotton industrialist.
12. Tribhovandas B. Sheth, Dar es Salaam. Merchant in groceries, sundries.
13. Jetha Lila, Zanzibar. Bankers.
14. Magan Umed Patel, Kisumu. Late businessman and farmer.
15. Messrs. J. H. Gidoomal, Nairobi. Trading partnership of the brothers Jethanand and the late Hiranand H. Gidoomal.

Notes

1. The initial staff is described in GMAS, *Souvenir Volume,* 2:40–41.
2. Roy. Tech. College, *Calendar 1957–58,* 10–12.
3. Ibid., 17–25. Kenya, *Educ. Dept. Annual Summary, 1956* (Nairobi: Govt. Ptr., 1957), 20. E.A. Govts., *Rept. of the Quinquennial Advisory Committee, 1960* (Nairobi: Govt. Ptr., 1960), 3. Kenya, *Rept. of the Working Party,* 5–6. Statement by C. H. Hartwell (Memb. for Educ. and Labour), *Kenya Leg. Co. Debates,* 6 Oct. 1953, col. 8. *E. Afn. Standard* (Nairobi), 6 July 1956, 9.
4. Some descriptions of the founding of University College, Nairobi, imply that the site was chosen because the Asians, swayed by commercial interest, had insisted on an urban site. See, e.g., Furley and Watson, *Hist. of Educ.,* 325. The available evidence does not support this claim.
5. Sheth's name is not among the contributors in the GMAS souvenir volumes. In the society's "Eighth Bulletin" Nazareth and Yajnik complained that donors had paid only £240,000 of a promised £300,000.
6. N. S. Mangat (pres., EAINC) to all presidents of Ind. orgs. in Kenya, 4 Feb. 1955 and 18 Dec. 1955, EAINC papers, SU microfilm 1929, reel 13. *E. Afn. Standard,* 16 May 1958, 1. For a sharp reply to Mangat, see "In Defence of the Roy. Tech. College" by "An Asian Correspondent," *Kenya Weekly News* (Nakuru), 23 May 1958, 35.
7. P. J. Rogers (chairman, gov. council) to pres., Ind. Assoc., Momb., 8 Jan. 1959, and enclosed memo by Rogers, "Roy. Tech. College of E.A.," 9 Jan. 1959, EAINC papers, reel 4.
8. The findings are summarized in Kenya, *Rept. of the Working Party,* 1. The

party is described in *E. Afn. Standard,* 13 July 1955, 2; and Singh, *Gandhi Memorial,* 11–12.

9. Quoted, Kenya, *Rept. of the Working Party,* 1; see also 6–7, and App. C, 37. Even Europeans criticized the site: e.g., Kendall Ward, "College in a City—1," *Kenya Weekly News,* 6 Dec. 1957, 39. Some Asians had hoped to establish the campus in Eldoret: ibid., 10 Oct. 1952, 46.

10. Paragraphs 82, 84, and 90 of the report of the working party; and paragraphs 8 and 20 of the white paper—quoted, Singh, *Gandhi Memorial,* 12–14.

11. "Speech delivered by Mr. J. M. Nazareth, Q.C., at Luncheon of Council of Univ. of Nairobi on 3rd Feb. 1977," 2, typescript sent to Gregory by Nazareth in 1985.

12. Ibid.

13. Kenya, *Rept. of the Working Party,* App. A and B. Singh, *Gandhi Memorial,* 19–22.

14. E.A. Govts., *Rept. of the Quinquennial Advisory Committee,* 10.

15. For the draft agreement between the society and the college and vital portions of the Roy. College Act of 1960, see Singh, *Gandhi Memorial,* App. D, 38–42.

16. The history of University College, Nairobi, is briefly described in its calendar, e.g., *Calendar 1967–68,* 45–49.

17. M. S. Khimasia (hon. sec., Fed.) to Chanan Singh (advocate, Nairobi), 18 Feb. 1958; Chanan Singh (Roy. Tech. College) to hon. sec., Fed., 22 Feb 1958—Federation papers, SU microfilm 1923, reel 3. N. G. Patel (hon. sec., Fed.) to J. M. Nazareth (leg. councillor, Nairobi), 28 Oct. 1958, ibid.

18. E.g., Kenya, *Rept. of the Working Party on Higher Educ. in E.A., July-Aug., 1958* (Nairobi: Govt. Ptr., 1959), 7; and Abreau, *Role of Self-Help,* 134.

19. Univ. College, Nairobi, *Calendar 1967–68,* 45.

20. *Univ. of Nairobi Calendar 1984–85,* esp. 18. Descriptions of the university in the Kenya government's annual education reports during the late 1950s and 1960s made no mention of the Gandhi memorial or Asian contributions. Nor is there any reference in important scholarly writings, such as Beaulah M. Ragu, *Educ. in Kenya: Probs. and Perspectives in Educational Planning and Admin.* (London: Heinemann, 1973), which has a chapter on higher education; and Kenneth James King, *Pan-Africanism and Educ.: Study of Race Philanthropy and Educ. in the Southern States of America and E.A.* (Oxford: Clarendon, 1971).

21. GMAS, *Souvenir Volume,* 1:47–48. *E. Afn. Standard,* 26 Apr. 1952, 1.

22. Singh, *Gandhi Memorial,* 27, 38, 43. The Asian contribution to the Chiromo purchase came from accumulated interest on the Endowment Fund lodged by the society with the college. J. M. Nazareth, letter to Gregory, May 1984.

23. Kenya, *Rept. of the Working Party,* 23.

24. Gifts each year are listed in the annual college *Calendar.*

25. GMAS, *Souvenir Volume,* 1:65.

26. Ibid., App. 7B, 75–76.

27. *Univ. of Nairobi Calendar 1984–85,* 548–50.

28. Univ. College, Nairobi, *Calendar 1967–68,* 179–81.

29. Nazareth to Gregory, May 1984.

30. Roy. Tech. College, *Calendar 1957–58,* 6. Actual attendance was somewhat

different: 132 Africans, 133 Asians, 6 Europeans, and 1 "Non-Native." Kendall Ward, "College at the Start of Its Road," *Kenya Weekly News,* 20 Dec. 1957, 41.
31. Furley and Watson, *Hist. of Educ.,* 326. Univ. College, Nairobi, *Calendar 1967–68,* 186, 188, 190. Nazareth to Gregory, May 1984.
32. GMAS, *Souvenir Volume,* 1:21–32, 78–79; 2:89.

8

Literature and the Arts

*The past has boiled itself over and we are the
steam that must flee.*
— Jagjit Singh, 1973

Although the British dependencies in East Africa evolved a managed economy in which the governments assumed a prominent
role in the ownership and administration of the means of production and distribution, the development of literature and the arts
was left largely to private initiative. Most of what the Asians
achieved in this respect was a result of Asian philanthropy. The
Asians formed their own communal and intercommunal drama,
dance, and literary societies, established their own theaters and
allied edifices, contributed generously to the organizations initiated by the governments and European communities, and, with
enthusiastic attendance, supported the plays, musical performances, and readings of poetry and other literature produced by the
Asian writers and artists. Most of the Asian authors and performers
donated their time and energy for the benefit of the public with little
or no recompense.

Contrary to popular opinion, the Asian community was not so
engrossed in material acquisition that it failed to make a contribution to the development of East African literature and art.[1] This is
not to say that the Asian achievement was particularly outstanding
or remarkable. Before independence the contribution of the European peoples, who were outnumbered approximately three to one
by the Asians, was considerably more impressive. After independence the budding Asian artists were quickly surpassed by the

161

Africans who, as the Europeans had earlier, enjoyed the favor of their governments, the local press, and the compilers, literary critics, and publishers outside the area. It was in the period of transition, the decade before independence and the decade after — perhaps the only time favorable to them — that the Asians made their contribution.

The Asian literary and artistic attainment has not been recognized. In most of the four dozen anthologies of African literature, and in some of those specifically on East Africa, the Asian authors have been overlooked or ignored. In the few in which they have been included, they have not been distinguished from Africans or Europeans, and the reader who is not familiar with Asian names would assume that they were black Africans. There seem to have been two schools of thought among the editors and critics. One, exemplified by David Cook, Wole Soyinka, and Ezekiel Mphahlele, is based on the view that the term *African* embraces all the peoples of East Africa regardless of racial and cultural origins and ties.[2] The Asians themselves fostered this view since in this period of transition from European to black African rule they were striving to be recognized as "Africans" and to be accorded a permanent place in the new social order. The other school, with Austin J. Shelton, Kofi Awoonor, and Adrian Roscoe as examples, obviously distinguished black Africans from the other peoples in Africa and wrote of them exclusively.[3] Neither school, because of its particular interest, could discuss the Asian contribution per se.

The fact that East Africa lagged behind West and South Africa in literary and artistic endeavor during the period of transition is an additional reason for the lack of attention to Asians. During the two decades while both Asians and Africans were developing a literature, creative writing by the Europeans greatly declined. In 1965 Ann Tibble remarked in her anthology that "the awakening came to the East of the continent in general later than to the South and the West."[4] It was that year when the Ugandan author Taban Lo Liyong wrote his much publicized letter entitled "East Africa, O East Africa, I lament thy literary barrenness."[5] Since then, as is generally recognized, "many flowers have blossomed."[6] That Asians were among these flowers has often been overlooked even by the Asians. In 1974 Rajat Neogy, one of the foremost Asian authors, exclaimed, "The Asian involvement in art and literature was pathetic." [7] In view of what actually was accomplished, however, this assessment seems unjustified.

Communal and Intercommunal Organizations

The Asians' concern for literature and the arts apparently was manifest from the time of their earliest settlement. It was first expressed in the activities of their communal organizations. The Asians met regularly in the Jamat Khana, the Muslim Association, the Gujarati Samaj, the Marathi Mandal, and other organizations to sing hymns, recite holy verses, and produce religious plays. An exception was the Goans, who, because of their Western orientation, suffered no religious restraints in their enjoyment of European arts and literature. As early as 1908 there was a Goan Drama Club in Nairobi, and in 1909 the Goan Union of Mombasa was presenting stage performances to audiences as large as three hundred.[8] Unique among the early Asians was the Mombasa Muslim Shariff Jaffer, who in 1908 was described as having the best collection of antique china in Africa.[9]

Not until after World War II was there much deviation from this pattern; then there was an increasing evidence of westernization. The Ismailis of Dar es Salaam may be taken as an example. In addition to meeting in the Jamat Khana for presentations of religious music, poetry, and drama, the Ismailis began to gather in private homes to sing popular and classical songs of a nonreligious nature. In Dar es Salaam these informal meetings, misnamed *ginan* (hymnal) parties, were often held in the home of the Tejpar family, which was noted for its interest in music. Aziz Tejpar offered regular Saturday evening *ginans* at which he played the harmonium. Many of those attending composed music, and V. D. Suliman was especially noted for his songs. Similar sessions for reciting *gwalis* (verses) were also held in private homes. A leader would recite the verse while the others served as a chorus. Since the Jamat Khana did not permit secular themes or the use of props or scenery, most Ismaili plays were presented in the new Diamond Jubilee Hall, which served as a clubhouse, and in the schools. By 1960 the Ismailis were regularly entering the competitions of the British Council by staging plays by Shakespeare and contemporary playwrights, including Noel Coward.[10]

As the Ismaili activity attests, the Asian contribution occurred mainly after World War II, when the community as a whole acquired a new prosperity. Not until then did a noticeable number acquire the financial security and find the time and interest to work toward a development of the arts. Though most of those involved dabbled in art and literature as an avocation, a few in the younger generation rebelled against the family business tradition, disregarded parental urgings, and pursued full-time literary careers. It was then also that the Asians began to establish organizations devoted to the arts, and some of the wealthy became patrons. This new direction in Asian life is explained not only by the community's increasing affluence and, perhaps, gradually declining economic opportunity, but also by a steady secularization of Asian interests, values, and activities. Most of the old art forms had been tied to religion. In East Africa the impact of westernization entailed a shift to a more worldly culture and an exposure to nonreligious art forms. The postwar literature of the community was thus characterized by experimentation with Western concepts as well as a revival of traditional Indian expressions.

The first important attempt to organize Asian dramatists, poets, and other artists and present their work to the public occurred in Nairobi in 1948 with the inauguration of the Oriental Art Circle (OAC). The stimulus came from India. Apa B. Pant, the Indian high commissioner, and his wife Dr. Nalini Devi met with young Asian political and cultural leaders and encouraged them to merge as representatives of various communal sects in endeavors that would develop Asian unity and further Asian cultural achievement. They also urged that the Asians combine with Africans in this activity. The main result of the Pants' effort was an intercommunal, multiracial artistic association under Asian direction. The OAC was at first made up of a small active group including M. M. Patel and Subos Inamdar, advocates, Shanti Pandit, a journalist-politician, Dr. Abdulali Esmail Samji, a dentist, and Mr. and Mrs. B. Billimoria, a Parsi couple who were fond of western music. Nalini Devi was the first president, and subsequently the wife of each succeeding high commissioner was honored with the position.

Within a few years the OAC membership had expanded to approximately six hundred.[11]

Situated in the Kenya Cultural Center next to the National Theatre, the OAC organized monthly presentations of Indian drama and poetry readings as well as music and dance, and it participated annually in the competitions sponsored by the National Theatre. Its first play, presented when the Indian navy visited East Africa, was an Indian version of *Charley's Aunt*.[12] Many of the plays were borrowed from India, and a few were locally written. Most were performed in Indian languages, especially Gujarati, Punjabi, and Hindi, but some, such as *Passage to India*, were in English. All were produced by local Asians. The actors included not only Asian men and women, but Africans and Europeans in accord with the characters portrayed, and Africans were invited to become honorary members of the OAC. An extension of the OAC's activities was the inauguration on Nairobi radio of a weekly Asian program of music and poetry.[13]

Although the Nairobi OAC was the largest and most enterprising of the early organizations designed to promote art and literature, there were many others. In Mombasa an active Arts Circle sponsored various activities including drama and musical ballet. In Kampala the Kala Nikitan fostered drama, dance, music, and poetry. Unlike the Nairobi and Mombasa organizations, however, its membership was confined to Gujaratis. A similar communal restriction applied to the active Goan, Ismaili, Hindu, and Sikh organizations begun in each of the three capital cities and to that of the Oshwal sect in Nairobi. Among these the most active was the Hindu Volunteer Corps of Dar es Salaam, which devoted the proceeds of its artistic presentations to charities, including the founding of a public library and hospital. During 1962–63, in a major attempt to unite the various communities in artistic endeavor, the Aga Khan and Nanji Kalidas Mehta each donated £5,000 toward the establishment of a National Cultural Centre in Kampala. Supported also by many other Asian as well as European donors, the center contained a national theatre, a language hall, and many offices for promotion of a variety of arts, including film production.[14] Another wealthy Ugandan, Indar Singh Gill, inaugurated Gill's Opera House Ltd. in Kampala in 1946 at a cost of £40,000.[15]

In the smaller urban centers, depending on local initiative, there were a few attempts to form intercommunal organizations similar to the OAC. In Tanga in 1947, for instance, Naval B. Rajay, an employee in the British civil service, combined with P. C. Dave, Chotu Somaia, N. Samat, and other young enthusiasts to form the Tanga Radical Society. Distressed by the communal friction following the partition of India that was destroying the Tanga Indian Association, the group hoped to bring Asian Hindus and Muslims together with Africans in various nonpolitical endeavors. With a membership of twenty, including seven Africans, they launched a literary magazine, *Today's View,* printed partly in English and partly in Gujarati, and organized debating and dramatic societies. Inviting participation by Asian and African secondary-school children, they were surprisingly successful in adding a new dimension to the isolated Tanga society.[16]

Drama and Poetry

Among the various art forms, drama received the most attention from the Asians. One inducement came from the British Council, which sponsored annual competitions in each capital for presentation of plays in English by the local European, African, and Asian schools. The Asians competed enthusiastically with plays of Shakespeare, Noel Coward, and other British playwrights. In the OAC, Kala Nikitan, and Mombasa Arts Circle, and in the Gujarati Samaj, Marathi Mandal, and the Muslim and Sikh Associations in each major city, plays written locally or borrowed from India were prepared for the East Africa Drama Festival, an annual event beginning in 1950 in Kampala. There was also a Kenya Drama Festival. These plays were presented in Indian languages as well as English, and they were often evaluated at the festivals by notable guest artists specially invited from India.[17] The activities of four of the foremost East African playwrights—Kuldip Sondhi, Ganesh Bagchi, M. M. Patel, and Peter Nazareth—well illustrate the Asian endeavor and success.

Sondhi has been described as a renaissance man for whom playwriting was but one of many interests and talents. He was born in Lahore in 1924 into a remarkable Hindu family. His father, a civil engineer who settled in Mombasa in 1932, quickly built a fortune in construction, warehousing, and a variety of businesses, and his mother, Kenya's foremost public servant among Asian women, served twenty-six years on the municipal council and was for more than thirty years president of the Mombasa Women's Association. Kuldip attended the prestigious Bishop Cotton School in Simla, received a B.Sc. from the Punjab University, briefly attended the Massachusetts Institute of Technology, then at Brooklyn Polytechnic completed a five-year course in three and one-half years to earn an M.S. in aeronautical engineering. After working two years for the Bristol Aircraft Co., he was invited by Jawaharlal Nehru to head the development of the Gnat fighter engine in Bangalore. He stayed only briefly in India and returned to Mombasa to run successively a contracting business, woodworking shop, concrete block factory, and a sawmill. In these activities, according to his brother, Sondhi quickly lost "a hell of a lot of money." [20] He eventually settled into administering the family's new posh hotel on the Mombasa coast.

Meanwhile Sondhi was writing essays, poems, and one-act plays, all in English. His first play, *Undesignated,* won first prize at the Kenya Drama Festival in 1963 and was later staged throughout Uganda by the Makerere Travelling Theatre. It portrayed the rivalry between two engineers, an African and an Asian, for a top governmental position in independent Africa. Subsequently Sondhi wrote perhaps a dozen other plays, six of which have been published. *With Strings,* revealing the problems faced by a young Asian and an African as they contemplate marriage, won the Kenya Drama Festival award in 1965 for the best original play of the year. *Encounter* presented the racial conflict and human bonds between a Mau Mau general and a British army lieutenant. *The Magic Pool* was the story of an African hunchback. *A Mile to Go, Sunil's Dilemma,* and *Devil in the Mixer* were written specifically as thirty-minute productions for radio, and at least two were broadcast by the BBC's African Theatre. Their themes were, in order, an Asian's frustrating attempt to leave Kenya, an Asian couple's conflict with two African secret police, and African-Asian superstition. All Sondhi's plays were complex, with large casts, and Africans were given as much prominence in them as Asians. *The*

Magic Pool had an all-African cast. The plays were, as his brother believed, perhaps "too open" for the East African audience. On the whole they were of a quality to afford their author a reputation as East Africa's foremost playwright.[19]

Ganesh Bagchi, who had emigrated from East Bengal to Uganda in 1942 at age twenty-six, combined playwriting with a teaching career. After two years as a teacher at the Government Secondary School in old Kampala, he was sent to England by the government for a postgraduate certificate in education at the University of London. On returning to Uganda, he rapidly advanced to the position of principal of the Kampala Teacher Training College. In 1950 he wrote his first play, *The Gold Diggers of Yaksha Town,* and submitted it as the first entry by an Asian to the East Africa Drama Festival. Yaksha is the god of wealth in Indian mythology, and the play was a parody on Kampala, with the local Asians portrayed as the gold diggers. Bagchi's entry received the award for best play of the festival. Subsequently he wrote and produced six more plays in Uganda: *Soma and Synthesis; Eggs for Breakfast; Of Malice and Men; The Deviant; A Recurrent Theme, Part One;* and *A Recurrent Theme, Part Two.* These plays, all of which were in English, were presented one each year from 1958 to 1964 at the Makerere University College Hall or the National Theatre, and all were broadcast by Uganda Radio. At least one, *Of Malice and Men,* was set in India. Asians were the main characters, the casts were small, and love and race relations were main themes. Bagchi also produced two Tagore plays in the Uganda National Theatre for the Tagore Centenary in 1961. In most of the plays he took a leading role as actor — his wife was also a talented actress — and for his performance in his last play, which won the prize for the best all-round production, he received the award for the best actor. Five of his seven plays won prizes.[20]

The third dramatist, M. M. Patel, a prominent Nairobi advocate, is less well known, primarily because his plays were all in Gujarati. He was born in the Gujarat in 1930, attended local schools, then Ahmedabad University, and received an L.L.B. from Bombay University. En route to Britain for further study in 1954, he visited East Africa and decided to stay. He became a partner in the well-known Nairobi firm of P. I. Patel and S. G. Amin and specialized in criminal law, earning a reputation, especially during the Mau Mau trials, as a defender of Africans. He also entered politics and bought a coffee farm in Ruiru. In India he had begun to act at age ten and, before emigrating, had written several plays and considerable poetry.

In East Africa Patel continued to write and act, introduced plays from India, and took a leading role among the young Asian artists in Nairobi. From 1966 to 1971 he was chairman of the OAC. Meanwhile he wrote four one-act plays. His first, *Na Aato Mari Maa Chhe* (Oh No, This Is My Mother), a satire on himself as an advocate, won first prize at the East Africa Drama Festival as the best one-act play locally written. His second, *Mahila Downer* (Looking Down at Women), was printed in the Nairobi *Colonial Times*. The third, *Krishna ni Sita* (Krishna's Sita) was presented on Nairobi radio. The fourth, *Rasik Gaya* (Rasik Passed Away), a tragedy involving a musician, still has not been produced. As these titles denote, some of Patel's writings were on religious themes, but most of his plays in India as well as Africa questioned concepts of morality and behavior as Asians were affected by modernization and westernization. Patel's roles as advocate and dramatist were enhanced by his wife, the former Hansa Gathani, who, while trained in law and a member of her husband's firm, enjoyed a language fluency and talent that enabled her to act in English, Hindi, and Gujarati plays.[21]

Peter Nazareth, East Africa's foremost Asian novelist and literary critic, began essentially as a dramatist. He wrote several plays, the most successful of which before 1975 was *Brave New Cosmos*. A study of the interaction between two African undergraduates and an African teacher, the play was the first by an East African author to be presented by the BBC African Service and was later produced by the Nigerian Broadcasting Corporation. Two other very successful plays, also written for radio, were *The Hospital* and *X*. Set in postcolonial Africa, they focused on the plight of individuals in a society that had little concern for human values. The one portrayed a person condemned to death in a callous, impersonal hospital, and the other described an individual who was increasingly turned into a cipher, conscious that he was being brainwashed at one level but completely unaware that he was also being seriously affected at another level.[22]

Nazareth had an outstanding literary career. A Goan, born in

Uganda in 1940, he attended the Senior Secondary School in Kampala where he was inspired by Ganesh Bagchi, his teacher. In his senior Cambridge examination Nazareth stood first in Uganda. At Makerere he was one of the founders and first editors of the English Department's magazine *Penpoint* (later *Dhana*). He also started the first jazz society and dance band at Makerere and helped begin the university newspaper, *The Makererean,* for which he was a sports editor. At Makerere he wrote *Brave New Cosmos.* After taking an English honors degree Nazareth taught school briefly, then moved to England to study and eventually receive a postgraduate diploma in English studies at Leeds University. In England he wrote the other two plays for the BBC. He then followed a typical Goan path by entering the Uganda civil service. For the next seven years he held a post in the Ministry of Finance, but he continued to write, and the publication of a novel led to a fellowship at Yale University.[23]

Among others involved in Asian theater, Vinay J. Inamdar, Sadru Kassam, Jagjit Singh, and Parvin Sayal deserve mention. Inamdar was the principal director and producer. In 1949, after finishing secondary school in Maharashtra, he left for Kenya to join his father, who was Pant's private secretary. While employed as an accountant, Inamdar became active in the OAC. The Indian play *Duniya ne Undha Chashma* (The World Is Wearing Spectacles Upside Down), which he directed, was so popular among Asian audiences that it was presented in Mombasa, Kampala, and Kisumu as well as Nairobi. Among his many other productions was Sondhi's prize-winning play *Undesignated.*[24] Kassam, a teacher who was born in Mombasa in 1941 and graduated from Makerere with honors in English, is unique for writing in Swahili. His humorous but politically pointed play *Mifupa* (Bones), about an African butcher who had to give "key money" to get his license renewed, was performed twenty times throughout Uganda in 1965, the first year of the Makerere Travelling Theatre. Kassam himself acted as the butcher.[25]

Jagjit Singh and Sayal, like most Asian dramatists, wrote plays in English. Jagjit, who was born in Uganda in 1949, won distinction while reading literature at the University of Sussex. His first play, *Sweet Scum of Freedom,* won third prize among six hundred entries in 1971 in the Second BBC African Service Competition for new half-hour radio plays. A frank writing, it viewed African corruption and Asian weakness through the eyes of a prostitute.[26] Sayal, who was primarily a poet, was born in Kenya in 1947. As a dramatist he is noted for *Through a Hand-cuff,* which won third position in a competition organized by the English department at the University of Nairobi.[27]

As a whole the Asian plays made a distinct and valuable contribution to the new and rapidly changing societies of East Africa. The contribution happened to be in greatest strength when most needed — during the decade overlapping the transfer of power — when the old values were being most critically examined and retained or rejected. Society was in transformation. While subtly damning the European arrogance and paternalism inherent in colonialsm, the Asian playwrights fearlessly condemned the corruption, discrimination, and duplicity manifest in the rising African elites. They also frankly portrayed the acquisitiveness and exclusiveness that the British and Africans so much resented in Asian society. These writers thus set a model for the emerging African dramatists to emulate.

It was not only on the audiences and prospective playwrights that the Asians made this impact, but on all those involved in the production of plays, from stagehands to actors. Nearly all the plays written in East Africa included roles for Africans, and in some, such as *Devil in the Mixer,* African characters were paramount. Whenever possible, Africans were assigned the African roles. In *Undesignated,* for instance, Jonathan Kariara, who later became the East African editor of Oxford University Press, Norbert Okari, who was subsequently a newscaster for Kenya television, and Vertisteen Mbeya, an American black, were assigned the leading African roles. Unfortunately, well-trained Africans were not always available. After a vain search the African lead in *With Strings,* as well as in *Encounter,* was given to Sondhi's sister Krishna.[28] African dramatists too were in short supply. In compiling a book of plays representative of East, South, and West Africa in 1968, Cosmo Pieterse, who was himself an African, decided to include only three from East Africa: two plays by Sondhi and one by Bagchi.[29] Five years later in selecting nine African plays for radio, Gwyneth Henderson and Pieterse included only one from East Africa — Sondhi's *Sunil's Dilemma* — and Sondhi was the only non-African among the nine authors.[30]

Poetry was next to drama among the Asians' literary interests, and like drama it apparently received the most attention in Nairobi and Kampala. The reciting of poems in small, select groups was one of the cultural activities carried to East Africa from India, where recitation was traditionally practiced in villages as well as urban centers. In East Africa it became more eclectic as Muslims and Hindus from various sects came together increasingly in the postwar years to write, read, and critique. Among the prominent poets in these circles were Haroun Ahmed, M. M. Patel, and Harshad Joshi in Nairobi; D. A. Patel and Rajat Neogy in Kampala; and Kuldip Sondhi and his brother Jagdish in Mombasa. Some were quite prolific. By 1973, for instance, M. M. Patel had written 160 poems. Publication was not emphasized, but some poems were read on radio, and many appeared in the Nairobi *Colonial Times* and other Asian newspapers as well as in the Kampala literary journal *Transition*.[31]

Before independence the most important group in Kenya was organized in the early sixties by Haroon Ahmed, a Bohra Muslim. Born in Bombay in 1914 and a resident of East Africa from an early age, Ahmed was mainly self-educated. Though interested in many subjects, he earned his living as a journalist. Successively editing the *Colonial Times, Daily Chronicle,* and *Africa Samachar,* he was a trenchant critic of British colonialism and was imprisoned in 1947 for sedition. His poetry group included about ten writers, all Asian, who wrote in English, Gujarati, and Hindi. The members, including M. M. Patel and Kuldip Sondhi, met monthly to read poems on a common theme determined at the previous meeting. In the mid-sixties Ahmed arranged a program on Nairobi radio for a regular recitation. After only six or seven broadcasts, however, the program fell victim to the anti-Asian wave of 1967–68.[32]

Despite lack of recognition in the anthologies on East Africa, the Asians' most successful poet in these years was probably Hubert Ribeiro. Unlike the others, he wrote from the beginning as an expatriate in isolation. He was born in 1942 into a well-known Nairobi Goan family. His grandfather was Nairobi's first medical doctor. After local schooling Ribeiro was sent to the Huddersfield College of Technology in Yorkshire, where, inspired by a professor, he developed a keen interest in the Irish poet William Butler Yeats. He then enrolled in Trinity College, Dublin, concentrated on English literature and metaphysics, and took up painting and photography as well as poetry. His plans for an academic career were terminated by tuberculosis, and in 1971 after two operations he returned to Goa to live splendidly but alone in the family's three-hundred-year-old home. His first volume of poetry, *El Peregrino* (The Wanderer), was rejected by an East Africa publisher as not East African. "But I am East African," Ribeiro argued. "My only commitment is to my art." Later he admitted, however, that all his sympathies were Anglo-Irish. "I write for them, not the Africans." The volume was soon published (1971) in California and went through three editions.[33]

By 1973 Ribeiro had written poems for two other volumes to be issued under the same title. His work poignantly reflects the mind of a dispossessed Asian who has not yet found happiness in another society. "I have a problem of self-identity," he confided. "I don't fit anywhere!" The following poem, one of his best known, was written three years before the beginning of Idi Amin's rule in Uganda:

MOMBASA

Think how a flower's martyrdom
Adds to the beauty of poinciana
Trees, and tell me if a people's
Slaughter gives a country glory.
For standing on this brilliant shore
My mind is vexed with prophecy:
Tangles and drifts of dark bodies
Turn in the loud waves; others, logged
On the sand, await an avenging tongue.
But now, only the wind, picking
At their delicate garments, sighs.[34]

Ribeiro eventually moved to Toronto, where under the pen name Hubert de Santana he wrote several articles, published a book on sports, and interviewed famous personalities for *Maclean's*.[35]

Other poets in Kenya included Amin Kassam, the dramatist Parvin Sayal, and Pheroze Nowrojee. Kassam, who was born in Mombasa in 1948, has been described as "best known as one of East Africa's most widely published poets, represented in almost every journal and anthology." [36] Before leaving for McGill University to study social science, Kassam was an assistant editor of *Busara,* the journal of the University of Nairobi's Department of Literature. Later he wrote for newspapers in Nairobi and became a correspondent in Delhi. Among his poems, which were written in English on a wide range of subjects mostly concerned with black Africans, "Waiting for the Bus" and "Martin Luther King" seem to have been the most widely cited and published.[37] Sayal began writing poetry in English and Hindi at age ten and won several prizes with poems such as "The Pot" and "Defeat" before he began medical studies in Nairobi.[38] Nowrojee, an advocate, is known for verse with sharp sarcasm and a rare humor. Typical is his ironic poem "Sonnett," a critical analysis of a dictator.[39]

In Tanzania Yusuf O. Kassam, U. K. Oza, and Sukhi Singh, and in Uganda a large number, including Bahadur Tejani, Rajat Neogy, Jagjit Singh, Michael Sequeira, Saroj Datta, Mohamed Virjee, Mohamed Talib, and Mo Tejani, achieved recognition as poets. Kassam and Bahadur Tejani are apparently the most widely published. Kassam began to write in 1964 at age twenty-one when studying at Makerere. Within a year he won a poetry prize at the Cardiff Commonwealth Arts Festival, and soon his poems were appearing in journals and anthologies. They were also broadcast on the BBC African Service. His poems "Maji Maji" and "The Recurrent Design" seem to have been the most favored.[40] Tejani was one of the first Asians able to apply himself full-time to literary endeavor. He taught in the University of Nairobi Department of Literature and then in the English Department of the University of Sokoto in Nigeria after reading literature at Makerere and then philosophy at Cambridge. At Makerere he was a classmate of Ngugi wa Thiong'o and with Peter Nazareth a sports editor for the first issues of *The Makererean.* Tejani quickly established a reputation as a novelist and critic as well as a poet. One of his best-known poems is "Wild Horse of Serengeti." [41]

Short Stories, Novels, and Nonfiction

Short stories did not receive the attention accorded drama and poetry, but the young Asian writers tended to experiment with all forms of literature. Kuldip Sondhi's story "Bad Blood," written almost as if it were a play, describes the vain attempt by a young half-caste to persuade a beautiful prostitute of similar blood to marry him. In the end she prefers her loose relationship with a brutish African police inspector.[42] The dramatists Sadru Kassam, Jagjit Singh, and Peter Nazareth also wrote short stories. Two of Kassam's stories were broadcast by Uganda Radio, and Nazareth by 1975 had published seven short stories.[43] Another Goan author from Uganda, Lino Leitau, wrote several stories set in East Africa that he included in an anthology, *Goan Tales*.[44] Though noted more for their poetry, Amin Kassam had short stories published in *Busara* and Tilak Banerjee in *Penpoint*.[45]

Before independence the production of novels and other books was conspicuously lacking. As Rajat Neogy has pointed out, there was no V. S. Naipaul in East Africa.[46] Some of the early Asian immigrants produced books, but they wrote almost entirely in Indian languages about subjects not related to East Africa and published in India. U. K. Oza, editor of *Tanganyika Opinion*, is an example. According to his son, Oza wrote twenty-five to thirty books, but apparently only two of these ever reached the U.S. Library of Congress. Another example is provided by the Kampala bicycle dealer Umakant Tribhovandas Patel, who by 1958 had written "many novels" in Gujarati, some of which were popular enough to be translated into Hindi.[47] By 1964 not one Asian had published a novel in English with an East Africa setting, a book of poetry or short stories, or an autobiography. The only scholarly volumes had been a history of Asian settlement and an Asian who's who in 1961 and 1963 by Shanti Pandit and Narayan Shrinivas Thakur. Pandit, an Asian of many talents, was among the founders of the Oriental Art Circle and the Shree Gujerat Lalit Kala Mandir (later the Kenya Eastern Arts), for each of which he served as president. Thakur was a talented journalist.[48]

During the decade after 1964, as their efforts in drama, poetry, and short-story writing reached an apex, some Asians did produce books. Peter Nazareth, Bahadur Tejani, and Mahmood Mamdani published novels. Nazareth's *In a Brown Mantle* is a political study of a Goan who joins Africans in developing a multiracial party but eventually discovers that he has been used, is distrusted as an Asian, and will soon be rejected. Despite the depressing theme, the novel is not an expression of Asian disillusionment. Nazareth intended the audience to be critical of his narrator. A testimony to his under-standing of the communal conflict in East Africa is the fact that the novel predicted not only Amin's coup, but also the Asians' expul-sion. The novel sold out its first printing and, as mentioned, led to Nazareth's Yale fellowship.[49] Bahadur Tejani's *Day after Tomor-row* is the story of an Asian who breaks from the tradition of his community by marrying an African nurse and forsaking a lucrative business to become a teacher. It too was widely read.[50] Mamdani's *From Citizen to Refugee* is a revealing account of the Uganda exodus and the Asians' initial experiences in Britain. With Mam-dani himself as the central character, the novel takes the form of an exciting autobiography.[51] In addition to these novels there were Hubert Ribeiro's book of poems and a volume of plays by Kuldip Sondhi.[52]

The Asians also produced several volumes of nonfiction. Peter Nazareth in 1972 published the first book by an Asian on literature, and he soon followed it with two others.[53] J. S. Mangat, a university lecturer in Nairobi, Makhan Singh, the veteran Kenya trade un-ionist, Nizar A. Motani, and Abdul Sheriff, professor of history in the University of Dar es Salaam, wrote separate histories.[54] The third Aga Khan, Ambu H. Patel, a Kenya journalist, Mahmood Mamdani, a Uganda political scientist, and Issa G. Shivji, a Tan-zanian professor of law, produced political studies.[55] A. B. Patel, Kenya's preeminent politician, compiled after his retirement to Pondicherry a treatise on world order.[56] Yashpal Tandon and Dharam Ghai, Kenya economists, wrote socioeconomic treatises on the Asian community.[57] Ladis da Silva on Zanzibar described his own East African community in a larger history of the Goans, and Nanji Kalidas Mehta, the Uganda industrialist, John Maxi-mian Nazareth, the Kenya advocate and political leader, and So-phia Mustafa, the Tanzania politician, issued autobiographies.[58] A considerable number of Asians, including Ghai, Mamdani, Mangat, Motani, Sheriff, Shivji, Tilak Banerjee, F. R. S. de Souza, Visho B. L. Sharma, and Shirin Walji, completed Ph.D. theses in the humanities and social sciences.

While many were conspicuous in literature and the performing arts, very few Asians have been noted for achievement in the visual arts. There was no prominent sculptor. Artists from India were commissioned to sculpt the statue of Gandhi in Nairobi and the busts of Allidina Visram and J. B. Pandya in Mombasa. In photography and painting, however, East Africa did produce at least two outstanding artists. John Shamsudin Karmali, the Nairobi Ismaili whose unique multiracial school is discussed in Chapter 9, became one of East Africa's foremost photographers and compiled two extraordinary photographic studies of East African birds. He was honored with a fellowship in Britain's Royal Photographic Society.[59] A. D. Oza, a Uganda Goan, concentrated on painting African peoples and landscapes and is noted for a portrait of Tagore.[60]

Transition

Among all the Asian writers and artists, including the dramatists and poets, the greatest contribution may have come from Rajat Neogy, the Bengali editor and founder of the Uganda literary journal *Transition*. He was born in Kampala in 1938, the son of a teacher who became principal of Uganda's largest primary school, the Kampala Government School. Although Rajat finished secondary school at the young age of thirteen, he was not an outstanding student and was unable to enter Makerere. He spent two years at the London Polytechnic and afterwards "fooled around," as he said, until he was eighteen, the minimum age to enter a British university. At last enrolling in the School of Oriental and African Studies at the University of London, he concentrated on anthropology but quickly decided that he wanted to become a writer. He left in 1958, a year short of his degree, to return to Uganda, help found the Uganda Action Group, a multiracial political organization, and establish Africa East Publications with the intention of beginning a literary magazine. He became "sidetracked into politics," as he later admitted, and although he wrote a lot for the press, the subjects were all political. He soon started a fortnightly, *Sport,* which failed financially after a dozen issues. In 1959 he returned to London, where he took more courses in anthropology, wrote news scripts for the BBC, and married a Swede. Then he spent a year in Sweden, where, as in England, he moved in a circle of young artists. In 1961 he visited Uganda with the intention of staying only two weeks and settling as a writer in Greece, but the excitement of emerging Africa caught him. He stayed and in November 1961 launched the first issue of *Transition.*[61]

Ironically, it is not so much what Neogy himself wrote as his editorship of *Transition* that forms the essence of his contribution. With Ganesh Bagchi, Ben Mkapa, Daudi Ocheng, and other young Ugandan artists and politicians in Kampala, with a similar group who had fled the Congo, and with lecturers and graduate students from Makerere — Europeans, Africans, and Arabs as well as Asians — Neogy made his journal a medium of expression for nearly all the avant-garde literati of East Africa. He also attracted outside talent from Europe, the United States, and West and southern Africa. He started a writer's fellowship to support such visitors as Saul Bellow and Naipaul, who would affiliate with the university, hold two or three seminars, and write for his journal. *Transition* became a clearing house, a focal point, for artists coming and going. It printed plays, poems, short stories, and literary essays as well as political and economic analyses. Maintaining a very high quality, it prospered with an ultimate paid circulation of 12,000. Its rise, however, coincided with that of Milton Obote, who became increasingly resentful of its explicit revelation of his growing authoritarianism. Meanwhile evidence was published indicating that Neogy had become involved with the U.S. Central Intelligence Agency. In October 1968 he was arrested, tried for sedition, and, though acquitted, imprisoned for six months. On his release, with citizenship revoked, he fled to the United States and thence to Ghana, where he briefly revived *Transition.* He eventually moved to Canada.[62]

Unfortunately, after so promising a beginning, the Asian literary and artistic endeavor proved to be short-lived. Despite the remarkable success of a few, the Asian involvement did not have a sound base. Part of the difficulty lay with the Asian community, which was unable or unwilling to make the financial commitment that would have ensured full-time professional careers and the organization and stability essential to an enduring contribution. Not one playwright or actor was able to assume such dedication. Moreover, the community's emphasis on material acquistion diverted talent to other occupations, and its attitude toward sex roles precluded the serious involvement of women. There was also, as Hubert Ribeiro so well illustrated, a problem of identity. Nearly all the talented young artists were in a process of adopting Western culture. Most were no longer comfortable writing in the Indian languages but were not yet proficient in Swahili. They were, in effect, constrained to write in a European language, take Africans as their subjects, and in other ways disregard their unique cultural heritage.[63]

These creative Asians were victims of an unusual circumstance. Their presence in East Africa was resented not only by the postwar colonial governments and the European settlers, but also by the new African governments and significant numbers of the African people. They received no official encouragement in their efforts to develop an East African literature. At best they were tolerated. After two years the Tanga Radical Society was forced to dissolve by a British government that apparently feared that the society would become political and saw danger in a joint Asian-African endeavor.[64] In Nairobi the Asians' time on the radio was gradually restricted.[65] The Makerere Travelling Theatre presented plays in Swahili, Luganda, Lwo, Runyoro/Rutoro, and English, but not in an Indian language.[66] The climate of opinion after independence, as one author observed, was no longer favorable to free expression.[67] In the end the greatest deterrents proved to be the measures taken by the new African governments to curtail the Asian business activity on which all those in literature depended. Even before Amin's expulsion order in Uganda, many of the Asian writers and artists had left East Africa. By 1973 in all the countries many of the organizations dedicated to literature and the arts were defunct.

The Asian literature will be remembered not so much for its quality, or even its quantity, as for its unique role in East African literary development. None of these plays, poems, novels, and short stories is likely ever to enjoy an enduring esteem in world literature. As Bahadur Tejani has noted, "The East African Asian authors wrote in a tense atmosphere and it affects the theme, style and form." [68] Nor was there a remarkable quantity of production. During the two decades characterized chiefly by the transfer of political power, however, the Asians filled a void in literature between an era of European supremacy and one of African ascendency. While continuing European models of form and style, some clung to subjects of Indian tradition, but many developed new, peculiarly African themes. A few, with perhaps Peter Nazareth and Kuldip Sondhi in the fore, identified and boldly exposed the delicate social issues and problems of independent Africa that were to be developed further by Africans such as Ngugi wa Thiong'o. In essence, the Asians provided what Rajat Neogy so aptly recognized and illustrated, a literary transition.

Notes

1. This chapter is an elaboration of an article by the author, "Literary Devt. in E.A.: The Asian Contribution, 1955–75," *Research in Afn. Literatures* (Winter 1981): 440–59.
2. David Cook, ed., *Afn. Lit.: A Critical View* (London: Longman, 1977). Wole Soyinka, ed., *Poems of Black Afa.* (London: Secker and Warburg, 1975). Ezekiel Mphahlele, *Afn. Writing Today* (Baltimore: Penguin, 1967).
3. Austin J. Shelton, ed., *Afn. Assertion: A Critical Anthology of Afn. Lit.* (London: Longman, 1976). Kofi Awoonor, *Breast of the Earth: A Survey of the Hist., Culture, and Lit. of Afa. S. of the Sahara* (Garden City, N.Y.: Anchor/Doubleday, 1975). Adrian Roscoe, *Uhuru's Fire: Afn. Lit. E. to S.* (Cambridge, Eng.: Cambridge Univ. Press, 1977).
4. Ann Tibble, ed., *Afn.-English Lit.: A Short Survey and Anthology of Prose and Poetry up to 1965* (London: Peter Owen, 1965), 79.
5. *Transition* (Kampala) 19 (1965): 11.
6. Andrew Gurr and Aangus Calder, eds., *Writers in E.A.: Papers from a Colloquium Held at the Univ. of Nairobi, June 1971* (Nairobi: E. Afn. Lit. Bureau, 1974), 1.
7. R. Neogy intv.
8. *E. Afn. Standard,* 8 Aug. 1908, 13; 9 Jan. 1909, 7.
9. Ibid., 20 June 1908, 9.
10. S. K. Velji intv.
11. M. M. Patel intv.
12. S. Thakore (OAC member) intv.
13. M. M. Patel intv. J. R. Sondhi (brother of Kuldip), intv.
14. M. M. Patel intv. D. N. Mehta (son of N. K. Mehta) intv. H. Pandya intv.
15. *Saben's Commercial Directory and Handbook of Ug., 1950–51* (Kampala: Saben & Co., 1951), 213.

16. N. B. Rajay intv.
17. Among the popular Indian plays were *Sundar Van* (Beautiful Forest) and *Abbi Abbi To Laye Ho* (You Have Just Come). M. M. Patel intv.
18. J. R. Sondhi intv. His parents were interviewed with him.
19. Ibid. Five of the plays were published in Kuldip Sondhi, *Undesignated and Other Plays* (New Delhi: Orient Longman, 1973). Two were included in Cosmo Pieterse, ed., *Ten One-Act Plays* (London: Heinemann Educ. Books, 1968); one in Gwyneth Henderson and Cosmo Pieterse, eds., *Nine Afn. Plays for Radio* (London: Heinemann, 1973); and another in Cosmo Pieterse, ed., *Short Afn. Plays* (London: Heinemann Educ. Books, 1972).
20. G. Bagchi intv. *Of Malice and Men* is in David Cook and Miles Lee, eds, *Short E. Afn. Plays in English* (London: Heinemann Educ. Books, 1968), 67–82. *The Deviant* is in Pieterse, *Ten One-Act Plays,* 167–90.
21. Hansa Patel was interviewed with M. M. Patel.
22. *Brave New Cosmos* is in David Cook, ed., *Origin E.A.: a Makerere Anthology* (London: Heinemann, 1965), 166–78. For the other two plays, see Peter Nazareth, *Two Radio Plays: The Hospital and X* (Nairobi: E. Afn. Lit. Bureau, 1976).
23. A detailed interview with Nazareth appears in Bernth Lindfors, *Mazungumzo: Interviews with E. Afn. Writers, Publishers, Editors, and Scholars* (Athens: Ohio Univ. Ctr. for Intl. Studies, 1980), 80–97.
24. V. J. Inamdar intv.
25. *Mifupa* was translated into English in Cook and Lee, *Short E. Afn. Plays in English,* 67–82.
26. Pub. in Gwyneth Henderson, ed., *Afn. Theatre: Eight Prize-Winning Plays for Radio* (London: Heinemann, 1973), 35–51.
27. David Cook and David Rubadiri, eds., *Poems from E.A.* (London: Heinemann, 1971), 200.
28. V. J. Inamdar and M. M. Patel intvs.
29. Pieterse, *Ten One-Act Plays.*
30. Henderson and Pieterse, *Nine Afn. Plays for Radio.*
31. R. Neogy, M. M. Patel, and J. R. Sondhi intvs.
32. H. Ahmed intv. Also, M. M. Patel intv.
33. A. Ribeiro intv.
34. The poem has been revised slightly since its publication in *El Peregrino* (Santa Barbara: Noel Young, 1971).
35. Letter from Peter Nazareth to Gregory, 14 Mar. 1981.
36. Gurr and Calder, *Writers in E.A.,* 21–22.
37. Ibid., 189. Kassam is the only Asian in *Who's Who in Afn. Lit.: Biogs., Works, Commentaries* (Tubingen: Horst Erdmann Verlag, 1972), 169.
38. Cook and Rubadiri, *Poems from E.A.,* 167–70, 200.
39. Nowarojee's poems are analyzed in Bahadur Tejani, "Themes from Indian-English Lit. from E.A.," *ACLALS Bulletin* 4, no. 3 (1975): 55–57.
40. For five of Kassam's poems, see Cook and Rubadiri, *Poems from E.A.,* 78–83.
41. Some of Tejani's poems are in Gurr and Calder, *Writers in E.A.,* 150; and Cook and Rubadiri, *Poems from E.A.,* 176–79. For Neogy's, see *Transition* 1 (Nov. 1961); 4 (June 1962); and 12 (Jan.–Feb. 1964). For Jagjit Singh's, see Cook, *Afn. Lit.,* 52; and Cook and Rubadiri, *Poems from E.A.,* 152–60.

Sequeira's poems were reported by Peter Nazareth to be published in one of Howard Sergeant's anthologies on Commonwealth poetry. Some of Datta's are in Cook and Rubadiri, *Poems from E.A., 35.* Virjee's, Talib's, and Mo Tejani's are discussed in B. Tejani, "Themes," 50-60 passim.

42. Mphahlele, *Afn. Writing Today,* 99-107.

43. For Kassam's, see David Cook, ed., *In Black and White: Writings from E.A. with Broadcast Discussions and Commentary* (Nairobi: E. Afn. Lit. Bureau, 1976), 7-10. For Tejani's, see *Penpoint* 7 (Mar. 1960); *E.A. Journal,* special lit. issue, ed. James Ngugi, Jan. 1968; *Ghala,* ed. Bethwell A. Ogot, 9, no. 1 (Jan. 1972); *Zuka,* ed. Johnathan Kariara, 6 (Jan. 1972); *Dhana* 2, no. 1 (Dec. 1972); ibid. 4, no. 1 (1974); and ibid. 4, no. 2 (1974/75).

44. Lino Leitao, *Goan Tales: a Collection of Short Stories* (Cornwall, Ont.: Vesta, 1977).

45. For Kassam, see Soyinka, *Poems of Black Afa.,* 362.

46. R. Neogy intv.

47. Cook, *In Black and White,* vii. Oza's two books catalogued by the Library of Congress are *Serfs of Kathiawar: Being Studies in the Land Revenue Administration of Smaller States in Kathiawar* (Kathiawar: Sadhama Services, 1945) and *Sheni and Vijanand, a Poem* (Bombay: National Info. and Pub., 1974). P. U. Oza (U. K. Oza's son) intv. For U. T. Patel, see Vaghela and Patel, *E.A. To-day (1958-59),* 611-12.

48. *Brief Hist. of the Devt. of Indian Settlement in E.A.* (Nairobi: Panco, 1961); and *Asians in E. and Cen. Afa.* (Nairobi: Panco Pub., 1963). The latter has a biography of Pandit, 201-2, and of Thakur, 268.

49. *In a Brown Mantle* (Nairobi: E. Afn. Lit. Bureau, 1972). For Nazareth's interpretation of his novels, see his article "Practical Probs. and Tech. Solutions in Writing My Two Novels," *Afriscope* (Sept. 1980): 49-51; and his interview in Lindfors, *Mazungumzo,* 80-97.

50. *Day after Tomorrow* (Nairobi: E. Afn. Lit. Bureau, 1971).

51. Pub. in London by Frances Pinter, 1973.

52. Ribeiro, *El Peregrino.* Sondhi, *Undesignated and Other Plays.*

53. *Lit. and Society in Modern Afa.* (Nairobi: E. Afn. Lit. Bureau, 1972); *Third World Writer (His Social Responsibility)* (Nairobi: Kenya Lit. Bureau, 1978); and *Afn. Writing Today,* ed., pub. as a special issue of *Pacific Quarterly Moana* (Hamilton, N.Z.: Outrigger, July/Oct. 1981). The first book was republished as *An Afn. View of Lit.* (Evanston: Northwestern Univ. Press, 1974). Nizar A. Motani, *On His Majesty's Service in Ug.: the Origins of Uganda's Afn. Civil Service, 1912-40* (Syracuse: Syracuse Univ. For. & Comp. Studies Program, 1977).

54. J. S. Mangat, *Hist. of the Asians.* Makhan Singh, *Hist. of Kenya Trade Union Movt. to 1952* (Nairobi: E. Afn. Pub. House, 1969). Nizar A. Motani, *On His Majesty's Service in Ug.: The Origins of Uganda's Afn. Civil Service, 1912-40* (Syracuse: Syracuse Univ. For. & Comp. Studies Program, 1977). Abdul Sheriff, *Slaves, Spices & Ivory in Zan.: Integration of an E. Afn. Commercial Empire into the World Econ., 1770-1873* (London: J. Currey, 1987).

55. Aga Khan, *India in Transition: a Study in Pol. Evolution* (London: P. L. Warner, 1918). Ambu H. Patel, *Struggle for "Release Jomo and His Colleagues"* (Nairobi: New Kenya Pub., 1963). Mahmood Mamdani, *Politics and Class Formation in Ug.* (London: Heinemann, 1976); and *Imperialism*

and Fascism in Ug. (Trenton, N.J.: Afa. World Press, 1984). Issa G. Shivji, *Silent Class Struggle* (Dar es Salaam: Tan. Pub. House, 1973); *Tourism and Soc. Devt.* (Dar es Salaam: Tan. Pub. House, 1973); *Class Struggles in Tan.* (N.Y.: Monthly Review Press, 1976); *Law, State and the Working Class in Tan., c. 1920–64* (London: J. Currey, 1986); *State and the Working People in Tan.* (Dakar: Codesria, 1986).
56. A. B. Patel, *Towards a New World Order* (Pondicherry: World Union Intl., 1974).
57. Yashpal Tandon, *Probs. of a Displaced Minority* (London: Minority Rights Group, 1973); Yash P. Ghai, *Taxation for Devt.: a Case Study of Ug.* (Nairobi: E. Afn. Pub. House, 1966); Dharam P. Ghai and Yash P. Ghai, eds., *Portrait of a Minority: Asians in E.A.* (London: Oxford Univ. Press, 1970).
58. Mehta, *Dream.* J. M. Nazareth, *Brown Man Black Country: a Peep into Kenya's Freedom Struggle* (New Delhi: Tidings, 1981). Mustafa, *Tang. Way.* For a collection of Uganda Asian writings that includes essays and poems as well as short stories, see E. A. Markham and Arnold Kingston, eds. *Merely a Matter of Colour: the Ugandan Asian Anthology* (London: 'Q' Books, 1973).
59. J. S. Karmali intv. The books are *Birds of Afa.* (London: Collins, 1980) and *Beautiful Birds of Kenya* (Nairobi: Westlands Sundries, 1985).
60. H. P. Joshi intv.
61. R. Neogy interview.
62. Ibid. For the trial, see *Times* (London), 1 Nov. 1968, 10; 23 Nov. 1968, 5; 10 Jan. 1969, 6; 3 Feb. 1969, 4. Also, Judith Nowinski, "Transition," Ph.D. diss., Columbia Univ., 1968.
63. Bahadur Tejani has testified to this: "The single factor most affecting the lives of the present generation of writers of Indian origin was the subjugation of their home languages in the school situation." See Tejani, "Themes," 46.
64. N. B. Rajay intev.
65. M. M. Patel intev.
66. Cook and Lee, *Short E. Afn. Plays,* x. David Cook, "Theatre Goes to the People," *Transition* 25 (1966): 23–33.
67. J. R. Sondhi intev. African writers' portrayal of Asians, which well illustrates the popular view, is described in Charles Ponnuthurai Sarvan, "Asians in Afn. Lit.," *J. of Commonwealth Lit.,* 11 (Dec. 1976): 160–70.
68. Tejani, "Themes," 49.

9

Contributions to Non-Asian Peoples

*The right we have to be in these parts is not
because we are here, but because of our ability
to be of real service to the Africans.*
—M. P. Chitale, 1944

*It is the pious duty of every member of the
Indian community to assist the African.*
—The Aga Khan, 1946

In their philanthropic considerations, the Asians were responsive to the needs of the other peoples in East Africa. As expressed in
Chapter 5, the Asians' contribution to education, reflecting their
charitable endeavors generally, expanded from an initial preoccupation with the needs of their separate ethnic groups, to a concern
for the entire Asian community, and finally in the later colonial
years to a humanitarian awareness of the educational needs of the
Africans. In the early years when their financial resources were
meager, the Asians had to concentrate on the welfare of their own
community. Later, especially after World War II, when they were
more affluent, they were able to contribute more to the other peoples. From the beginning of their settlement, however, the Asians
appear to have contributed generously to the needs of the non-
Asians.

Support of European and African Fund Drives

Throughout the colonial period the Asians were asked to contribute to a number of funds and institutions organized by the

British. Among those for which there was an annual fund drive were Empire Day (subsequently Commonwealth Day), the British Legion, the British Red Cross Society, the Baden-Powell Fund, the Kenya Girl Guides, the Kenya Society for the Blind, the Sailors' Fund, the East African Overseas Troops Christmas Fund, and the Royal Society for the Prevention of Cruelty to Animals. During World War I the East Africa Protectorate established a Patriotic Fund for the support of the war effort and an East Africa War Relief Fund for Africans incapacitated by illness or wounds during military service. In World War II Kenya set up a War Relief Fund. Earlier, to commemorate one of its most popular governors, Sir Robert Coryndon, the government instituted a memorial fund that culminated in the building of the Coryndon Museum. After the death of King George VI it formed a committee to collect money for a memorial fountain in Mombasa. In time of need the government sought contributions for a Kenya Famine Relief Fund, and at four-year intervals in support of athletes it solicited money for the Kenya Olympic Association.[1]

Other organizations sponsored by the British governments included the UN Children Fund, the Uganda Foundation for the Blind, the Kenya Heart Foundation, the annual Mombasa Exhibition, the United Kenya Club, the Nairobi Ex-prisoners' Aid Society, the Joy Town School for the Handicapped, the Thika Salvation Army School for the Blind, and various sports funds organized by the individual provinces.

After independence the African governments followed the British example by urging the Asian communities to contribute to new general welfare organizations, such as the Kenya National Fund, and to special drives in aid of the destitute and the disabled of East Africa and of Congo refugees. They also encouraged the Asians to support a variety of self-help ventures, including the Harambee projects.[2]

Despite a deep-seated resentment against the governments, whether British or African, for the discrimination practiced against them, the Asians donated to all these causes. In their quest for equal rights, they felt constrained to manifest an unswerving loyalty to the Crown or a succeeding African government. It is obvious, however, that the Asians also believed that the charities sponsored by the governments were worthy of support. The administrators relied heavily on their participation in any officially sponsored campaign and, with rare exception, appointed Asian leaders to the planning committees. In response to a particular request, Asian political associations and chambers of commerce sent letters to their members endorsing the campaign and soliciting contributions. After collecting the money, they forwarded it to the appropriate agency. In many instances they organized "flag-day" or "poppy-day" campaigns in which the Asian women and children sought gifts from individuals on the streets. Often the Asians gave far more than expected and provided valuable initiatives. As part of the celebrations for the visit of Princess Margaret in November 1956, for instance, the Mombasa Asians devoted Shs. 5,000 to the erection of a spectacular triumphal arch of simulated elephant tusks over the Makupa Causeway.[3]

Apparently, the Asians were only once accused of not giving their due share, during World War II with reference to the Kenya War Welfare Fund.[4] In 1939, shortly after the outbreak of war, the British inaugurated the fund, the proceeds of which were to be used not only in Kenya, but throughout the empire as need arose. As congress president Shamsud-Deen explained, however, many Asians were initially reluctant to support the war effort because of Britain's deferral of independence for India. "It is without doubt," he remarked, "the Whiteman's quarrel in which it is humanely impossible for the Indians to be involved with any zeal, enthusiasm or desire."[5] The Asians were also disturbed by the Kenya government's declared intention to evacuate, as a wartime measure, all Asians from the coast to an area near Lake Victoria. The proposed forced move was, the Asians believed, a manifestation of a lack of trust in their community. Though opposing a European suggestion of a £2 contribution by everyone in Kenya, the Asians in time liberally supported the war effort. Many Asian organizations created special War Welfare Fund committees and energetically collected money. Prince Aly Khan created in his own name a war fund, which by December 1942 amounted to over Shs. 140,000.[6]

Unfortunately, the Asian contributions to the governments' many fund drives are difficult to ascertain. The total collected for a particular benefit was seldom mentioned in the press or recorded in the extant government records, and the Asian organizations, while preserving a full record of their incoming correspondence, usually did not make copies of the letters that accompanied the remittances to other organizations. Detailed records for nearly all the charities are no longer available.

One of the major government-sponsored drives for which records have been preserved is the Coryndon Museum Building Fund. Soon after Coryndon's death in 1924 a committee was formed to consider the erection of a suitable memorial. It decided on a natural history museum to serve all East Africa. Although not enthusiastic about Coryndon, who as governor had strongly favored European interests, the Asians joined with Europeans in the campaign, with the result that the museum opened in 1930. The one building, however, proved too small, and in 1949 at the urging of the curator, Dr. L. S. B. Leakey, the trustees launched a fund drive for construction of a wing that would nearly triple the building's size. Their plan, devised after consultation with Asian leaders, was to include two major halls in the wing, one in honor of Churchill, the other in honor of Gandhi, and to establish separate funds for the purpose. The government made an initial grant of £5,000 and agreed to add £1 for every £3 donated by the public.[7]

Again, despite the fact that no one from their community had ever been appointed a trustee or been employed in any way by the museum, the Asians responded generously. India's high commissioner to East Africa, Apa B. Pant, was appointed to the fund drive's management committee. In a colony-wide broadcast for public support, Pant emphasized the value of the museum for all races. Then an unfortunate division occurred. The Ismailis refused to participate in a drive to honor Gandhi. Eventually a compromise was effected whereby a third fund for the construction of a separate hall in honour of the Aga Khan would be established. Under the new arrangement Muslims as well as Hindus joined the campaign. Among the many Asian organizations that responded was the Nairobi Indian Youth League, which declared a flag day and collected Shs. 4,929. In April 1950 the Asians organized and conducted at the site a grand fete, with food, drink, and entertainment, which alone returned Shs. 44,920 to a general fund. In the end the Asians contributed an additional Shs. 101,506 for the Gandhi Memorial Hall and Shs. 170,000 for the Aga Khan Hall. Their total was Shs. 315,436. The European community raised Shs. 82,754 for the Churchill Memorial Gallery, and the government granted Shs. 300,000.[8] The new wing opened in February 1952. After independence, although the whole was renamed the Kenya National Museum, the separate halls retained their Asian and European identities.

Some idea of the Asians' involvement in philanthropy as compared to that of Europeans can be gained from the lists of their societies. For instance, in Tanganyika the registered societies for each community in 1960, when the Asians were four times as numerous as the Europeans, reveal numbers considerably in the Asians' favor:[9]

	Asian	European
Cultural and scientific	14	9
Religious and charitable	147	22
Social betterment	57	16
Totals	218	47

Multiracialism in Asian Schools

Though designed initially to serve the educational needs of their own community, most Asian schools eventually adopted a multiracial admissions policy. The liberal evolution of the Mombasa Institute of Muslim Education, described in Chapter 5, is typical. The Asian institutions generally began through communal philanthropy as small schools restricted to one sex and one race and often to a single creed or caste. In time the governments became the chief patrons, and the schools were opened to both sexes and to Africans and other peoples as well as Asians of different faiths. The British colonial governments were factors of change in that, for all the schools they administered or aided, they stimulated expansion by subsidy and, with few exceptions, required a policy of admitting all peoples within a racial category. A cornerstone of British rule, however, was segregation of the races. The governments expected the Asian schools, like the European and African schools, to serve the educational needs of only their own community.

Near the end of the colonial period many of the restricted schools began to admit and assist Africans. The Allidina Visram High School became fully integrated in the early sixties, hired its first African faculty in 1965, and received its first African headmaster in 1970. Meanwhile it introduced Swahili as a language of instruction on a par with English. In 1965 its Drama Club, with Swahili productions of *Julius Caesar* and *The Merchant of Venice,* attained first place in the Coast Festival of Arts.[10] The transformation of the Allidina school was typical of that of other Asian institutions. By 1973 the Burhaniya Primary School in Mombasa had 152 Africans among its 581 students, the Bohra Primary Schools in Nairobi 49 among 147, the Arya Nursery School in Nairobi 107 among 207, the Guru Nanak Primary School in Mombasa 106 among 272, and the Goans' St. Xavier's Primary School in Nakuru 149 out of 325.[11]

The racial liberalization of most Asian schools occurred in the late fifties or very early sixties when it became apparent that a transfer of power was imminent, and one of the first educational measures taken by the new African governments, as expected, was to order an end to all racial discrimination in the schools. The liberalization of many Asian schools, therefore, can be ascribed to outside compulsion as distinct from Asian humanitarianism.

Some Asian schools differed from the norm in having an open admissions policy from the start, and many that began with restrictions moved to a more liberal policy well before an impending transfer of power was apparent. Because of their Prophet's emphasis on the brotherhood of all believers, the Muslim Asians were less racially restrictive than most non-Muslims. The traditional Koranic schools, many of which were administered by Bohras, usually served Arab and African Muslims as well as Asians, but since they offered only religious education and were refused all aid by the colonial governments, they were relatively unimportant to African education. Among the Asians who founded modern schools the Sunnis seem to have been the most concerned with African education. In 1929 they opened in Kisumu a Koranic school for Africans and Arabs as well as Asians, and since the boys were sons of poor laborers, the school charged no fees. By 1937 about 90 percent of the students were Africans. The Sunnis' Nairobi Muslim Girls' School, founded in 1930, was nonracial from the beginning and by 1954 had fifty-five African students.[12] The Ithnasheri Muslims also admitted Africans. Their Nairobi primary school, which opened in 1951, was about 10 percent African by 1958.[13]

The Ismailis seem to have been more restrictive, although they have claimed that their schools were always open to all races and creeds. The requirement that all students participate in a daily Muslim religious ceremony deterred non-Muslim Asians from enrolling, and the Ismailis' relatively high school fees, the instruction in Gujarati until 1952 in the lower classes, and the Asian milieu made the mission and government schools more attractive to Africans. Thus even after independence, in locations where alternative schools were available, the Ismaili schools included only a token number of non-Ismaili students. In the few schools where non-Ismaili students were numerous, such as in Kisii and Sultan Hamud, there was considerable friction.[14]

Among the non-Muslims several Asian communities demonstrated a genuine concern for African education. The Shahs were probably foremost. From the beginning of their intensive educational program in 1952 they freely admitted African students to their nursery and primary schools. As in the Ismaili schools and for similar reasons, however, the number of Africans in these schools was never large before independence.[15] In 1927 the Arya Samaj of Nairobi started a night school for Africans, which, incidentally, soon had to close because of European missionary opposition.[16] In 1956 the Kutch Gujarati girls' primary school in Nairobi began to admit Africans, and many others about this time removed all racial restrictions.[17]

Within the Asian communities there were a number of individuals who developed a close association with Africans and contributed significantly to their education. The contributions of the wealthy planter-industrialists to their African employees were extraordinary when considered within the context of world capitalism, but they have received very little publicity. Some other Asians, whose financial means did not permit so extensive a munificence, also promoted African education but have received no public recognition.

Nanji Kalidas Mehta, the Uganda planter-industrialist, was remarkable in his contributions to the education of both Africans and
Asians. At his sugar factory in Lugazi, where by 1950 he employed
as many as ten thousand Africans and two hundred Asians, Mehta
established racially integrated nursery, preprimary, primary, and
secondary schools. The nursery school cared for approximately
one hundred African girls. The preprimary, mixed schools, of
which there were eleven, enrolled annually from twelve to thirteen
hundred African and Asian children. In addition to forming and
maintaining these schools, Mehta paid for approximately one
dozen scholarships granted annually by the Ministry of Education
for the secondary level. Each year he sent several African students
to India, primarily to the Porbandar Girls' Institution he had
founded in his home city, but also, beginning in 1957, to various
Indian universities for higher education. In 1964, for instance, he
gave scholarships to five Uganda girls for study in the Porbandar
school. After matriculation one of the five returned to Uganda, but
two began midwifery training in Bombay, and the other two entered universities in Baroda and Ahmedabad, all with continuing
support. After Mehta's death in 1969 his sons continued this extraordinary educational program in their father's name.[18] As explained in other chapters, Mehta also donated generously to the
founding of schools throughout East Africa, especially those of the
Arya Samaj, and to the support of institutions of higher education.
    The Madhvani family, which rivaled the Mehtas in its commer-
cial, agricultural, and industrial empire, also contributed substantially to African education. In the late forties, after completing his
legal training and beginning to assist in the direction of the family
group of companies, Jayant persuaded his father, Muljibhai, to
open estate schools for their African workers. During the early
fifties at Kakira, where twelve thousand employees worked for the
Muljibhai Madhvani Sugar Works Ltd., the family thus established
a set of schools very similar to those of the Mehtas at Lugazi.
Perceiving the need for the training of Africans in technical skills
and business management, Jayant encouraged his father to found,
in addition, a technical school and a commercial college. The latter,
which opened in Kampala in 1950 as the Muljibhai College of
Commerce, became eventually the Uganda College of Commerce.

Jayant brought many of the graduates of this college and the technical school into high-level positions in the Madhvani companies. After his father's death in 1958 he founded the Muljibhai Madhvani Foundation Trust, the income of which was disbursed annually in scholarships and other educational grants. In 1971, following Jayant's early death, the family, as explained, established the Jayant Madhvani Foundation. The new trust supported students in agriculture, commerce, economics, and science at the secondary and university levels, and Africans were the main beneficiaries.[19]

Though lacking the financial resources of the Mehtas and Madhvanis, John Shamsudin Karmali, the Ismaili pharmacist who was introduced in Chapter 8, made a unique contribution to multiracial education. While developing their pharmaceutical and photographic businesses, Karmali and his wife Joan became distraught over the prospect of educating their children in Kenya's segregated schools, and they decided to form their own multiracial school. They encountered an enthusiastic response from Apa Pant and his wife Nalini, and also encouragement from three Kenya administrators — Mitchell, the governor; Sir Charles Mortimer, member for lands and settlement; and Sir Ernest Vasey, member for education — with whom they associated socially.[20]

The Karmalis' school, the first truly multiracial institution in East Africa, opened as a nursery school in Pant's home in 1949 with six Asian and four European children. An annual grant was obtained from the government consisting of £97 for each European student, £34 for each Asian, and £4 for each African, and additional funds and assistance with teachers were provided by the International School at Geneva. After six months the school moved into the Karmalis' home, and a year later into an army hut that was purchased by the Asian parents and placed on land in Parklands donated by Mortimer. Subsequently Africans were added to the growing number of Asian and European pupils, and it was obvious that larger facilities were necessary.[21]

The government came to the Karmalis' aid. Mitchell promised to assist with buildings and approached the Colonial Office for a grant. Getting any support for a multiracial school, however, was difficult in colonial Kenya. Mitchell hesitated to bring the subject before the Legislative Council. He did not want to give "people of ill will," he confided, "an opportunity of wrecking the thing at the start." [22] Though Mitchell left office before the issue was resolved, his successor, Sir Evelyn Baring, provided a group of spacious buildings, former dormitories adjacent to Government House. He also continued negotiations with the Colonial Office, which awarded an initial grant of £7,000, another £3,000 for refurbishing the buildings, and £4,000 for recurrent expenditure.[23]

With its new official support the Karmalis' school, renamed at its new site the Hospital Hill School and directed by an Asian head-mistress, acquired a novel reputation. Beginning with twenty stu-dents, it quickly developed into a full-fledged primary school and filled its new buildings to capacity with an enrollment of three hundred. Within five years it was the top primary school in the colony-wide examinations, and Europeans, who earlier had faced social ostracism in supporting the school, were eagerly seeking admission for their children. On the eve of independence, when Kenya's nine European primary schools suffered a drastic decline in enrollment, the Karmalis applied to take them over. In the end they were accorded one, the Parklands School, which became the new Hospital Hill School. In the larger facility the school expanded to include 670 students and 21 teachers. In 1974, when most of its students were Africans, twenty-five years after its humble begin-ning, the school was taken over by the Kenya government.[24]

Financial Aid to Africans and Arabs

Many other Asians exhibited a humanitarianism similar to that of the Karmalis by contributing a much-needed financial support. The Aga Khan, after reorganizing his East African Muslim Welfare Society in 1945, donated Shs. 3 million to "African, Arab, and Somali" Muslims.[25] N. K. Mehta and Jayant Madhvani, as men-tioned, provided scholarships as well as schools for their workers. Kakubhai K. Radia, a leading Kampala ginner, devoted each year during the fifties about Shs. 10,000 to the educational needs of his employees and other Africans whom he knew personally. He con-tributed books, clothing, and travel expenses as well as scholarships for their study in India.[26] Girdhar Purshotan Mehta emigrated to

East Africa from Rajkot in 1920 and by 1939 had established his own wholesale and retail textile firm, Girdhar Purshotan & Co., in Kampala. He dealt particularly with the Ganda, whose language he is reputed to have spoken more fluently than any other Asian, and he mixed with them socially. Though not wealthy, he arranged many scholarships for higher education abroad for the children of his Ganda friends by soliciting money from other Asians.[27]

Lakhamshi R. Shah, the Nairobi industrialist, personally subsidized the education of about twenty Africans with whom he became well acquainted. One of them, B. Mareka Gecaga, was a clerk of a European doctor who cared for Shah's ill wife. In the late forties Gecaga received Shs. 4,000 from Shah to study at the London Inns of Court. He became an advocate and eventually chairman of the British American Tobacco Co. in Kenya.[28]

Another African, Abdulla A. Suleiman, has testified to the munificence of Sir Yusufali A. Karimjee. In 1953 Suleiman was one of several Africans who, after screening by the Zanzibar Indian National Association, received a Karimjee scholarship for study in India. Enrolled at Hislop College, he encountered in India about sixty fellow Africans from East and Central Africa with scholarships for higher education. Most were from Kenya and Uganda, and five came from Zanzibar. Having formed an All African Student Association, they assembled in Delhi in December 1953 at a meeting attended by Kenya's future president, Daniel arap Moi, and it future UN representative, Ojara Jaro. Suleiman returned to Zanzibar for a career in journalism.[29]

Zarina Patel, a remarkable Asian woman, differed from these other philanthropists by taking four African children into her home. A grandaughter of A. M. Jeevanjee and a physiotherapist, she was unique among Muslims in her marriage to a Hindu. Zarina and her physician husband, however, had no children, and she busied herself with humanitarian work for the Mombasa YMCA and then the Nairobi Lions Club and the National Christian Council of Kenya. One day the African servants in the Patels' beach home brought their children to Zarina to ask if she would help educate them. She eventually took three children from her own servants and one from the servant of a neighbour, brought them into her home, outfitted them, and enrolled them in the St. Augustine School, an expensive institution of United States origin which she considered the best in Mombasa. She was committed to educating these children through all levels as if they were her own.[30]

In addition to personal contributions of this kind, the Asians supported African and Arab students through their political, economic, and social organizations. The Indian Associations, Merchants' Chambers, and Chambers of Commerce situated in the larger towns helped needy Africans as well as Asians. The same was true of the Asian Social Service Leagues in Nairobi, Mombasa, Kampala, and Dar es Salaam. The Lions and Rotary Clubs, many of which were initiated and dominated by the Asians, provided a similar aid to students irrespective of race. There were also the Indian Women's Associations which in the larger urban centers subsidized African education. The Association in Kampala, for instance, formed in 1948 a school for African adult education and offered instruction particularly in English and family planning.[31]

To augment their support of African and Arab education, the Asians enlisted financial aid from the government of India. In September 1946 the East Africa Indian National Congress, cognizant of African educational needs, passed a resolution: "This Congress is of the opinion that it is vitally necessary to promote full understanding between the African, Arab and Indian communities and that periodical steps should be taken as early as possible to create an organization to work for their general advancement." [32] Pursuant to this resolution the Congress executive called a meeting with African leaders to discuss the means of implementation. The Africans, stressing an urgent need for higher education, made two suggestions: (1) that scholarships be created for African students in universities in India for studies in arts and sciences; and (2) that special facilities also be provided for African students for technical, commercial, and agricultural studies in India. At the suggestion of the Congress leaders, the Africans then composed a letter to Nehru, vice president in India's interim government, and forwarded it through India's high commissioner to South Africa, Raja Sir Maharaj Singh, who in late 1946 was on an official visit to East Africa. "As the dominance of illiteracy in our midst," the Africans stated, "has retarded our progress in all spheres of life, immediate efforts to raise our standard of education would be most sincerely appreciated by our people." [33] Nehru responded favorably:

> I agree with you that cordial relations should be established between the people of Africa and the people of India, and I reciprocate fully the sentiments of the resolution passed by the East Africa Indian National Congress which you have conveyed to me. . . . I like the idea that African students should come to the universities and technical institutes of India.[34]

At Nehru's direction the government of India promptly devised an educational program in which the Indian government and private institutions would combine with wealthy Asians of East and Central Africa in offering scholarships for study in India. The scheme was announced early in 1949 in a thirty-one-page pamphlet issued by Apa Pant as the new high commissioner. There were to be eight Indian government scholarships annually for indigenous students from British East and Central Africa. Seven would be general awards to serve the interests of the particular students, and one would be specifically for the study of Indian culture. In addition, a number of private organizations in India would offer scholarships. The Charutar Mandal Vallabhvidyenagar of the Gujarat, for instance, would donate two scholarships for Africans from East Africa for the study of commerce and engineering. Moreover, several Indian universities and technical schools would grant free tuition and maintenance. Each scholarship would guarantee free tuition as well as a monthly stipend of Shs. 300, but students would be expected to provide their own travel costs.[35]

The pamphlet also listed the financial aid that would be provided to Africans and Arabs by the local Asians. From Kenya Meghji Pethraj Shah would offer five scholarships of one-year each for mechanical and electrical engineering, and Hemraj Nathoobhai Shah would bestow a four-year scholarship in agriculture. From Uganda Muljibhai Madhvani would provide two scholarships, one general and one in engineering for the durations of the courses, Chandulal Kalidas Patel and Narain Dass Raja Ram would each offer a four-year scholarship in agriculture, and the Uganda Commercial Co., an Asian concern, would support a five-year scholarship in engineering. Although there were no offerings from Asians in Tanganyika and Zanzibar, there were three from Nyasaland, two from Southern Rhodesia, and one from Northern Rhodesia.[36]

Beginning in 1947 African students from East and Central Africa, increasing in number each year, went to India on scholarship for a higher education in academic or technical subjects. In 1947 the number from East Africa was only 5, but by 1960 there were 31 new awards annually— 15 for Kenya, 7 Uganda, 6 Tanganyika, and 3 Zanzibar — and the African students then studying in India included 73 Kenyans, 66 Ugandans, and 32 Tanganyikans.[37] Although these numbers are not large in proportion to the Africans' need, they are very significant in comparison to the aid to Africans from other sources. In 1955 when the Indian government was supporting 39 Kenya Africans, the Kenya government was providing bursaries totalling £5,774 to only 13 Africans for overseas education, and the United Kingdom, through its Colonial Development and Welfare Fund, was aiding only 15. Apart from the government's bursaries, and an insignificant provision for loans, the only non-Asian aid from Kenya for higher education overseas was the support of 8 students by the African District Councils. There were in 1955 a total of 110 Kenya Africans in higher education abroad, with 48 in India and Pakistan, but only 45 in the United Kingdom, 1 in South Africa, and 16 in other countries.[38] Apparently, the Kenya government, in common with the other East African territories, was relying on Makerere College in Kampala to serve the higher education needs of the Africans. In 1955 there were 194 Kenya Africans at Makerere.[39]

Although it would be an exaggeration to aver that the Asian community of East Africa in combination with the government of India provided the principal support for African higher education in the colonial period, the aid certainly was extensive in comparison with that from other sources. It definitely exceeded that which came directly from the United Kingdom. During the closing years of colonialism as the Africans were permitted a share in administration, the local governments greatly increased their aid to Africans for higher education, but India did the same. In 1960, for instance, India awarded 140 scholarships to students in 47 countries. Among the recipients were 10 Africans from Kenya, 7 from Uganda, 6 from Tanganyika, and 3 from Zanzibar.[40] Moreover, beginning in 1956, Pakistan followed India with a similar, though more modest program of scholarships for Africans. The number of Kenya Africans on scholarship in Pakistan increased from 1 in 1956 to 7 in 1958.[41]

Even in Tanganyika where the Asian community was the least affluent, the Indian aid to higher education was impressive. In 1960/61, the last year before independence, the Tanganyika government, with a greatly expanded program, supported 159 Africans at Makerere and 6 at the Royal Technical College in Nairobi. It also supported 90 Africans in higher education overseas, mainly in Britain. The United Kingdom that year granted scholarships to 21 Tanganyika Africans through its Colonial Technical Training Scheme and its Commonwealth Scholarships. Local Christian missions, none of which, incidentally, was based in Britain, aided 57 Africans for overseas study mainly in theology. The government of India granted Tanganyika Africans 22 scholarships, Pakistan provided 10, and the Ahmadiyya Muslim Mission 1, a total of 33 for study in South Asia. Unlike in Kenya and Uganda, there were no wealthy Tanganyika Asians who subsidized the Africans' higher education. The Aga Khan and A. Y. A. Karimjee provided many scholarships — 29 and 14 respectively in 1960-61 — but only for Asians. Presumably, there were Asians in Tanganyika who, like those in Kenya and Uganda, contributed privately to the Africans' study abroad, but their gifts do not appear in the statistics.[42]

When all is considered, the Asians' contribution in schools and scholarships to the development of East Africa appears very considerable. Whether the schools were restricted in enrollment or were multi-racial now appears somewhat irrelevant. Eventually all the schools, more than two hundred throughout East Africa, with their buildings, grounds, equipment, and teaching and administrative personnel were converted fully to the service of the new nations. In 1958 in Kenya alone there were 151 of the Asian schools accommodating 47,400 students in contrast to 49 European schools with 11,500 students, and 12 Arab schools with 2,700 students.[43] The Asian schools, and the many forms of financial aid with which the students were supported, obviously were important to the evolution of a learned and skilled citizenry.

Notes

1. The government's requests for funds and the Asians' response are scattered through the records of the EAINC (SU microfilm 1929), the Nairobi Cen. Chamb. of Commerce (film 1924), the Nairobi Ind. Assoc. (film 1929), and the Mombasa and Kisumu Ind. Assocs. (films 1926 and 2232). Some are also in the *E. Afn. Standard* (film 1627) and the *Kenya Daily Mail* (film 2283).
2. D. N. Mehta intv. Other Asians have testified to this.
3. A. V. Ratcliffe (town clerk) to S. T. Inamdar (hon. sec., Mombasa Ind. Assoc.), 25 Oct. 1956, and other corresp., Momb. Ind. Assoc. records, film 1926, reel 4.
4. *E. Afn. Standard,* 29 Mar. 1940, 7; 5 July 1940, 8; 16 Oct. 1940, 4. See also comments by B. Martis and A. A. Jeevanjee on editorial of 22 April accusing Asians of exploiting the British in wartime by requesting independence: *E. Afn. Standard,* 1 May 1940, 7. Suraj Perkash Talwar to editor, ibid., 14 Feb. 1940, 7. S. H. Fazan (prov. commr., Nyanza) to dist. commrs., Nyanza, 16 Apr. 1942, Kisumu Ind. Assoc. records, film 2232, reel 3.
5. *EAINC: Presidential Address Delivered by the Hon'ble Shamsud-Deen at the 16th Ses. Held at Nairobi, Kenya Colony, on 14th, 15th and 16th Jan. 1944* (pamphlet, Nairobi: Mercury Press, 1944), 22.
6. *E. Afn. Standard,* 4 Oct. 1940, 7; 6 Nov. 1940, 7; 9 Nov. 1940 (two), 7; 20 Oct. 1940, 7; 22 Nov. 1940, 14; 25 Dec. 1942, 5.
7. Benarsi Dass (hon. gen. sec., Ind. Youth League, Nairobi) to gen. sec., EAINC, 1 Nov. 1949, EAINC records, film 1929, reel 11. *Museum's Trustees of Kenya: Coryndon Museum Nairobi Annual Rept. for 1953.*
8. *Kenya Daily Mail* (Momb.), 25 Mar. 1949, 1; 23 Dec. 1927, 2, 12. *E. Afn. Standard,* 17 Feb. 1950, 11; 3 Mar. 1950, 5; B. Jamna Dass to editor, 18 Apr. 1950, 4.
9. Tang., *Annual Rept. of the Regstr. General's Div., 1960,* 51.
10. Naronha, *Fifty Years,* 49, 53.
11. Abreau, *Role of Self-Help,* 76, 78, 102, 116, 180.
12. Ibid., 80.
13. Ibid., 72.
14. Ibid., 66–70.
15. L. R. Shah intv.
16. Abreau, *Role of Self-Help,* 101.
17. Ibid., 127.
18. D. N. Mehta intv. K. N. K. Mehta intv.
19. Edwin de Souza, "Jayant Madhvani—the Educationist," chap. 14 in Joshi, Kotecha, and Paumo *Jayant Muljibhai Madhvani,* 26-27. *Uganda Argus* clippings, c. 11 Sep. 1971 and c. 23 Aug. 1971, ibid., 319. Supplemented by H. P. Joshi intv.
20. J. S. Karmali intv.
21. Ibid.
22. Mitchell to Oliver Lyttelton (sec. of st. for cols.), 14 Feb. 1952, file "C.D.&W.

Grant for an Inter-racial Kindergarten & Primary School in Nairobi, Kenya, 1952-53," C.O. 822/691.
23. J. S. Karmali intv.
24. Ibid.
25. Shanti Pandit, ed., *Asians in E. and Cen. Africa* (Nairobi: Panco, 1961), 66.
26. Radia, intv.
27. S. G. Mehta (son of G. P. Mehta) intv.
28. L. R. Shah intv.
29. A. A. Suleiman intv.
30. Z. Patel, intv.
31. Mrs. D. Kotecha, intv.
32. Quoted, *E. Afn. Standard,* "India Supplement," 20 Feb. 1960, iv.
33. Quoted, ibid.
34. Quoted, Commr. for Govt. of India in Brit. E.A., *Scheme of Cultural Scholarships for Brit. E. and Cen. Afn. Territories* (Nairobi: Zenith, 1949).
35. Ibid.
36. Ibid.
37. *E. Afn. Standard,* "India Supplement," iv.
38. Kenya, *Educ. Dept. Annual Summary 1955* (Nairobi: Govt. Ptr., 1957), 22.
39. Ibid., 21. In 1958 there were 826 students at Makerere—316 from Kenya, 216 Tang., 272 Ug., 16 Zan., and 6 other countries. Among them were 48 Asians, 10 Arabs, and 4 Europeans. Kenya, *Rept. of the Working Party on Higher Educ. in E.A., July-August, 1958* (Nairobi: Govt. Ptr., 1959), 19.
40. *E. Afn. Standard,* "India Supplement," iv.
41. Kenya, *Educ. Dept. Annual Summary 1956* (Nairobi: Govt. Ptr., 1957), p. 21; *1958,* 14.
42. Tang. Dept. of Educ., *List of Students Studying outside the Territory 1960/61* (Dar es Salaam: Govt. Ptr., 1961).
43. Kenya, *Educ. Dept. Annual Summary 1958* (Nairobi: Govt. Ptr., 1959), 4–8.

10

Conclusion

> *Generosity starts at home and spreads out to our relations, then to our friends, then to our immediate community, then to society as a whole. . . . Business . . . provides a way to benefit society by spreading the economic and human benefits generated by our enterprises throughout the peoples of the world.*
> —Shamil Chandaria, 1985

The past century has been the most important in the history of East Africa. It was a period of momentous change as the Africans adopted many aspects of the Western culture that had evolved during Europe's modern age. It was also a time of intense racial conflict as Europeans, Asians, Arabs, and Africans vied for a dominant position. Much of the transformation, both positive and negative, can be ascribed to the impact of European colonialism, and much to African, and possibly Arab, initiatives. But the Asians were important catalysts in producing the more positive economic and social changes associated with development. For this reason, not only from the view of their own history, but also from that of the African transformation, there is some justification for calling this century the Asian era of East Africa. As the foregoing chapters reveal, there is reason also to characterize it as East Africa's age of philanthropy.

This history has had to be limited mainly to the nature and magnitude of the contributions. Little specific information is available on the financial holdings of the Asian companies. Nearly all the Asians' financial organizations were private rather than public, and the colonial and succeeding independent governments did not require or maintain detailed statistics on the private concerns. Moreover, in the colonial and postcolonial environments, where the governments impeded private enterprise with many fees and regulations and where there was open discrimination in favor first of the European residents and then of the Africans, the Asians concealed as much of their business activity as possible. Most kept their accounts in Gujarati and, on retiring or leaving East Africa, nearly always destroyed their records.

The Asians' participation in the development of East Africa is usually assessed in economic and political terms. Though only now achieving recognition, the economic contribution was appreciable. As the main people engaged in commerce, the Asians contributed to the development of importing-exporting and retailing-wholesaling. They developed an extensive system of credit for the benefit of their business associates and customers. They not only provided most of the economic enterprise in the towns and cities, but they also expanded this activity into the rural areas often beyond the sphere of government protection. In furtherance of trade the Asians pioneered in the development of road transport, which quickly became more economical than the government-owned railways. Through road transport they helped open the African areas to the importation of foreign manufactures and the exportation of cash crops. As the principal artisans through most of the colonial period, the Asians provided a vital service in mechanics and construction, and they became the main contractors and builders. They occupied the important middle level of the racially tiered civil service. They participated significantly in the development of industry and estate agriculture, and they were among the principal professional workers as doctors, lawyers, accountants, and teachers. Perhaps above all, the Asians through mutual service, training, and example assisted Africans in forming alternatives to the colonial system of wage labor.

The Asians' political contribution also deserves more recognition than it has received. Their chief political aim may be characterized as a quest for equality. The Asians formed local political associations and chambers of commerce and, territory-wide, a congress of associations and a federation of chambers to campaign for removal of the various forms of racial discrimination and the implementation of a common electoral roll. They established newspapers to publicize their demands and organized trade unions for political as well as economic action during the years when political parties were prohibited. In these endeavors the Asians joined with Africans in seeking a general reform of colonial society. By example and direct aid they stimulated the rise of African nationalism. During the last colonial decade a majority of the Asian politicans, fearing a continuation of anti-Asian discrimination after independence, wavered in their support of African political aspirations, but an optimistic minority continued a close association with African leaders and vigorously campaigned for a transfer of power. In all the East African territories the achievement of independence should be ascribed to Asian as well as African initiatives. Perhaps even more to the Asians' credit is that they were primarily responsible for thwarting two concerted moves—the first during the twenties and the second during the decade following World War II—to federate East Africa under the European community's control and form a new white dominion on the model of the Union of South Africa.

Clearly, although it is accorded even less recognition than these economic and political attainments, the Asians' philanthropy must be considered an important contribution. Foremost was the Asians' role in creating the University of Nairobi, East Africa's first nonracial institution of higher education. But the many communal organizations that served the Asians' social and economic needs; the religious, social-service, and medical establishments; the primary and secondary schools, museums, libraries, and recreational facilities; the support of literature and the arts; and the contributions to European charities and to African and Arab education and welfare—all attest to the Asians' munificence.

Through philanthropy the Asians provided a valuable supplement to the welfare undertakings of the colonial administrations. This took the form not only of provision for institutions, facilities, and activities needed by their own peoples, but also of aid to Europeans, Africans, and Arabs in realms that were inadequately served by the state. From the time of their creation many of the projects were designed for all peoples without distinction of race or creed, but even most of those that originally were intended to fill an Asian need ultimately were to serve all segments of African society. In addition to these more tangible evidences of their philanthropy, the Asians exhibited a social responsibility and a methodology for its implementation, in effect a pattern of benevolence useful to others. They also provided, as evident especially in their support of literature and the arts, a vital transition between the significant European expression, which declined in the late colonial era, and the impressive African achievement after independence.

Unlike in Western societies, where philanthropy, at least in the industrial age, has been associated with a relatively few, affluent members of society, philanthropy among the Asians tended to be general through the society. It was not confined to any one religious community, nor to people in any distinct level of capital accumulation. On the whole, it was practiced by both rich and poor. It was as though everyone had assumed an obligation to give, and to give according to his means. Thus Asian philanthropy is explained not so much by factors that determined the unique motivation of individuals, as by those that affected the society as a whole.

The principal determinants of the Asians' philanthropy appear to have been their religious and communal heritage from South Asia and the British colonial environment in East Africa. As noted in the introduction, the Asians were representatives of South Asian cultures that placed a high value on charity. Throughout the subcontinent the sharing of wealth with the needy was incorporated at an early time in the traditional religious beliefs and practices. In the northwest, especially in the Gujarat, Kutch, Sind, and the Punjab, where inconsistent weather patterns, infertility, and high densities of population fostered poverty and insecurity, there was a particular need for the development of patterns of mutual service and benevolence, not only to care for the less fortunate, but also to promote the general welfare. Thus the Asians who left the farms, towns, and cities of northwest India, no matter how poor, brought with them to East Africa long-standing traditions of communal charity.

In explaining their philanthropy, most Asians have stressed the influence of their religions, particularly Hinduism, Islam, Jainism, and Sikhism. Others have argued that the colonial conditions of

East Africa, which offered unique opportunities for economic gain and emphasized Western culture, including the rationalism inherent in the Western world's modern age, eroded the traditional beliefs and practices, with the result that the Asians became less religious and more materialistic than their kinsmen in India. The Western influences in colonial East Africa, however, also prompted among the Asians a desire to reject the forces of change and to preserve and reinforce many facets of South Asian culture. The negative impact on the Asians' religious beliefs and practices was largely superficial. Most Asians learned to speak English, adopted Western dress, acquired automobiles, and gave other evidence of materialistic values, but nearly all remained deeply spiritual. Nearly every Hindu home had its family shrine, and Muslims faithfully attended the local mosques and observed Ramadan. Certainly, religion was an important determinant of Asian philanthropy.

The colonial milieu was perhaps even more important. As explained in Chapters 1 and 2, the environment offered a unique economic opportunity for the accumulation of wealth. Despite a land policy and taxation system that favored the European settlers, the Asians until late in the colonial period lived in a relatively free economy. With habits of industry and thrift, which were essential for their survival in India, with some experience in shopkeeping and trade, and accustomed to colonial rule, the early immigrants seized the opportunity to become middlemen in a trade, at one end, with the peoples in Africa and, at the other, with industrial and commercial concerns in India. Thus most chose not to resume an agricultural way of life, but to engage in some type of entrepreneurship in the general business of importing-exporting and retailing-wholesaling. Others turned to various forms of artisanry to serve the local needs. On the whole, the Asians prospered. In time they formed the bulk of East Africa's middle class, and some became very wealthy. There was thus a high potential for the development of philanthropy.

The welfare policies of the colonial governments created the essential need. During the colonial years the British administrations of Kenya, Tanganyika, and Uganda, and perhaps even Zanzibar, concentrated on promoting the economic and social interests of the European and African communities, with the result that the Asians, and to some degree the Arabs, were left to develop their own employment opportunities and provide for their own social needs. The colonial welfare state, unlike its counterparts in Europe, was racially selective. In this situation the Asians responded by forming communal organizations to promote their own economic and social interests, and mainly through these organizations they established their own educational, medical, and social facilities. Increasingly, as they became more affluent and were drawn into common economic and political endeavor, the Hindus, Jains, Muslims, Sikhs, and Christians combined to promote the welfare of the Asians in general. Eventually they extended their philanthropy to other peoples — to Africans, Arabs, and Europeans. Although this three-stage, chronological pattern is evident for the Asians as a whole, there were many exceptions. The Asians contributed to some European charitable causes very early in their settlement, and some of their initial philanthropic projects were designed for all, without distinction of race or creed.

That the Asians moved beyond a concern for their own needs to assume a responsibility for the care of other peoples is evident in many aspects of their history. The nonracial provisions in the foundation of the University of Nairobi, the open admissions policy of the Pandya Memorial Clinic and the Karmalis' school, the universal concern of the Nairobi Social Service League, and the African scholarships for study abroad are perhaps the foremost examples, but there are many others that could be cited.

The motivation behind these contributions of a humanitarian nature appears complex. The Asian religions, the egalitarian features of the Western Enlightenment, the natural human inclination to assist the less fortunate, and the example of the European peoples were important determinants. Self-interest was also a factor in that there were political advantages to be gained from cooperation with the peoples in power. It was logical to assume that support of European-sponsored fund drives early in the colonial period and of African related charities later would induce favorable responses from the colonial and postcolonial governments. Tax considerations, however, were not a factor.

Unlike Britain and India, East Africa offered no tax advantages for philanthropy. The Income Tax Ordinances, which were first introduced in Kenya in 1937 and in Tanganyika, Uganda, and Zanzibar a few years later, contained no provision for deductions from income of any money given for charitable purpose. In 1952 the imperial government decided to coordinate income tax by drafting one law for all the territories and assigning the management and collection of income tax to the newly formed East Africa High Commission. An Income Tax Committee was appointed in Kenya to review and suggest amendments to a new East African Income Tax (Management) Act. Chaired by P. J. Gill, the committee included five members, only one of whom, the Ismaili advocate K. R. Paroo, was an Asian. A. B. Patel, the Asians' foremost political leader, and J. D. Byramjee, the initiator of the Nairobi Social Service League, were among the four Asians interviewed, and the Asians' main economic organizations—the Nairobi Indian Chamber of Commerce, the Mombasa Indian Merchants' Chamber, and the Federation of Indian Chambers of Commerce and Industry in Eastern Africa—submitted written testimony. Presumably, they were among those who argued for a charitable deduction.[1]

Reporting in 1954, the Income Tax Committee recommended against any change in favor of philanthropy. It rejected deductions for charitable donations "arising out of the social customs of certain communities" because they could not "properly be regarded as voluntary" and were "more in the nature of obligatory payments." It also held that there were "practical difficulties" in viewing "voluntary contributions to a voluntary social organization as on the same plane as compulsory contributions in the form of income tax which goes to finance state services, including state social services." With these arguments it rejected the view, so long accepted in Britain, that there was in East Africa "room for voluntary as well as state social services."[2] The committee's recommendations in this respect determined the course of income tax law in subsequent years for all East Africa. Apparently, none of the independent governments introduced any changes in recognition of philanthropy.[3]

Within the colonial context, in which the rationalization for European administration was predicated on the transmission of the finer points of Western civilization to the "backward" peoples, and in view of their own humble beginnings in East Africa, the Asians' philanthropy appears remarkable. It far surpassed that of the local Europeans. It can be argued that the Asians were three times as numerous as the Europeans and that in comprising most of the middle class they were on the whole more affluent. Admittedly, some were very wealthy, but even in the last colonial decade, when the community was the most prosperous, the wealth of the average Asian appears to have been considerably less than that of the average European.[4] If the large British and multinational companies are considered, there was a potential for a sizeable European contribution.

Apparently, the very environmental conditions that fostered Asian philanthropy served to diminish that of the Europeans. The colonial state's emphasis on European settlement was an important factor. Primarily in Kenya, but also in the adjacent territories as far as possible, it created an economic and social structure to further the interests of a European planter class engaged in the production of export crops of particular value to commercial and industrial interests in the home country. The transportation and communications network, the customs, excise, and income taxes, the measures to provide and ensure a plentiful and inexpensive supply of farm labor, the segregation system, and the provision of medical, educational, and recreational facilities—all were designed to this end. In its association with the various peoples, despite occasional pronouncements to the contrary, the state applied a policy of European paramountcy. In this situation, far different from that in Britain or the United States, the Europeans had slight need, as far as their own interests were concerned, for either a welfare state or a system of philanthropy. Without such a system it was more difficult for them than for the Asians to devise private programs of assistance to Africans. This is not to say that the local Europeans did not engage in philanthropy. It is obvious in the foregoing chapters that they supported numerous charities, but much of their effort was on behalf of organizations, such as the Red Cross, that had no special concern with the local society.

Asian philanthropy itself diminished as the environment changed. After World War II the British governments in all East

Africa abandoned the relatively free economy that had prevailed until then in favor of what historians have recognized as a managed economy. In conformity with policies emergent in Britain, the imperial authorities decided that development in the dependencies would be achieved most expeditiously by government initiatives, control, and ownership. In the closing colonial years new regulations on private business combined with the development of cooperatives, government agencies, and parastatal companies in which the government retained a controlling interest increased the size of the bureaucracy, necessitated huge increases in taxation, and effectively terminated the free economy.

During the sixties and early seventies the new African governments retained all forms of the managed economy, adopted new policies of racial discrimination, and virtually destroyed the foundation essential for Asian philanthropy. Nearly all Asian activity on the Zanzibar islands ceased with the African coup of 1964. In mainland Tanzania the Asians were gradually excluded from government, trade unionism, and independent journalism after the 1960 election, but it was the Arusha Declaration of 1967 renouncing multiracialism, industrialization, and all forms of private business that heralded the end of the Asians' separate political, economic, and social identity. In Kenya the various forms of Asian political and economic organization dissolved in 1966 and 1967, when severe restrictions were placed on the Asians' business activity. In Uganda Obote's Africanization policies beginning in 1962 and his subsequent "move to the left" considerably diminished Asian political and economic activity, and in 1972–73 Amin's expulsion order effectively terminated the Asian settlement.[5]

Meanwhile, as these measures curtailed the Asians' economic, political, and social activity, other policies directly reduced their philanthropic potential. In common with the trend in other parts of the world, the governments assumed responsibility for social welfare, discouraged individual action, and welcomed private philanthropy only within organizations that they either initiated or sponsored. The individual entrepreneur, such as Allidina Visram, A. M. Jeevanjee, Nanji Kalidas Mehta, Muljibhai Madhvani, M. P. Shah, Indar Singh Gill, A. Y. A. Karimjee, or the Aga Khan, who had provided leadership for Asian philanthropy in the colonial era, was anathema in the new societies dedicated to African socialism. A few whose services were especially valued, notably the Madhvanis, Mehtas, and Chandarias, were allowed to continue some of their economic activities and philanthropy, but nearly all had moved their headquarters to other countries.

The policies varied from country to country. In Tanzania independence brought an end to all the private benevolent organizations. It was not only the Indian Associations and chambers of commerce that had to close, but even organizations such as the Dar es Salaam Social Service League, nearly all of which were directing most of their services to Africans. Under Nyerere's guidance TANU from its inception opposed all racial organizations, even the philanthropic, and after taking over the government it tried to channel all collective charitable activity into new, semigovernment service clubs. Even the local Indian Women's Associations and the Central Tanganyika Council of Women were merged into a new organization, the United Women of Tanzania, established as a branch of TANU. In Uganda during the decade preceding Amin's expulsion order, the many Asian organizations deleted "Indian" or "Asian" from their titles, solicited African membership, and continued, but with less enthusiasm, many of their charitable activities.[6]

In Kenya, as a similar transformation began during 1964, the government assumed a prominent role in social welfare by establishing the Kenya National Council of Social Services. Asians were encouraged to participate, and the Ismaili advocate Badrudeen Rajabali Suleman Verjee ("Jimmy"), beginning in 1967, served a long term as chairman. Through Verjee's efforts Kenya became a member of the International Council on Social Welfare, and Nairobi in 1974 was the site for the council's annual conference.[7] Although Kenya remained the least oppressive, its increasing restrictions on Asian enterprise combined with its system of state welfare to discourage and weaken the Asians' private philanthropy.

So the Asians departed from Kenya in large numbers as they did from the other countries, and Asian philanthropy as an important factor in African development was effectively terminated. By the mid-seventies the Asian population throughout East Africa had been reduced by two-thirds, and those who remained were mostly the very young and the old, the least productive segments of the Asian society. The Asians with the greatest potential for enterprise and accumulation, and for a continuing philanthropy, had moved mostly to Britain and Canada. Only in Kenya were there still glimmerings of an Asian philanthropy. From London the Chandarias have continued to administer their two Kenya charitable foundations, and the remaining local Asians have occasionally launched a fund-raising campaign for some public project. In 1988, to commemorate Kenya's twenty-fifth year of independence and Moi's tenth year of rule (the *Nyayo*), the Sikhs in several centers, for instance, erected monuments, the most impressive of which was the giant arch now spanning the main thoroughfare in Eldoret.[8] But these activities are insignificant in comparison with those of the colonial period. No one year stands out to mark the end of this history of Asian philanthropy in East Africa, but perhaps 1980 is most appropriate as signifying the end of the last important decade.

Though regarded at the time as a tragedy for the Asians, the exodus now appears less consequential in its harmful effects on the community. In Uganda and Zanzibar the Asians lost nearly all their property, savings, and means of employment. They were expelled with scarcely any of the capital they had worked so long and hard to accumulate. In Kenya and Tanzania the Asians left voluntarily in search of a more favorable economic, political, and social environment, but they too had to abandon their homes, land, businesses, and many personal possessions as well as a cherished way of life. Yet within a generation in the new environments most Asians, beginning in many instances with no investment capital, but applying what they had learned in East Africa and again stressing industry, thrift, family, and community, regained a position of financial security. In commerce, manufacturing, and land-holding some have acquired great wealth.

For East Africa the loss of some 260,000 Asians had more serious, long-range effects. The area no longer enjoyed the contribution to development stemming from Asian economic activity, political leadership, and philanthropy. Uganda, it has been said, was set back fifty years, and Tanzania's startling decline can also be ascribed, at least in part, to the absence of a flourishing Asian community. It may be argued, too, that Kenya's development was diminished not only by the policies that curtailed Asian enterprise, but also by the sizeable contraction of the Asian community.

Although detrimental in these ways, the Asians' departure may have conferred a benefit in improved race relations. During the late colonial years the Africans were increasingly resentful of the presence not only of Asians throughout East Africa, but also of Europeans, especially in Kenya, and of Arabs in Zanzibar. During 1961–63 the attainment of political independence successively by Tanganyika, Uganda, and Kenya considerably diminished the resentment against Europeans, and the coup of 1964 removed both Asians and Arabs from Zanzibar. During the ensuing decade, however, the popular resentment against Asians intensified on the mainland and culminated in the discriminatory measures that prompted the Asians' departure. Then the situation changed. The Asians who remained were no longer perceived as sufficiently numerous or influential to provide a serious economic threat to African aspirations. In fact, as their economies declined, the Tanzania and Uganda governments invited the Asians to return. Having adapted to their new environments, the emigrés, with few exceptions, ignored these invitations, but the Asian communities of East Africa have recently begun a moderate growth with the arrival of new immigrants from India and Pakistan. The racial problem is no longer evident.

In common with this problem, East Africa's era of philanthropy coincided with the rise and fall of Asian influence and may be viewed as terminating with the Asian exodus. The Europeans' philanthropic role, which was relatively insignificant after the transfer of power in the early sixties, concluded approximately a decade earlier than that of the Asians. The Arabs', though considerable in the early colonial decades, became insignificant after World War II with the decline of the community's wealth and prestige. To their detriment, the Africans were not permitted to succeed these peoples in philanthropy. The potential for an African contribution was curtailed in Tanzania and Uganda by the socialistic policies of presidents Nyerere and Obote, and in Kenya, though perhaps socialism is not the right word, by the managed economy and state welfare systems developed successively by presidents Kenyatta and Moi. It is true that in Kenya the Africans were involved in some

charitable endeavors. They donated their labor and money generously to the Harambee projects, and Moi initiated a charitable
President's Fund supported by private as well as government contributions. Since independence, however, neither in Kenya nor in
Tanzania or Uganda have Africans been able to form even one
private philanthropic foundation. Unfortunately, the retarding
policies adopted in East Africa have been applied in nearly all the
world's newly independent countries.

This study thus should be assessed in terms not only of what it
reveals pertinent to the history of East Africa and of the South
Asian peoples, but also of what it indicates generally about non-
Western peoples and cultures. The Asians' history clearly shows
that philanthropy is not solely a creation of the Western world. It is
obvious that the non-European peoples, when permitted an economic environment conducive to the accumulation of private capital, can develop an impressive system of philanthropy.

Notes

1. Kenya, *Rept. of the Income Tax Committee Kenya* (Nairobi: Govt. Ptr., 1954),
   1-2, 112-14.
2. Ibid., 42-43.
3. For Kenya this was confirmed in A. Shah (Avinash Shah & Co., certified public
   accountants) to Bachulal T. Gathani, 27 Nov. 1990, with copy forwarded to
   Gregory. Although the income of a charitable trust was exempt from income
   tax, the donations of the trust were not. See "Income Tax," *Laws of Kenya:
   Rev. 1986,* cap. 470, p. 117, sec. 10.
4. Asian per-capita income in Uganda in 1963 was £288 for Asians, £990 for
   Europeans, whereas total Asian income was £24.0 million for Asians, £9.7
   million for Europeans. R. R. Ramchandani, *Ug. Asians: The End of an Enterprise* (Bombay: United Asia Pub., 1976), 241. In Kenya in 1962 the percentage
   of taxpayers with annual incomes of over £400 was 68.4 for Asians and 92.2 for
   Europeans. Dharam P. Ghai and Yash P. Ghai, eds., *Portrait of a Minority:
   Asians in E. Afa.* (Nairobi: Oxford Univ. Press, 1970), 109.
5. These measures are explained in the author's forthcoming volume, *South
   Asians in E. Afa.: An Econ. and Soc. Hist.*
6. Mrs. U. Jhaveri, N. Dastur, G. H. Hemani, and Sir Amar Nath Maini
   intvs.
7. B. R. S. (Jimmy) Verjee intv.
8. Robert M. Maxon, professor of history at West Virginia University, contributed this information on return from a year (1989-90) of research and teaching at Moi University.

Bibliography

The following includes a full list of the government records, Asian private records, and newspapers that were used in the overall study of the Asians. There is also a full list of the major publications by Asian authors. Since the Asians were involved with almost all aspects of East African history in the period covered, it was necessary to be selective in citing other sources. An attempt was made to include only writings that provide information useful to understanding the Asians' philanthropy and to restrict the interviews to those cited in the notes.

Published Government Records: East Africa

Annual reports (Blue Books) (title varies): Initially published in Britain as Command Papers, they began to be issued in Kenya and Uganda in 1912–13. The first of Tanganyika, covering the period from the Armistice to 1920, was published in 1921.
Annual reports of the various departments of the central governments
Legislative Council Debates: beginning in Kenya in 1906, Uganda 1920, and Tanganyika and Zanzibar 1926
Official Gazettes: first published in Kenya in 1899, Uganda 1908, and Tanganyika 1919
Reports of local commissions and legislative committees

Published Government Records: Great Britain

Annual reports (Blue Books) for the East Africa and Uganda Protectorates through 1911–12
Reports of Royal Commissions and parliamentary committees, published variously as Command Papers, Colonial Reports, or House of Commons or Lords Papers
Statements of official British policy, published as Command Papers

Statistical abstracts on Britain, India, and the British Empire 1890– ,
    published as Command Papers

Unpublished Government Records: Kenya

Annual, Quarterly, Handing-Over Reports: Syracuse Univ. microfilm
    (SUM) 2801
Daily Correspondence of Provincial and District Officers
    Central Province: Syracuse Univ. microfilm (SUM) 4751
    Coast (Seyidie) Province: SUM 1995, 4759
    Northern Province: SUM 4753
    Nyanza Province: SUM 1949, 2800
    Rift Valley Province: SUM 4752
    Southern Province: SUM 2804
Intelligence Reports: SUM 2805
Local Authority Records: SUM 2246
Miscellaneous Correspondence: SUM 2802
Registry of Trade Unions: SUM 2081
Secretariat Circulars: SUM 2807

Unpublished British Government Records: Tanganyika

Secretariat Files, 1916–53
Provincial Files
    Central Province (Dodoma)
    Eastern Province (Morogoro)
    Lake Province (Mwanza)
    Northern Province (Arusha)
    Tanga Province (Tanga)
    Western Province (Tabora)
District, Area, and Regional Files

Bagamoyo	Karagwe	Mbeya
Bukoba	Lindi	Pangani
Iringa	Lushoto	

Unpublished Government Records in Britain

Kenya

C.O. 533: original correspondence, 1905–
C.O. 630: sessional papers, 1903–

Tanganyika

C.O. 691: original correspondence, 1916–
C.O. 736: sessional papers, 1918–

Uganda

C.O. 536: original correspondence, 1905–
C.O. 537: railway original correspondence, 1895–1905
C.O. 685: sessional papers, 1918–

Zanzibar

C.O. 618: original correspondence, 1913–
C.O. 688: sessional papers, 1909–

General

C.O. 822: (East Africa) original correspondence, 1927–
F.O.   2: (Africa) original correspondence, 1895–1905
F.O. 84: (Africa) slave trade, 1880–92
F.O. 367: (Africa: New Series) original correspondence, 1906–13

Asian Unpublished Records

East Africa Indian National Congress: SU microfilm (SUM) 1929
Congress Supplemental Records: SUM 2085
Federation of Indian Chambers of Commerce and Industry of Eastern
    Africa: SUM 1923
Kisumu Indian Association: SUM 2232
Mombasa Indian Association: SUM 1926
Mombasa Indian Merchants' Chamber: SUM 1922
Nairobi Central Chamber of Commerce: SUM 1924
Nairobi Indian Association: SUM 1929
Nakuru Indian Association: SUM 2081
Zafrud-Deen Papers: SUM 2174

Newspapers

East African Standard (Nairobi)
Colonial Times (Nairobi)
Dar es Salaam Times
Democrat (Mombasa)
East Africa and Rhodesia (London)
Kenya Daily Mail (Mombasa)
Kenya Weekly News (Nakuru)
Leader of East Africa (Nairobi)
Samachar (Zanzibar)
Tanganyika Standard (Dar es Salaam)
Tanganyika Times (Dar es Salaam)
Tribune (Nairobi)

Writings by Asians

Aga Khan. *India in Transition: A Study in Political Evolution.* London: P. L. Warner, 1918.

Amiji, Hatim. "The Bohras of East Africa." *Journal of Religion in Africa* 7 (1975): 27–61.

———. "Some Notes on Religious Dissent in Nineteenth-century East Africa." *International Journal of African Historical Studies* 4 (1971): 603–16.

Chandaria, Ratilal Premchand, comp. "Chandaria Foundation, Chandaria Supplementary Foundation: Analysis of Donations, 1956–1983." Unpublished typescript, London, 1984.

Chandaria, Shamil. *Chandaria Family: An Introduction to the Foundation Stones of the Unique Integrated Modus Vivendum of the Family.* Geneva: Comcraft Publishing Corporation, 1985.

Desai, R. H. "The Family and Business Enterprise among the Asians in East Africa." *East African Institute of Social Research Conference Papers—Jan. 1965.* Kampala: Makerere Univ., 1965.

Gandhi Memorial Academy Society, *Souvenir Volume.* 2 vols. Nairobi: GMAS, 1956.

Ghai, Dharam, and Yash P. Ghai, eds. *Portrait of a Minority: Asians in East Africa.* Nairobi: Oxford Univ. Press, 1970.

Ghai, Yash P. *Taxation for Development: A Case Study of Uganda.* Nairobi: East African Publishing House, 1966.

Ghai, Yash P., and Dharam Ghai. *Asian Minorities of East and Central Africa (up to 1971).* London: Minority Rights Group, 1971.

Jamal, Vali. "Asians in Uganda, 1880–1972: Inequality and Expulsion." *Economic History Review* 29 (1976): 602–16.

Jeevanjee, A. M. *An Appeal on Behalf of the Indians in East Africa.* Bombay: n.p., 1912.

Karmali, John Shamsudin. *Beautiful Birds of Kenya.* Nairobi: Westlands Sundries, 1985.

————. *Birds of Africa.* London: Collins, 1980.

Maini, Sir Amar Nath. "Asians and Politics in Late Colonial Uganda: Some Personal Recollections." Chap. 8 in *Expulsion of a Minority: Essays on Uganda Asians,* ed. Twaddle.

Makhan Singh. *Kenya's Trade Unions 1952–56.* Nairobi: Uzima, 1980.

————. *Kenya's Trade Union Movement to 1952.* Nairobi: East African Publishing House, 1969.

Mamdani, Mahmood. *From Citizen to Refugee.* London: F. Pinter, 1973.

————. *Imperialism and Fascism in Uganda.* Trenton, N.J.: Africa World Press, 1984.

————. *Politics and Class Formation in Uganda.* London: Monthly Review Press, 1976.

Mangat, J. S. *History of the Asians in East Africa, c. 1886 to 1945.* Oxford: Clarendon, 1969.

————. "The Immigrant Communities (2): The Asians." Chap. 12 in *History of East Africa,* ed. Low and Smith.

Mehta, Nanji Kalidas. *Dream Half Expressed: An Autobiography.* Bombay: Vakils, Feffer & Simons, 1966.

Mohamed, H. E. *The Asian Legacy in Africa and the White Man's Colour Culture.* New York: Vantage, 1979.

Motani, Nizar A. *On His Majesty's Service in Uganda: The Origins of Uganda's African Civil Service, 1912–40.* Syracuse: Syracuse Univ. Foreign and Comparative Studies Program, 1977.

Mustafa, Sophia. *Tanganyika Way: A Personal Story of Tanganyika's Growth to Independence.* London: Oxford Univ. Press, 1962.

Narain Singh, ed. *Kenya Independence-Day Souvenir: A Spotlight on the Asians of Kenya.* Nairobi: Kenya Indian Congress, 1963.

Naronha, Francis. *Fifty Years: A History of Allidina Visram High School, 1923–72.* Mombasa: Huseini Packaging & Printing, 1972.

Nazareth, J. M. *Brown Man Black Country: A Peep into Kenya's Freedom Struggle.* New Delhi: Tidings, 1981.

Nazareth, Peter. *African Writing Today.* Special issue of *Pacific Quarterly Moana.* Hamilton, N.Z.: Outtrigger, July/Oct. 1981.

————. *In a Brown Mantle.* Nairobi: East African Literature Bureau, 1972.

————. *Literature and Society in Modern Africa.* Nairobi: East African Literature Bureau, 1972.

————. *Third World Writer: His Social Responsibility.* Nairobi: Kenya Literature Bureau, 1978.

————. *Two Radio Plays: The Hospital and X.* Nairobi: East African Literature Bureau, 1976.

Rizvi, Seyyid Saeed Akhtar, and Noel Q. King. "Some East African Ithna-Asheri *Jamaats* (1840–1967)." *Journal of Religion in Africa* 5 (1973): 12–22.
Sheriff, Abdul. *Slaves, Spices & Ivory in Zanzibar: Integration of an East African Commercial Empire into the World Economy, 1770–1873.* London: J. Currey, 1987.
Shivji, Issa G. *Class Struggles in Tanzania.* New York: Monthly Review Press, 1976.
———. *Law, State and the Working Class in Tanzania, c. 1920–64.* London: J. Currey, 1986.
———. *Silent Class Struggle.* Dar es Salaam: Tanzania Publishing House, 1973.
———. *Tourism and Social Development.* Dar es Salaam: Tanzania Publishing House, 1973.
———, ed. *The State and the Working People in Tanzania.* Trenton, N.J.: Africa World Press, 1989.
Sondhi, Kuldip. *Undesignated and Other Plays.* New Delhi: Orient Longman, 1973.
Tandon, Yashpal. *Problems of a Displaced Minority.* London: Minority Rights Group, 1973.
———, ed. *Technical Assistance Administration in East Africa.* Stockholm: Almqvist Wiksell, 1973.
Tandon, Yashpal, and Dilshad Chandarana, eds. *Horizons of African Diplomacy.* Nairobi: East African Literature Bureau, 1974.
Tejani, Bahadur. *Day after Tomorrow.* Nairobi: East African Literature Bureau, 1971.
Varghese, Mary I. Noozhumurry. "The East African Indian National Congress, 1914 to 1939: A Study of Indian Political Activity in Kenya." Ph.D. diss., Dalhousie Univ., 1976.
Walji, Shirin Remtulla. "Ismailis on Mainland Tanzania, 1850–1948." Ph.D. diss., Univ. of Wisconsin, 1969.

Other Writings Pertinent to the Asians

Abreau, Elsa. *Role of Self-Help in the Development of Education In Kenya, 1900–73.* Nairobi: Kenya Literature Bureau, 1982.
Bahadur Singh, I. J., ed. *The Other India: The Overseas Indians and Their Relationship with India: Proceedings of a Seminar.* New Delhi: Gulab Vazirani for Arnold-Heinemann, 1979.
Becker, Robert, and Nitin Jayant Madhvani, eds. *Jayant Madhvani.* London: W. & J. Mackay, 1973.
Bennett, Charles. "Persistence amid Adversity: The Growth and Spatial

Distribution of the Asian Population of Kenya, 1903–63." Ph.D. diss., Syracuse Univ., 1976.

Bharati, Agehananda. *Asians in East Africa: Jaihind and Uhuru.* Chicago: Nelson-Hall, 1972.

Chattopadhyaya, Haraprasad. *Indians in Africa: A Socio-Economic Study.* Calcutta: Bookland, 1970.

Clark, W. E. *Socialist Development and Public Investment in Tanzania, 1964–73.* Toronto: Univ. Press, 1978.

Cliffe, L., and J. S. Sayl, eds. *Socialism in Tanzania.* Dar es Salaam: East African Publishing House, 1973.

Cook, David, ed. *African Literature: A Critical View.* London: Longman, 1977.

————, ed. *In Black and White: Writings from East Africa with Broadcast Discussions and Commentary.* Nairobi: East African Literature Bureau, 1976.

————. *Origin East Africa: A Makerere Anthology.* London: Heinemann, 1965.

Cook, David, and David Rubadiri, eds. *Poems from East Africa.* London: Heinemann, 1971.

Cook, David, and Miles Lee, eds. *Short East African Plays in English.* London: Heinemann Educational Books, 1968.

Coulson, Andrew, ed. *African Socialism in Practice: The Tanzanian Experience.* Nottingham: Spokesman, 1979.

Delf, George. *Asians in East Africa.* London: Oxford Univ. Press, 1963.

Don Nanjira, Daniel D. C. *Status of Asians in East Africa: Asians and Europeans in Tanzania, Uganda, and Kenya.* New York: Praeger, 1976.

Fieldhouse, D. K. *Black Africa, 1945–80: Economic Decolonization and Arrested Development.* London: Allen & Unwin, 1986.

Frankel, S. Herbert. *Capital Investment in Africa: Its Course and Effects.* London: Oxford Univ. Press, 1938.

Gregory, Robert G. *India and East Africa: A History of Race Relations within the British Empire, 1890–1939.* Oxford: Clarendon, 1971.

————. "Literary Development in East Africa: The Asian Contribution 1955–75." *Research in African Literatures.* Winter 1981: 440–59.

————. *Quest for Equality: Asian Politics in East Africa, 1900–73.* New Delhi: Orient Longman, forthcoming 1991–92.

————. *South Asians in East Africa: An Economic and Social History, 1890–1980.* Boulder: Westview, forthcoming 1991–92.

Gupta, Anirudha. *Reporting Africa.* Bombay: People's Publishing House, 1969.

Gupta, Anirudha, ed. *Indians Abroad: Asia and Africa: Report of an International Seminar.* New Delhi: Orient Longman, 1971.

Gurr, Andrew, and Aangus Calder, eds. *Writers in East Africa: Papers from a Colloquium Held at the Univ. of Nairobi, June 1971.* Nairobi: East African Literature Bureau, 1974.

Harlow, Vincent, and E. M. Chilver, eds. *History of East Africa,* vol. 2. Oxford: Clarendon, 1965.

Henderson, Gwyneth, and Cosmo Pieterse, eds. *Nine African Plays for Radio.* London: Heinemann, 1973.

Henderson, Gwyneth, ed. *African Theatre: Eight Prize-Winning Plays for Radio.* London: Heinemann, 1973.

Hollingsworth, L. W. *Asians of East Africa.* London: Macmillan, 1960.

Honey, Martha. "History of Indian Merchant Capital and Class Formation in Tanganyika, c. 1840–1940." Ph.D. diss., Univ. of Dar es Salaam, 1982.

Hopkins, A. G. "Big Business in African Studies." *Journal of African History* 28 (1987): 119–40.

———. "Imperial Business in Africa, Part I: Sources," and "Part II: Interpretations." *Journal of African History* 18 (1976): 29–48, 167–90.

Hyden, Goran. *Beyond Ujamaa in Tanzania: Underdevelopment and an Uncaptured Peasantry.* Berkeley: Univ. of California Press, 1980.

Iliffe, John. *Tanganyika under German Rule, 1905–12.* Cambridge, Eng.: Cambridge Univ. Press, 1969.

International Bank for Reconstruction and Development. *Economic Development of Kenya.* Baltimore: Johns Hopkins Press, 1963.

———. *Economic Development of Tanganyika.* Baltimore: Johns Hopkins Press, 1961.

———. *Economic Development of Uganda.* Baltimore: Johns Hopkins Press, 1962.

Joshi, H. P., Bhanumanti V. Kotecha, and J. V. Paun, eds. *Jayant Muljibhai Madhvani: In Memorium.* Nairobi: Emco Glass Works, 1973.

Kabwegyere, T. B. "The Asian Question in Uganda, 1894–1972." Paper, History Assoc. of Kenya Annual Conference, 1973.

Kaplinsky, Raphael, ed. *Readings on the Multinational Corporation in Kenya.* Nairobi: Oxford Univ. Press, 1978.

King, Kenneth, *African Artisan: Education and the Informal Sector in Kenya.* London: Heinemann, 1977.

King, Kenneth, and Ahmed Salim, eds. *Kenya Historical Biographies.* Nairobi: East African Publishing House, 1971.

Kirkpatrick, Colin, and Frederick Nixson, "Transnational Corporations and Economic Development," *Journal of Modern African Studies* 11 (1981): 367–99.

Kitching, Gavin. *Class and Economic Change in Kenya: The Making of an African Petit Bourgeoisie, 1905–1970.* New Haven: Yale Univ. Press, 1980.

———. "The Role of a National Bourgeoisie in the Current Phase of

Capitalist Development: Some Reflections." Chap. 2 in *The African Bourgeoisie.* Ed. Lubeck.

Leitao, Lino. *Goan Tales: A Collection of Short Stories.* Cornwall, Ont.: Vesta, 1977.

Lindfors, Bernth. *Mazungumzo: Interviews with East African Writers, Publishers, Editors and Scholars.* Athens, OH: Ohio Univ. Center for International Studies, 1980.

Low, D. A., and Alison Smith, eds. *History of East Africa,* vol. 3. Oxford: Clarendon, 1976.

Lubeck, Paul M., ed. *The Afn. Bourgeoisie: Capitalist Development in Nigeria, Kenya and the Ivory Coast.* Boulder: Lynne Rienner, 1987. Includes chaps. by Kitching and Swainson.

McCormack, Richard T. *Asians in Kenya.* Brooklyn: T. Gaus's Sons, 1971.

Marett, Paul. *Meghji Pethraj Shah: His Life and Achievements.* Bombay and London: Bharatiya Vidya, 1988.

Markham, E. A., and Arnold Kingston. *Merely a Matter of Colour: the Ugandan Asian Anthology.* London: 'Q' Books, 1973.

Mehta, Surendra, and G. M. Wilson. "The Asian Communities of Mombasa." Chap. 6 in "Mombasa Social Survey, Part I," ed. Wilson.

Morris, H. Stephen. *Indians in Uganda.* Chicago: Univ. of Chicago Press, 1968.

———. "Indians in East Africa: A Study in a Plural Society." *British Journal of Sociology* (Sept. 1956): 194–211.

Munro, J. Forbes. *Britain in Tropical Africa, 1880–1960: Economic Relationships and Impact.* London: Macmillan, 1984.

Murray, Robin. "The Chandarias: The Development of a Kenyan Multinational." Chap. 7 in *Readings on the Multinational Corporation in Kenya.* Ed. Kaplinsky.

Naseem, Abdul Waheed. "Nature and Extent of the Indian Enterprise along the East African Coast and Subsequent Role in the Development of Kenya, 1840–1905." Ph.D. diss., St. John's Univ., 1975.

Patel, Hasu H. *Indians in Uganda and Rhodesia: Some Comparative Perspectives on Minority in Africa.* Vol. 5, no. 1, *Studies in Race and Nations,* Center on International Race Relations. Denver: Univ. of Denver, 1973.

Pieterse, Cosmo, ed. *Short African Plays.* London: Heinemann Educational books, 1972.

Pieterse, Cosmo, ed. *Ten One-Act Plays.* London: Heinemann Educational Books, 1968.

Pratt, Cranford. *The Critical Phase in Tanzania, 1945–68: Nyerere and the Emergence of a Socialist Strategy.* Cambridge, Eng.: Cambridge Univ. Press, 1976.

Rai, Kauleshwar. *Indians and British Colonialism in East Africa, 1883–1939.* Patna: Associated Book Agency, 1979.

Ramchandani, R. R. *Uganda Asians: The End of an Enterprise*. Bombay: United Asia, 1976.
Rothchild, Donald. *Racial Bargaining in Independent Kenya*. New York: Oxford Univ. Press, 1973.
Spencer, I. R. G. "The First Assault on Indian Ascendency: Indian Traders in the Kenya Reserves, 1895–1929." *African Affairs* 80, no. 320 (July 1981): 327–43.
Swainson, Nicola. *Development of Corporate Capitalism in Kenya, 1918–77*. London: Heinemann, 1980.
———. "Indigenous Capitalism in Postcolonial Kenya." Chap. 2 in *The African Bourgeoisie*. Ed. Lubeck.
Twaddle, Michael, ed. *Expulsion of a Minority: Essays on Ugandan Asians*. London: Athlone, 1975.
Walji, Shirin Remtulla. "Ismailis on Mainland Tanzania, 1850–1948." Ph.D. diss., Univ. of Wisconsin, 1969.
Wilson, G. M. "Mombasa Social Survey, Part 1." Unpub. typescript, Nairobi, n.d. (1950s). Syracuse Univ. microfilm 2081, reel 12.
Working Party, Dept. of Christian Education and Training. *Who Controls Industry in Kenya*. Nairobi: East African Publishing House, 1968.
Zarwan, John Irving. "Indian Businessmen in Kenya during the Twentieth Century: A Case Study." Ph.D. diss., Yale Univ., 1977.

Writings on Philanthropy in South Asia

Aptekar, Herbert H. "Mahatma Gandhi's Contribution to Social Work." Ch. 5 in *Soc. Work in India*. Ed. Khinduka.
Banerjee, Gauri Rani. *Papers on Social Work: An Indian Perspective*. Bombay: Tata Institute of Social Science, c. 1972.
Chowdhry, D. Paul. *Handbook of Social Welfare*. Delhi: Atma Ram & Sons, 1966.
———. *Profile of Social Work and Development in India*. New Delhi: M. N. Publishers, 1985.
———. *Voluntary Social Work in India*. New Delhi: Sterling Publishers, 1971.
Dasgupta, Sugata. *Towards a Philosophy of Social Work in India*. New Delhi: Popular Book Services, 1967.
De Mel, V. S. M., ed. *The De Soysa Charitaya or History Pertaining to the Lives and Times of Charles Henry de Soysa J. P. and Other Members of the de Soysa Family*. Colombo, Sri Lanka: De Soysa & Co., 1986.
Ghosh, Grish. *Ramdoolal Dey, the Bengalee Millionaire*. Calcutta: Riddhi-India, 1978.
Gupta, Sumitra. *Social Work in India*. Allahabad: Chugh, 1989.

Hindery, Roderick. *Comparative Ethics in Hindu and Buddhist Traditions.* New Delhi: Motilal Banarsidass, 1978.

Khinduka, S. K., ed. *Social Work in India.* Allahabad: Kitab Mahal, 1956.

Kohli, Madhu. *Voluntary Action in India: Some Profiles.* New Delhi: National Institute of Public Cooperation and Child Development, c. 1982.

Kulkarni, V. M. *Voluntary Action in a Developing Society.* New Delhi: Indian Institute of Public Admin., 1969.

Lala, R. M. *Heartbeat of a Trust: Fifty Years of the Sir Dorabji Tata Trust.* New Delhi: Tata McGraw-Hill, 1984.

Manshardt, Clifford. "Social Work during the British Period," chap. 3, in Wadia, *History and Philos.*

Mazumdar, Ammu Menon. *Social Work in India: Mahatma Gandhi's Contributions.* Bombay: Asia Publishing House, 1964.

Naidu, Usha Sidana. *Altruism in Children: A Cross-sectional Study of Boys in a Welfare Residential Institution.* Bombay: Tata Institute of Social Science, 1980.

Parekh, Bhikhu. *Colonialism, Tradition and Reform: An Analysis of Gandhi's Political Discourse.* London: Sage, 1989.

Planning Commission, Govt. of India. *Social Welfare in India.* New Delhi: Govt. of India Publications Div., 1960.

Saklatvala, B. Sh., and K. Khosla. *Jamsetji Tata.* New Delhi: Govt. of India Publications Div., 1970.

Shri Brihad Bharatiya Samaj: Inaugural Souvenir, Oct. 1963. (Bombay: Jaya Art Printers, 1963).

Tripathi, Divijendra. *Dynamics of a Tradition: Kasturbhai Lalbhai and His Entrepreneurship.* Ahmedabad: Manohar, 1981.

Voluntary Service in India. New Delhi: Central Institute of Research and Training in Public Co-operation, 1967.

Wacha, D. E. *Life and Work of J. N. Tata.* Madras: Ganesh, 1914.

Wadia, A. R., ed. *History and Philosophy of Social Work in India.* 2d ed. Bombay: Allied Publishers, 1968. Includes chap. by Marquardt.

Reference Works

Altbach, Philip G. "Literary Colonialism: Books in the Third World." *Harvard Education Review* 45 (1975): 226–36.

Derrickson, Margaret Chandler. *Literature of the Nonprofit Sector: A Bibliography with Abstracts,* vol. 1. New York: Foundation Center, 1989.

Hodson, H. V. *International Foundation Directory.* London: Europa, 1974.

Kenya, Uganda — Tanganyika and Zanzibar Directory: Trade and Commercial Index. Published annually or biannually, 1936–60. Nairobi: East Africa Directory Co.

Layton, Daphne Niobe. *Philanthropy and Voluntarism: An Annotated Bibliography.* New York: Foundation Center, 1987.

Pandit, Shanti, ed. *Asians in East and Central Africa.* Nairobi: Panco, 1961.

Sharan, Serving the Poor: Resource Directory. New Delhi: Sharan Voluntary Agency, 1986.

Vaghela, B. G., and J. M. Patel, eds. *East Africa To-Day (1958–1959): Comprehensive Directory of British East Africa with Who's Who.* Bombay: Overseas Information Publishers, 1959.

Wilson, E. G., ed. *Who's Who in East Africa, 1965–66.* Nairobi: Marco, 1966.

Interviews

The names in parentheses are those of the interviewers: Charles Bennett, Robert Gregory, Martha Honey, and Dana Seidenberg.

Acharya, Mahendra Bhanubhai. Nairobi, Baroda, London travel agent. 5 July 1973, Baroda (Gregory).

Ahmed, Haroon. Nairobi journalist. 3–5 July 1973, Nairobi (Seidenberg).

Bagchi, Ganesh. Kampala teacher, playwright. 22 July 1973, New Delhi (Gregory).

Bhatia, Lutof Ali. Saw miller, industrialist, son of Alibhai. 17 Sep. 1973, Dar es Salaam (Honey).

Bhatt, Gunvantrai Jayanatilal. Fort Portal physician. 22 May 1973, Nairobi (Bennett).

Bhatt, Hariprasad. Kampala auto parts dealer. 9 July 1973, Ahmedabad (Gregory).

Bhatt, S. M. Nairobi businessman, publisher. 18 Jan. 1973, Nairobi (Gregory).

Byramjee, Jamshed Dinshaw. Company director, social worker, civic leader. 24 Jan., 5, 13, 22 Feb. 1973, Nairobi (Gregory).

Chandaria, Devchand Premchand. Nairobi industrialist. 27 Apr. 1973, Nairobi (Gregory).

Chandaria, Keshavlal Premchand. East Africa industrialist. 9–12, 14 May 1973, Addis Ababa (Gregory).

Chandaria, Manu Premchand. East Africa industrialist. 31 Jan. 1973, Nairobi (Gregory).

Chandaria, Ratilal Premchand. East Africa industrialist. 16 Oct. 1984, 5 May 1985, London (Gregory).

Chande, Jayantilal Keshavji. Dar es Salaam industrialist; business, civic, and political leader. 7 Aug. 1973, Dar es Salaam (Honey).

Dastur, Nergis. Dar es Salaam councilor. 18 Sep. 1973, Dar es Salaam (Honey).

Datoo, Rajabali Gulamhussein. Nairobi glassware merchant, property owner, civic and Ithnasheri leader. 22 Nov. 1972, Nairobi (Gregory).

Desai, Ramesh Manilal. Nairobi businessman, Hindu civic leader. 14 June 1985, Nairobi (Gregory).

De Souza, Fitzval R. S. Nairobi advocate, politician, civic leader. 30 Jan., 6 Feb. 1973, Nairobi (Gregory).

De Souza, Francis Anthony. Kenya civil servant, M.B.E. 28 June 1973, Porvorim, Bardez Goa (Gregory).

D'Souza, Jose Pio. Nairobi accountant. 26 June 1973, Porvorim, Bardez Goa (Gregory).

Fazal, Abdulla. Bukoba merchant, manufacturer. 22 Nov. 1973, Upanga (Honey).

Figueiredo, Henry Souza. Kampala businessman, politician, Portuguese consul. 27 June 1973, Saligao, Bardez Goa (Gregory).

Gathani, Bachulal Tribhovan. Nairobi businessman, politician, business and communal leader. 20 Nov. 1972, 8 Mar. 1973, 6 June 1985, Nairobi (Gregory).

Gill, Indar Singh. East Africa industrialist, planter. 4 May 1973, Nairobi (Bennett).

Haji, Saleh. Iringa general merchant, political leader. 27 June 1973, Iringa (Honey).

Hemani, G. H. Dar es Salaam bookstore proprietor. 11 Jan. 1974, Dar es Salaam (Honey).

Hindocha, Devjibhai Karamshi. Kisumu industrialist, planter. 20 Apr. 1973, Miwani (Bennett).

Hirjee, Abdulla Rahimtulla Waljee. Nairobi businessman, property owner. 18 Apr. 1973, Nairobi (Bennett).

Inamdar, Vinay J. Nairobi insurance agent, arts leader. 31 Jan. 1972; 21 May 1973, Nairobi (Gregory).

Jaffer, Sultan Habib. Kampala insurance agent, civic leader. 9 Apr. 1973, Nairobi (Bennett).

Jetha, Hassanally Mussa. Mombasa businessman, Ismaili and Muslim leader. 18 Apr. 1973, Mombasa (Seidenberg).

Jhaveri, Mrs. Urmila. Dar es Salaam women's leader. 24 Jan. 1974, Dar es Salaam (Honey).

Jivan, Ibrahim Mohamed. Arusha merchant, sisal planter. 16 Feb. 1973, Arusha (Honey).

Joshi, Hariprasad Poonamchandra. Jinja teacher. 6 July 1973, Baroda (Gregory).

Kakad, L. V. East Africa manager, Madhvani branch operations. 4 July 1973, Bombay (Gregory).

Kapadia, Farrokh. Under-secretary, Ministry of Commerce. 23 July 1973, New Delhi (Gregory).

Karia, Natoo T. Kampala politician, businessman. 13 July 1973, Porbandar (Gregory).

Karimjee, Abdulkarim Yusufali Alibhai. Tanzanian planter, businessman, political and civic leader. 20 Feb., 20 Mar. 1973; 19 Sep. 1974, Dar es Salaam (Honey, Gregory).

Karmali, John Shamsudin. Nairobi pharmacist, photographer, educator. 10, 13 June 1985, Nairobi (Gregory).

Karve, Dr. Shankar Dhondo. Mombasa medical doctor, civic leader, politician, O.B.E. 26 Feb. 1973, Mombasa (Gregory).

Khimasia, Mulchand Somchand. Kenya businessman, industrialist, planter. 19 Apr. 1973, Nairobi (Bennett).

Kotak, H. M. Dar es Salaam accountant, civic leader. 18 July 1974, Dar es Salaam (Honey).

Kotecha, Mrs. Dogar. Kampala civic leader, educator. 13 July 1973, Porbandar (Gregory).

Kotecha, Kalidas Jinabhai. Uganda ginner, industrialist, exporter, planter. 9 July 1973, Ahmedabad (Gregory).

Kothari, Shantibhai D. Nairobi accountant, civil servant. 10 July 1973, Rajkot (Gregory).

Kurji, Feroz. Graduate student. 28 Feb. 1974, Dar es Salaam (Honey).

Ladak, Gulamhusein Rajpar. Kigoma merchant, industrialist, civic leader. 14, 18 Jan. 1974, Dar es Salaam (Honey).

Lakha, Aziz R. Kassim. Mombasa hotelier, planter, industrialist. 9 May 1973, Mombasa (Bennett).

Lal, A. T. First secretary, Indian High Commission, Tanzania. 22 Feb. 1973, Dar es Salaam (Gregory).

Lalji, Manubhai K. Mombasa journalist. 1 Mar., 28 July, 27 Dec. 1973, Mombasa (Gregory).

Madhvani, Nitin Jayant. East Africa industrialist, planter. 12 June 1985, Nairobi (Gregory).

Maini, Sir Amar Nath. Uganda advocate, politician, civic leader, O.B.E., C.B.E. 22 Nov. 1984, London (Gregory).

Mamujee, Akbarali Adamjee. Nairobi hardware dealer, Bohra leader. 19 July 1973, Nairobi (Honey).

Mehta, Dhirendra Nanji. Lugazi industrialist, eldest son of N. K. Mehta. 13–14 July 1973, Porbandar (Gregory).

Mehta, Jagnet. High Commissioner for India, Tanzania. 8 Sep. 1973, Dar es Salaam (Honey).

Mehta, Khimjibhai Nanji Kalidas. Uganda industrialist, planter, son of N. K. Mehta. 30 Apr. 1973, Nairobi (Bennett).

Mehta, Mahendra Nanji. Uganda industrialist, planter, parliamentarian, son of N. K. Mehta. 1 May 1973, Nairobi (Bennett).

Mehta, Mrs. Medha Dhirendra. Kampala civic leader, educator, wife of D. N. Mehta. 13 July 1973, Porbandar (Gregory).

Mehta, Surendra Girdhar. Kampala advocate. 10 July 1973, Rajkot (Gregory).
Munawar-ud-Deen. Karatina sawmiller, son of Zafrud-Deen. 9 Jan. 1973, Karatina (Gregory).
Naranji, Dwarkadas Kanji. East Africa industrialist, planter, civic leader. 18 May 1973, Nairobi (Bennett).
Nazareth, John Maximian. Nairobi advocate, politician, communal leader, Q.C. 12 Nov., 17, 20 Dec. 1972; 1, 14 Feb., 10 Mar. 1973, Nairobi (Gregory).
Neogy, Rajat. Kampala journalist. 8 Feb. 1974, Syracuse (Gregory).
Oza, Pushkar U. Dar es Salaam journalist, politician. 2 July 1973, Bombay; 8 May 1981, Syracuse (Gregory).
Pandya, Anant Jagannath. Mombasa politician, businessman, civic leader. 17 Nov. 1973, Karen; 27 Feb. and 1, 4 Mar. 1973, Mombasa; 5 May 1980, Syracuse (Gregory).
Pandya, Hansa. Mombasa social worker, wife of A. J. Pandya. 7 July 1977, 10 Aug. 1980, Syracuse; 13, 34 Oct. 1984, 1 Aug. 1985, London (Gregory).
Pant, Apa Bala. Indian high commissioner to East and Central Africa. 2, 3 Oct. 1985, Syracuse (Gregory).
Paroo, Kassamali Rajabali. Nairobi businessman, politician, Ismaili leader (count). 1 Mar. 1973, Nairobi (Gregory).
Paroo, Mrs. Kassamali Rajabali. Associated with the Waljee Hirjee and Rahimtullah families. 10 May 1973, Mombasa (Bennett).
Patel, A. Kalidas. Uganda ginner, insurance agent, planter. 6 July 1973, Baroda (Gregory).
Patel, Hansa. Nairobi advocate, actress, daughter of B. T. Gathani, wife of M. M. Patel. 8 Mar. 1973, Nairobi (Gregory).
Patel, I. S. Nairobi headmaster. 29 Jan. 1973, Nairobi (Gregory).
Patel, M. M. Nairobi advocate, playwright, actor. 8 Mar. 1973, Nairobi (Gregory).
Patel, Usha. Kampala resident. 20 Oct. 1984, London (Gregory).
Patel, Dr. Vithalbhai Raojibhai. Nairobi medical doctor. 5–6 July 1973, Baroda (Gregory).
Patel, Zarina. Mombasa, Nairobi social worker. 22 Jan. 1973, Nairobi (Gregory).
Pirbhai, Yusufali. Dar es Salaam hardware dealer, brush manufacturer. 25 Feb. 1974, Dar es Salaam (Honey).
Puram, Dr. Prabhakar Ramchandra. Tanzania medical doctor. 24 June 1973, Poona (Gregory).
Radia, Kakubhai K. Kampala ginner, builder, O.B.E. 12 July 1973, Porbandar (Gregory).
Raishi, Amritlal. Nairobi businessman, Shah leader. 25, 29 Jan. 1973, 7, 10 June 1975, Nairobi; 18 Aug. 1984, London (Gregory).
Rajay, Naval Bavant. Tanga industrialist, journalist, arts and civic leader. 24 Feb. 1973, Tanga (Gregory).

Rattansi, Hassan. Kenya businessman, planter. 3 May 1973, Nairobi (Bennett).

Ribeiro, Dr. Ayres Lourenco. Kenya govt. pathologist, civic leader. 12 Nov. 1972, Nairobi (Gregory).

Ribeiro, Hubert. Nairobi poet. 26 June 1973, Porvorim, Bardez Goa (Gregory).

Rizvi, Seyyid Saeed Ashtar. Dar es Salaam Ithnasheri priest, scholar. 18 Feb. 1974, Dar es Salaam (Honey).

Sachoo, Abdulrasul. Tanzania industrialist, planter. 29 Oct. 1973, Dar es Salaam (Honey).

Shah, C. P. East Africa manager, Bank of Baroda. 4 July 1973, Bombay (Gregory).

Shah, Dhiru Premchand. Nairobi industrialist. 10 Mar. 1973, Nairobi (Gregory).

Shah, Gulabchand Devra. Nairobi industrialist, businessman. 12 July 1973, Jamnagar (Gregory).

Shah, Jeshand Punja. Kitale shopkeeper. 11 July 1973, Jamnagar (Gregory).

Shah, Kantilal Punamchand. Nairobi shopkeeper, industrialist, property owner, politician. 7 Feb., 16 Apr. 1973, Nairobi (Gregory).

Shah, Kashi. Mombasa social worker. 4 Mar. 1973, Mombasa (Gregory).

Shah, Mrs. Kauchan J. Nairobi teacher. 29 Jan. 1973, Nairobi (Gregory).

Shah, Khetshi N. Thika industrialist, communal leader. 27 Apr. 1973, Thika (Bennett).

Shah, Lakhamshi R. Nairobi textile merchant, East Africa industrialist, business and civic leader. 27 Nov. 1972, 8–9 Mar. 1973, Nairobi; 30 June 1973, Bombay (Gregory).

Shah, M. L. Dar es Salaam businessman. 10 Jan. 1974, Dar es Salaam (Honey).

Shah, Maganlal Meghji Rupshi. Nyeri dealer in building materials. 12 Apr. 1973, Nyeri (Bennett).

Shah, Somchand Manek Chand. Nairobi provisions dealer. 6 Apr. 1973, Nairobi (Bennett).

Shah, Veljee Devji. Nairobi advocate. 19 Apr. 1973, Nairobi (Bennett).

Shah, Vemchand Khimchand. Nairobi shopkeeper. 11 July 1973, Jamnagar (Gregory).

Shah, Vinodrai Bhimji. Kisii hardware merchant. 11 July 1973, Jamnagar (Gregory).

Shah, Zaverchand K. Kenya retailer, wholesaler, exporter. 26 July 1973, Nairobi (Bennett).

Sheriff, Ali Mohamedjaffer. Arusha businessman, Ithnasheri leader. 22 Oct. 1973, Arusha (Honey).

Sheriff, Yusuf. Arusha, Moshi merchant, industrialist. 4 Jan. 1974, Malindi (Honey).

Sheth, Amritlal T. B. Dar es Salaam merchant. 19 Feb. 1974, Dar es Salaam (Honey).

Sondhi, Jagdish R. Mombasa builder, civic leader. 2, 3 Mar. 1973, Mombasa (Gregory).

Suleiman, Abdulla Amour. Zanzibar journalist. 31 Jan. 1974, Dar es Salaam (Honey).

Thakkar, Madhusudn Jethalal. Madhvani company manager. 19 May 1973, Addis Ababa (Gregory).

Thakore, Ramanlal Trimbaklal. Nairobi architect, estate agent, dramatist. 7 Feb. 1973, Nairobi (Gregory).

Thakore, Sharad. Nairobi businessman, arts leader. 8 Feb. 1973, Nairobi (Gregory).

Trivedi, D. S. Mombasa accountant, communal leader. 28 Feb. 1973, Mombasa (Gregory).

Vasanji, Gordhendas. East Africa sundries merchant, textile manufacturer. 9 May 1973, Mombasa (Bennett).

Vasey, Sir Ernest. Kenya European financial leader, politician. 6 Feb. 1973, Nairobi (Gregory).

Velji, Shirin Kassam. Dar es Salaam airlines employee, wife of Noorali. 4–5 Jan. 1980, Honolulu (Gregory).

Vellani, Akbar. Zanzibar clove grower, exporter, Ismaili leader. 13–4 Feb. 1974, Zanzibar (Honey).

Verjee, Badrudeen Rajabali Suleman (Jimmy). Nairobi advocate, businessman, Ismaili leader. 10 Apr. 1973, Nairobi (Seidenberg).

Versi, Bashir A. S. Dar es Salaam advocate. 4 Mar. 1974, Dar es Salaam (Honey).

Vohora, Krishan Lal. Arusha banker, coffee planter. 23 Dec. 1973, Arusha (Honey).

Index

A. M. Jeevanjee & Co., 52
Abdullah Shah Library, Nairobi, 104
Acharya, Bhanubhai, 78
Acharya, Mahendra, 78
Acharya Travelling Agency, 78
Actors: African, 171; Asian, 171, 179
Adams, Walter, 134
Africa East Publications, 177
Africa Samachar, Nairobi, 172
African Almoners' Fund, 58
Africanization, 79, 179, 211, 214
Africans: competition with Asians,
    32, 203; definition of, 162, 173;
    education, 109–10, 117–18,
    122; literature and art, 161–62;
    marriage with Asians, 32–33;
    philanthropy, 186, 214–15; re-
    ligious conversion by Asians, 32;
    reverence for Gandhi, 128, 143;
    study in India and Pakistan,
    196–99; trade with Asians, 22,
    26, 57
Aga Khan, 30–2, 40 n., 53–54, 57,
    92, 101, 105, 113–15, 120–22,
    165, 176, 185, 188, 194, 199, 211
Aga Khan Academy, Nairobi, 112,
    115
Aga Khan Hall, Coryndon Mu-
    seum, 189
Aga Khan Hospitals: Dar es Salaam,
    101; Kampala, 101–2; Nairobi,
    98, 101

Aga Khan Ismaili Provincial Coun-
    cil, 128
Aga Khan Kenya Secondary School,
    Mombasa, 112
Aga Khan schools, 115
Aga Khan Special School, Mom-
    basa, 58
Agarkar, Gopal Ganesh, 6
Ahmad, Mirza Ghulam, 32
Ahmed, Haroon, 172
Ahmadiya Muslim Mission, 199
Ahmadiyas, 32–33
Aid-India Fund, 81, 86
All African Students' Association,
    India, 195
All India Village Industries Associa-
    tion, 6
Allidina Visram & Co., 51
Allidina Visram High School,
    Mombasa, 52, 62, 112, 120–22,
    190
Aly Khan, Prince, 92, 187
American Council of Learned Soci-
    eties, 10
Amin, Idi, 79, 173, 176, 179, 211–12
Amin, Shivabhai Gordhanbhai,
    130–31, 168
Amins, 27
Anjuman Himayat Islam, 48
Antiques, collection, 163
Arabs, 17, 26, 29, 81, 92, 95, 102,
    203, 208; association with

Jivanjee, Mohammedali A. Karim-
jee, 49
Jivanjee, Sir Tayabali, H. A., 49
Jivanjee, Sir Yusufali A. Karimjee,
49
Jivanjee family, 49–51
John Mukungar Limuru Boys
Center, 59
Joshi, Harshad, 172
Joshi, Kashibai, 107 n.
Journalists, Asian, 35, 52, 172, 175;
African, 195
Joy Town School for the Handi-
capped, 186
Jubilee Insurance Company, 30
Juma, Khamius bin Mohomed bin,
122

Kabir, Prof. Humayun, 132–33
Kaderbhai, A. M., 118
Kaderbhoy, Abdulhussein H., 107 n.
Kadva Patels, 40
Kakira sugar estate, 55, 192
Kakuswi Harambee Secondary
School, 59
Kala Nikitan, Kampala, 165–66
Kampala Teacher Training College,
168
Kariara, Jonathan, 171
Karim, Shah, 30
Karimjee, Abdulkarim Y. A., 32,
49, 50, 106, 113, 199, 211
Karimjee, Hassanali A., 119
Karimjee, Tayabali Hassanali A., 49
Karimjee, Sir Yusufali A., 50, 113,
195
Karimjee Jivanjee & Co. Ltd., 49
Karmakar, V. P., 142
Karmali, Joan, 193–94, 208
Karmali, John Shamsudin, 177,
193–94, 208
Karman, Popatlal, family of, 107 n.
Karve, Dr. Shankar Dhondo, 47,
99, 100, 102, 107 n.
Kassam, Amin, 174
Kassam, Sadru, 170, 175
Kassam, Yusuf O., 174
Kassum, Alnoor, 114
Kathiawar, 16–7, 39 n., 83

Katz, Stanley N., 10
Kenya: Asian exodus, 212–14; gov-
ernment, 123, 148–55 passim,
186–88, 193–94, 198; indepen-
dence, 191; mutiny (1964), 76
Kenya African Union, 128
Kenya Aluminium Co., Mombasa,
87 n.
Kenya Business Aid Society, 62
Kenya Congress, 62
Kenya Cultural Center, 165
Kenya Drama Festival, 166–67
Kenya Eastern Arts, 175
Kenya Extract & Tanning Co.,
Thika, 87 n.
Kenya Famine Relief Fund, 186
Kenya Freedom Party, 35
Kenya Girl Guides, 186
Kenya Heart Foundation, 186
Kenya Indian Congress, 85
Kenya Muslim League, 45
Kenya National Council on Social
Services, 212
Kenya National Fund, 186
Kenya National Museum, 189
Kenya National Theatre, 165
Kenya Olympic Association, 186
Kenya Rayon Mills Ltd., 78
Kenya Society for the Blind, 186
Kenya Tanning Extract Co., 59
Kenya Technical and Commercial
Institute, 132
Kenya War Welfare Fund, 187
Kenyatta, Jomo, 101, 113, 214
Kenyatta Hospital, Nairobi, 98
Kenyatta University College, 113
Khan, Sir Syed Ahmed, 5
Khimasia, Mulchand S., 58–59
Khimasia family, 57–58
Khira Steel Works Ltd., 78
Khoja Mosque, Nairobi, 92
Khojas, 30
Khumbars, 33
Kikira sugar estate, 55
King George VI memorial founda-
tion, Mombasa, 186
King's African Rifles Hospital,
Mombasa, 97
Kisii, 25; schools, 112, 191

Kisumu, 25, 34; schools, 115, 129
Koknis, 33
Koran, the, 3–4, 32
Koranic schools, 190–91
Kotecha family, 102, 107 n.
Krishnan, Prem, 150
Kurji, Feroz, 40 n.
Kutch, 16, 28–30, 32–33, 39 n., 40 n., 50, 72, 206
Kutch Gujarati girls' primary school, Nairobi, 191
Kutchi Patels, 40 n.
Kutch-Mandavi, 49

Laborers, Asian, 33
Ladak, Gulamhusein Rajpar, 21
Lady Crauford Charities, 58
Lady Grigg Maternity Hospital, 96
Lakha, Rhamtulla Kassim, 78
Lalchand Moolchand & Bros., 113
Lamu, 18, 25; schools, 112
Lancaster House Conferences, 76
Language: English, 34, 117–8, 122, 166, 169, 172, 174, 179, 207; Gujarati, 29, 95, 165–66, 169, 172, 175, 204; Hindi, 95, 165, 169, 172, 174–75; Indian, 175, 179; Kutchi, 19, 31; Luganda, 32, 179, 191; Lwo, 179; Marathi, 29; Portuguese, 34; Punjabi, 165; Runyoro/Rutoro, 179; Swahili, 29, 31–2, 95, 128, 179, 190
Leakey, Dr. L. S. B., 188
Leitau, Lino, 175
Legislative Council, Kenya, 52, 102, 131, 193
Leper Society, 6
Libraries 54, 71, 84–85, 95, 103–6, 115, 205
Library and Free Reading Room, Mombasa, 103
Limuru Tanning Co., 87 n.
Lions Clubs, 29, 46, 196; Kampala, 46; Mombasa, 63, 195; Nairobi, 65
Literary societies, 161, 163–66
Liyong, Taban, Lo, 162
Lockwood, Dr. J. F., 150

Lohana (East Africa) Education Trust, 63
Lohana Welfare Youth Organization, 48
Lohanas, 28, 31, 64
Lotteries, Asian, 48
Lugazi sugar estate, 54, 138, 192
Lumumba, Patrice, 77

M. J. Doshi Charitable Trust, 106 n.
M. M. Shah Primary School, Mombasa, 60
M. M. Shah School, Kisumu, 60
M. P. Shah All India Talking Book Centre, Bombay, 84
M. P. Shah Charitable Trust, 105
M. P. Shah Dispensary, Mombasa, 60
M. P. Shah High School and Primary School, Thika, 60
M. P. Shah Hospital, Nairobi, 69, 96, 97, 100–1
M. P. Shah Junior College, Bombay, 84
M. P. Shah Medical College, Jamnagar, 84
M. P. Shah Primary School, Mombasa, 60
M. P. Shah Wing, Nurses' Home, Kenyatta National Hospital, Nairobi, 60
Madhvani, Jayant Muljibhai, 55–56, 151, 192–94
Madhvani, Muljibhai Prabhudas, 55, 62, 75, 83, 85, 113, 137, 192, 197, 211
Madhvani, Nanjibhai Prabhudas, 55
Madhvani, Nitin Jayant, 56
Madhvani family, 28, 36, 53–55, 62, 80, 102, 192–93, 212
Magazines, 5, 166, 170, 172–74, 177–78
Mahajan, 74–75
Maharana Mills Ltd., 74
Maharashtra, 16, 170; famine, 81
Maharashtra Amateurs, 107 n.
Mahatma Gandhi Memorial Committee, 131, 135–36
Mahatma Gandhi Memorial Hall, Mwanza, 130

Visram, Allidina, 43, 50–51, 64, 94, 104, 106 n., 211
Vithaldas Haridas & Co., 55, 60
Vithaldas Haridas Pavilion, Jinja, 56
Vivekananda, Swami, 5
Voluntary service, definition, 2
Vyas, Shambu Shankar, 95

Wadia, A. R., 3
Walji Hirji & Sons, 94
Walji, Shirin, 177
War Relief Fund, 186
War Welfare Fund committees, 187
Water fountains, 85
Welfare state, 7–9, 208, 210
Westernization. See Modernization
Willoughby, G. P., 131–32, 135, 138
Women, Asian, 31, 33–34, 36, 48, 63, 71–72, 110, 114, 116, 119, 167, 169, 176, 188, 195–96, 212
Working Party on Higher Education in East Africa: first (1955), 149; second (1957–58), 149–50
World Bank, 11
World Council, International Travel Fund, 63
World Council of Young Men's Service Clubs, 63

World Health Organization, 11
World War: I, 15, 19, 29, 37, 44–45, 186; II, 61, 70, 73, 99, 106, 115, 119–21, 149, 163–64, 185–87, 210

Yajnik, Dr. Ramanlal Kanaiyalal, 136–39, 141, 143, 148, 150, 156
Yeats, William Butler, 173
YMCA, 6; Dar es Salaam, 56; Mombasa, 195
YWCA: Kisumu, 61, Mombasa, 58, 63

Zakat, the, 4
Zaire, 77
Zambia, 77
Zanzibar, 17–18, 20, 26, 28–31, 32–33, 45, 49, 130, 143, 198; coup (1964) 76, 79, 211, 213–14; government, 123; libraries, 103, 106, 108 n., 114; schools, 114, 124 n.
Zanzibar Indian National Association, 195
Zoroaster, 36